Region, State and Identity in
Central and Eastern Europe

D1473904

THE CASS SERIES IN REGIONAL AND FEDERAL STUDIES
ISSN 1363-5670
General Editor: John Loughlin

This series brings together some of the foremost academics and theorists to examine the timely subject of regional and federal issues, which since the mid-1980s have become key questions in political analysis and practice all over the world.

The Political Economy of Regionalism
edited by Michael Keating and John Loughlin

The Regional Dimension of the European Union: Towards a Third Level in Europe? *edited by Charlie Jeffery*

Remaking the Union: Devolution and British Politics in the 1990s
edited by Howard Elcock and Michael Keating

Paradiplomacy in Action: The Foreign Relations of Subnational Governments
edited by Francisco Aldecoa and Michael Keating

Ethnicity and Territory in the Former Soviet Union: Regions in Conflict
edited by James Hughes and Gwendolyn Sasse

Region, State and Identity in Central and Eastern Europe

Editors

JUDY BATT

and

KATARYNA WOLCZUK

FRANK CASS
LONDON • PORTLAND, OR.

First published in 2002 in Great Britain by
FRANK CASS PUBLISHERS
Crown House, 47 Chase Side, Southgate, London N14 5BP

and in the United States of America by
FRANK CASS PUBLISHERS
c/o ISBS, 5824 N.E. Hassalo Street
Portland, Oregon 97213-3644

Website: www.frankcass.com

Copyright © 2002 Frank Cass & Co. Ltd.

British Library Cataloguing in Publication Data

Region, state and identity in Central and Eastern Europe.
– (The Cass series in regional and federal studies)
1. Regionalism – Europe, Central 2. Regionalism – Europe,
Eastern, 3. Nationalism – Europe, Central 4. Nationalism –
Europe, Eastern 5. Europe, Central – Politics and
government – 1989– 6. Europe, Eastern – Politics and
government – 1989–
I. Batt, Judy, 1955– II. Wolczuk, Kataryna
320.8′0943

ISBN 0-7146-5243-1 (cloth)
ISBN 0-7146-8225-X (paper)
ISSN 1363-5670

Library of Congress Cataloging-in-Publication Data:

Region, state and identity in Central and Eastern Europe/
edited by Judy Batt and Kataryna Wolczuk.
    p. cm. – (The Cass series in regional and federal studies
ISSN 1363-5670)
Includes bibliographical references and index.
  ISBN 0-7146-5243-1 (hard) – ISBN 0-7146-8225-X (pbk.)
1. Regionalism–Europe, Central–Case studies.
2. Regionalism–Europe, Eastern–Case studies. I. Batt, Judy.
II. Wolczuk, Kataryna. III. Series.
  JN96.A38 R4365 2002
  320.943–dc21   2002007002

This group of studies first appeared in a Special Issue of *Regional and Federal
Studies* (ISSN 1359-7566), Vol.12, No.2 (Summer 2002),
published by Frank Cass and Co. Ltd.

Printed in Great Britain by
Antony Rowe Ltd., Chippenham, Wilts.

Contents

Acknowledgements

The research on which this volume is based was financed by the Economic and Social Research Council's *One Europe or Several?* Programme, for which the editors express their gratitude. Special thanks are due to the energy and enthusiasm of the Programme Coordinator, Professor Helen Wallace.

All the chapters except that of Bialasiewicz were produced by the project *'Fuzzy Statehood' and European Integration in Central and Eastern Europe* (ref. no. L213 25 2001) based at the University of Birmingham, while that of Bialasiewicz was produced by the project Regional Identity and European Citizenship (ref. no. L213 25 22031) based at the University of Durham.

The editors would like to thank Wanda Knowles for her assistance in preparing the final manuscript for publication.

MAP 1

STATES AND REGIONS IN CENTRAL AND EASTERN EUROPE

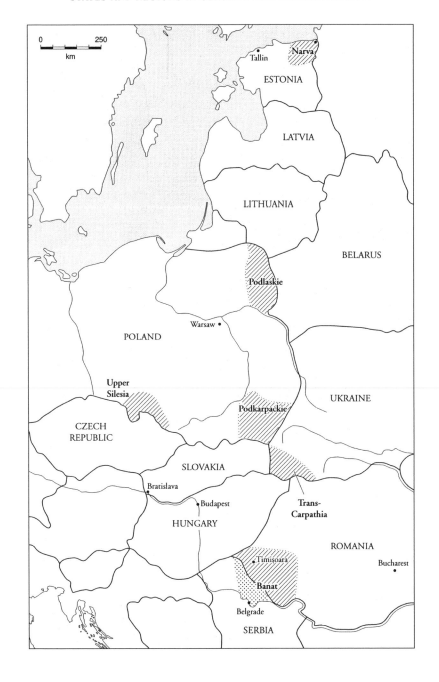

MAP 2

TWO EUROREGIONS

Acronyms and Abbreviations

ARC	Autonomous Republic of Crimea
AWS	Electoral Action Solidarity
CER	Carpathian EuroRegion
CHCA	Carpathian Hungarian Cultural Association
CSCE	Commission on Security and Cooperation in Europe
CPU	Communist Party of Ukraine
DPL	Democratic Party of Labour (Estonia)
DS	Slovak Democratic Party
ESSR	Estonian Soviet Socialist Republic
FIDESZ	Federation of Young Democrats
FIDESZ-MPP	FIDESZ-Hungarian Civic Party
FKGP	Independent Smallholders' Party
GOP	Upper Silesian Industrial District
HZDS	Movement for a Democratic Slovakia
IRBR	Interregional Block for Reforms
KDH	Slovak Christian Democratic Party
KDNP	Christian Democratic People's Party
MDG	Interregional Group of Deputies
MDF	Hungarian Democratic Forum
MSZP	Hungarian Socialist Party
NES	Narva Estonian Society
NKVD	People's Commissariat for Internal Security (later the KGB)
PDSR	Party of Social Democracy of Romania
PKWN	Committee of National Liberation
PRM	Greater Romania Party
RMDSZ	Democratic Union of Romanian Magyars
RSFSR	Russian Soviet Federal Socialist Republic
SDL	Slovak Democratic Left Party
SLD	Democratic Left Alliance
SMK	Hungarian Coalition Party
SNS	Slovak National Party
SOP	Civic Understanding Party
SZDSZ	Alliance of Free Democrats
TUC	Trade Union Centre
UkrSSR	Ukrainian Soviet Socialist Republic
UMO	Union of Cities and Towns in Slovakia
UNR	Ukrainian People's Republic (1917–20)
UPA	Ukrainian Insurgent Army
URCN	Union of Russian Citizens of Narva
UW	Freedom Union
VUC	[a regional level of territorial self-government in Slovakia]
ZMOS	Association of Towns and Villages of Slovakia
ZRS	Association of Workers in Slovakia

Introduction:
Region, State and Identity
in Central and Eastern Europe

JUDY BATT

...[N]ations living in this region lacked what was naturally, clearly precisely and concretely present in the everyday life and community consciousness of nations in Western Europe: A reality in their own national and state framework, a capital city, a harmony between economy and politics, a unified social elite etc ... In Eastern Europe ... a national framework was something that had to be created, repaired, fought for, and constantly protected, not only against the power factors existing in the dynastic state, but also from the indifference exhibited by a certain proportion of the country's own inhabitants, as well as from the wavering state of national consciousness (Bibó, 1946: 38).

The democratic revolutions of 1989–91 reawakened the historical aspirations of the peoples of Central and Eastern Europe for 'national self-determination'. The events were readily interpreted as the culmination of two centuries of struggle against imperial rule in various guises: the Habsburg, Ottoman, Prussian and Tsarist Russian empires up to the early twentieth century, thereafter followed by the Nazi Third Reich and, finally, Soviet 'socialist internationalism'. The opportunity to win or recover independent statehood was accompanied by a resurgence of nationalism, fuelled by the extraordinary demands of reconstituting the state out of the post-communist debris. Questions of identity were propelled to the fore by the very nature of 'democratic transition' itself: after all, democratic self-government presupposes the existence of a consensual community with shared understandings not only of *what* the state is for and *how* it is to function, but also of *where* its borders are and *who* it is for – who belongs to the community to which it is to be held accountable (Keens-Soper, 1989: 694). The rules of democracy do not by themselves provide answers to these questions, nor do they offer any prescription for delineating the state's external borders and its internal territorial structure.

Clifford Geertz, one of the leading political anthropologists working on the politics of post-colonial states in the Third World, has pinpointed the question of identity as the primary challenge facing state-builders 'the Day After the Revolution': 'It consists in defining, or trying to define, a collective subject to whom the actions of the state can be internally connected, in creating, or trying to create, an experiential "we" from whose will the activities of government seem spontaneously to flow' (Geertz, 1993: 240).

In Central and Eastern Europe, where national identities have had to be painfully constructed and fought for, and territorial borders have been chronically insecure and frequently changing, democratization rapidly exposed the fact that nothing could be taken for granted. All three multi-national communist federal states – the USSR, Czechoslovakia and Yugoslavia – disintegrated between 1989 and 1992, leading to the formation of a set of new states based on the demand for 'national self-determination'. Three of these – Ukraine, Estonia and Slovakia – are included in this volume. Each of these new states has faced the problem not only of consolidating its external borders and redefining its relations with its neighbours, but also of integrating the diverse ethnic and regional communities among its own population into a coherent 'body politic'. Moreover, even longer-established states have found coming to terms with newly exposed regional and ethnic minority identities far from straightforward, and the questions of whether and how such identities should receive institutional recognition in the constitutional structure of the state continue to be matters of contestation. As the Polish and Romanian case studies in this volume show, regional politics are still marked by the experience of territorial gains and losses in the course of the twentieth century.

The regional dimension has received relatively little coverage so far in the literature on 'democratic transition', despite the fact that the ethnic and regional diversity of Central and Eastern Europe is a widely known legacy of its history of belated state-formation and frequent border changes. The suddenness of the changes in 1989 and 1991, for which the Western academic community was ill-prepared both conceptually and in terms of area expertise, may account for this. Decades of communist centralization had done much to obliterate the evidence of local and regional identities, and the fact that (after the collapse of the three federations) all Central and East European states became unitary states helped propel the focus of research towards politics at the state centre as the primary locus of power. Moreover, the dominant paradigm of political science in the study of 'transitions to democracy' was derived from the experiences of southern Europe and Latin America in the 1970s, where questions of borders and national identity were (with the exception of Spain) less salient than they have been in Central and Eastern Europe (see O'Donnell et al., 1986; Linz and Stepan, 1996). Thus attention has been focused overwhelmingly on national-level politics and elite reconfigurations, on the institutional design of legislatures and executives, the development of political parties, and electoral outcomes. In turn, the 'political culture' approach stimulated an industry of public opinion surveys to gauge the extent to which democratization was supported by popular values and beliefs. The data collected produced aggregated results for each country as a whole in order to facilitate cross-country comparisons, with little attention to sub-state differentiation (see for example Rose and Haerpfner, 1998; Fuchs and Roller, 1998).

Studies of the sub-state level so far have tended to focus on 'top down' institutional change, and the dominant approach has been to assess a single, unidimensional process of reforms of regional and local institutions, where the starting point is communism and the end goal is democracy and 'Europeanization' (see for example, Hanson and Gibson, 1996; Surazska et al., 1997; Coulson, 1995; Kirchner, 1999; Hughes et al., 2001). In this literature only passing references to the underlying dynamics of identity politics can be encountered, despite the fact that institutional reforms in Central and Eastern Europe were not only preceded by heated debates on the nature of nationhood, national unity, and minority rights, but were also accompanied by strenuous efforts to gain recognition as rightful members of the 'European family', and by an upsurge of ethnic-minority and regional assertiveness.

In Clifford Geertz's view, the basic dynamic of identity politics in new states can broadly be understood in terms of the interaction between two partly competing, partly complementary and 'intimately related' motives. The first is to promote and express what he calls the 'Indigenous Way of Life': 'to look to local mores, established institutions, and the unities of common experience – to "tradition", "culture", "national character", or even "race" – for the roots of a new identity' (Geertz, 1993: 240). The second is to align with the 'Spirit of the Age': 'it is a demand for progress, for a rising standard of living, more effective political order, greater social justice, and beyond that of "playing a part in the larger arena of world politics", of "exercising influence among the nations"' (Geertz, 1993: 258).

Translated into the political idiom of post-communist Central and Eastern Europe, the assertion of the 'Indigenous Way of Life' is most evident in the agenda of ethnic nationalism, reviving a long tradition in the region which defines national identity primarily in terms of pre-political, cultural, religious and linguistic markers. But, as our case studies show, regional identities can also be understood as an assertion of an 'indigenous way of life' distinct from that of the rest of the state, and often linked with ethnic minority identities or a local pattern of multi-culturalism that is at odds with the prevailing nationalist discourse. On the other hand, aligning with the 'Spirit of the Age' in contemporary Central and Eastern Europe is connected above all with the aspiration to 'return to Europe'. The latter concept is multifaceted: it operates at the psychological level of asserting the essentially 'European' character of the national identity; at the level of domestic politics, it means establishing the social, political and economic frameworks for a way of life similar to those enjoyed in Western European countries; at the international level, it means acquiring the benefits associated with membership of international bodies such as the Council of Europe, the OSCE, and above all, the EU and NATO.

What these in turn imply for the internal structuring of the state, and in particular its provisions for regions and ethnic minorities, is, however, far from obvious. The problem is a deeper one than simply the lack of any detailed and definitive 'European norms' of either territorial-administrative structures or minority rights. There are also looming questions about what it means to be a 'modern' state in contemporary Europe. At first it seemed obvious: recovering a 'lost' European identity meant recovering national self-esteem as a member of the family of free, independent, sovereign *nation-states*. But many in the West have begun to argue that the nation-state is in decline, and that the 'end of sovereignty' is nigh (Horsman and Marshall, 1995; Camilleri and Falk, 1992). In an era of accelerating economic and communications globalization, deepening European integration, and an accompanying resurgence of regional and minority national identities, traditional understandings of state sovereignty, and of 'nations' as territorially and culturally cohesive political communities, have generally come into question. Thus while the idea of 'returning to Europe' has been central to the transformation of post-communist states, 'Europe' itself now turns out to be not only an ambiguous target, but a moving one.

The focus of this volume is on the debates provoked by these perplexities in Central and East European countries as they set about administrative-territorial reform, a key element of modernizing and democratizing state structures. This analysis uncovers lively encounters between divergent interpretations of national, regional, ethnic-minority and 'European' identities and their implications for the future shape of the state. Our aim has been to move on from the earlier research agenda, preoccupied with how the legacies of communism would be overcome, and how the Central and East European cases would fit into the existing comparative framework of 'democratic transition'. It now makes sense to set the state transformation in Central and Eastern Europe in the more general context of new pressures evident right across the continent. The peculiarities of Central and Eastern European history and endemic geopolitical vulnerability render this part of the continent acutely sensitive to the current general uncertainties surrounding the nature of statehood in Europe. For that very reason, these case studies may also contribute to wider understanding of the challenges facing statehood across the continent as a whole by throwing them into sharper relief.

THE CONTEXT

It is often argued that globalization and deepening European integration at the turn of the twenty-first century pose wholly new challenges to states. By blurring the distinction between the internal and the external dimensions of politics, they undermine the basis of territorial sovereignty that has been the defining characteristic of modern states, and erode the cultural and political cohesion of the nations that are the central reference point of their democratic legitimacy. But for Central and Eastern Europe, this predicament is by no means a new one. Indeed, it has been an enduring theme of the area's history over the past two centuries. It was only after the First World War that most of Central and Eastern Europe finally escaped the grasp of dynastic empires, and that 'nation-states' became established, on a model drawing heavily on French republican and Napoleonic traditions. The latter's unitary, centralized form was widely regarded as the epitome of modern statehood, encapsulating the aspirations to streamlined, rational administration of a homogeneous 'body politic' comprising equal, undifferentiated individual citizens.

From the start, however, questions hovered over the viability of these new states in Central and Eastern Europe, deriving not only from the legacies of socio-economic underdevelopment and post-war economic dislocation and crises, but also from unresolved 'national questions' that cut across borders and impeded the consolidation of unified, stable, consensual polities. These difficulties rendered them vulnerable to the revived ambitions of the great powers to their west and east, Nazi Germany and the Soviet Union. It was not just nostalgia for a vanished world that prompted many (now neglected) political thinkers from the region to argue for various forms of supra-national federation to replace the failed Austro-Hungarian order, but a very real appreciation of Central and Eastern Europe's enduring security problem, which, they warned, made the dogged nationalist pursuit of sovereign nation-statehood self-defeating (see Romsics and Király, 1999).

The inter-war Republic of Poland was an amalgam of territories that had, since the late eighteenth century, been under either Prussian, Habsburg or Russian imperial control, and thus inherited quite different administrative traditions and political cultures in the regions. The insistence of Polish national-democrats on the primacy of the

Polish ethnic nation within a unitary state provoked German minorities in the west, and Ukrainian and other eastern Slav minorities in the east, eventually prompting Nazi Germany and the Soviet Union to conspire in 1939 to dismember Poland and reclaim 'lost' territories and slighted ethnic kinsfolk. Inter-war Czechoslovakia's relatively tolerant approach to the sizeable ethnic German minorities along its western borders did not extend to granting them regional self-government, and the limitations of the unitary model of the first Czechoslovak Republic offended not only the German minority but also the Slovak 'partner' in the composite 'Czechoslovak' nation, eventually inducing their collaboration with Hitler in dismembering the state in 1938–39. Hungary, having lost two-thirds of its territory in the 1920 Treaty of Trianon, became ethnically homogeneous, but Hungarians were far from content with the 'nation-state' thus created, because its borders left outsideover 3 million Hungarian kinsfolk, living as frustrated and resentful minorities in southern Slovakia and its easternmost tip, Sub-Carpathian Ruthenia; in Transylvania and Banat, both handed to Romania; and inthe newly formed Kingdom of Serbs, Croats and Slovenes (later Yugoslavia), itself a highly unstable amalgam of territories and ethno-national identities that, like Czechoslovakia, would fall apart under the Nazi onslaught, in which Hungary connived to regain at least part of its losses.

The Holocaust of the Second World War decimated the Jewish communities, and post-war population transfers dramatically reduced the German minorities in Central and Eastern Europe. The victorious Western Allies reconstituted the area in the aftermath of the war along 'nation-state' lines, with little attention to the views of those most affected. The subsequent slide into Cold War saw the security question once more dealt with by force: the states of Central and Eastern Europe became part of the Soviet-dominated communist bloc. Any semblance of state sovereignty was in practice lost, most obviously in the case of Estonia, which was fully incorporated into the Soviet Union as a constituent republic of the socialist federation. Elsewhere, the imposition of communist regimes, directly subordinate to Moscow, signified a more far-reaching erosion of the distinction between the external and internal dimensions of politics than ever. National, regional and ethnic minority identities were submerged under the *Gleichschaltung* of 'socialist internationalism'.

While the form of the 'nation-state' was preserved, only in the case of Hungary was the pre-Second World War territorial *status quo* fully restored. Romania's western border was reconfirmed, but the eastern province of Bessarabia was annexed by the Soviet Union, forming the new Soviet Republic of Moldova. The most radical territorial changes affected Poland, whose borders were shifted 200 km westwards in 1945.

The result was that Poland became about 95 per cent ethnically Polish, and to that extent came closer to the inter-war nationalists' objective, but, ironically, only at the expense of dependence on the Soviet guarantee of its hold on the newly acquired former German territories up to the Oder-Neisse line in the west. Moreover, the loss to Soviet Ukraine of much of the eastern *Kresy*, the ethnically mixed borderlands, was a bitter blow to many Poles, who followed the inter-war leader Piłsudski in cherishing Poland in its historic rather than ethnic frontiers. The changed borders meant that the task of internal territorial integration had to be started over again. Regional and minority identities would nevertheless reappear disconcertingly after 1989, as the studies by Kisielowska-Lipman and Bialasiewicz in this volume show.

Czechoslovakia was put back together after the Second World War, thus leaving the 'Slovak question' unresolved until 1993, while Slovakia's 'Hungarian question' still hovers over the contemporary regional reforms that are the subject of Bitušíkova's study. Czechoslovakia ceded its easternmost province, Sub-Carpathian Ruthenia, to the Soviet Union in 1945, whereupon it was absorbed into the Ukrainian Soviet Socialist Republic as the Transcarpathian *oblast*. But, as Batt's study outlines, its claims to a distinctive regional identity would once again be heard when Ukraine, 'robbed' of independent statehood in the years 1917–21, seized its chance, along with Estonia and the other republics, in 1991, to break away from the Soviet Union. Meanwhile, in the course of the Soviet period, as Wolczuk's case study of Ukraine, and Smith's of Estonia show, large influxes of Russian and Russian-speaking migrant workers into the cities and industrial regions came to challenge the cultural hegemony of the titular nations, with enduring consequences that have burdened state transformation and regional reform in both cases.

The installation of communist regimes in Central and Eastern Europe in the late 1940s froze international borders, and effectively sealed them. Travel between states within the Soviet bloc became almost as difficult as travel to the West. Thus in many ways, the communist period, rather than merging nations in a 'socialist brotherhood', actually helped to solidify nationhood within the imposed state borders. While minorities within states were given their own cultural organizations, these were tightly policed; cross-border contacts between minorities and 'mother countries' were prevented as far as possible. Within state borders, the monopoly of power of hierarchically organized communist parties ran in parallel with, and thoroughly penetrated, formal state structures that still bore strong traces of the centralized territorial-administrative model characteristic of the inter-war 'nation-state' constitutions. One exception was Yugoslavia, which broke away from the Soviet bloc in 1948 and instituted its own form of decentralized 'self-managing' federation that included, eventually, far-reaching concessions to the six constituent national republics and Serbia's two autonomous regions. Another exception was Czechoslovakia, where federation of the state in late 1968 created two separate Czech and Slovak Republics following the Soviet model of ethnic federation. In both these cases, federalization under communist auspices served to consolidate rather than mitigate national feeling by attaching it to state structures. In all cases, below the level of the nation-state or national republic, local or regional identities were ignored, and battered by frequent, arbitrary changes of territorial-administrative structures: 'Communist leaders had little sense of the historical accretion that forms territorial units: the administrative boundaries were drawn and redrawn according to various problems at hand and regardless of regional coherence. Most often historic regions were split up, traditional districts dissolved, localities divided and amalgamated in a casual manner' (Surazska *et al.*, 1997: 439).

However, the late communist period, despite (and in part because of) its rigid formal centralization, saw an ever-growing disintegration of the polity as central elites proved less and less able to enforce plan directives and party discipline over increasingly assertive and often corrupt local subordinates. A recurrent pattern of local, regional and national-republican communist *nomenklatura* elites capturing territorial-administrative institutions at the corresponding level can be found in the last stages of regime collapse (see Brubaker, 1996; Zaslavsky, 1992). Exploiting the symbolic, as well as the economic and political resources afforded by control of these institutions, the *nomenklatura* hoped either to stave off reforms launched from the centre, or to position themselves to preserve their status and power in whatever way they could, and, in the process, to take full advantage of the opportunities for self-enrichment that the situation offered.

The end of communism thus found the states of Central and Eastern Europe in considerable, if not terminal, disarray, of which the break-up of the multi-national federal states was only the most obvious symptom. 'Democratization' called for a resuscitation of the local and regional levels in order to promote and secure democratization beyond the centre, to eliminate communist legacies and entrenched power networks, and to revive much-attenuated pre-communist traditions of self-government. Effective management and implementation of the economic transformation also called for well-organized administration capable of translating central government policies into action at the regional and local levels. The demands of 'returning to Europe', in the sense of EU accession, included enhancing 'administrative capacity' at the regional level in order to handle the anticipated transfers from the Structural Funds. The question of how these objectives were to be met immediately raised fundamental questions about the structure of the state – the allocation of power and authority between its various levels and the latter's territorial delimitation – that opened up the political space into which resurgent ethnic and regional identities stepped once the ideological and political straightjacket of communist regimes was removed, as all of our regional studies show.

'RETURNING TO EUROPE' – THE REGIONAL DIMENSION

As always in Central and Eastern Europe, the internal dimension of post-communist state transformation would not be easily separable from the external: domestic political and economic transformation was accepted not only as a good in itself, but as a means of demonstrating fitness for full membership in European institutions. The latter would provide the overarching security framework that had for so long eluded Central and Eastern Europe, which in turn would guarantee the irreversibility of the domestic transformation. What room this virtuous circle would leave for the exercise of the 'sovereignty' that the states of Central and Eastern Europe had only just recovered was at first passed over as unproblematic. But as the 'return to Europe' has progressed from a utopian vision to a practical – and vastly ambitious – project, the implications are becoming clearer. The domestic transformations in Central and Eastern Europe are accompanied by ever deeper penetration of 'Europe' into the domestic sphere, both as an *idea* mobilized in domestic political discourse by national, regional and ethnic minority leaders to legitimize proposals for change and reform; and as a practical *actor*, chiefly in the form of the European Commission, recommending the member-states to extend or withhold the promises of membership to this or that state; exhorting and advising applicant governments; monitoring reforms; offering financial assistance; and conducting accession negotiations. The extraordinary engagement of the Commission with the candidate countries can be explained by the sheer scale of the tasks of transformation in Central and Eastern Europe, and the corresponding need for substantial external support. In the process, however, the Commission is becoming involved in policy areas – including constitutional reforms – that have hitherto been the jealously guarded 'sovereign' terrain of the member states (see Grabbe, 2001). The case of territorial-administrative and regional reform, on which the studies collected in this volume focus, is one such area.

While a trend towards strengthening the regional tier of government has been evident throughout the EU's member-states over the past two decades, and there has been a certain amount of mutual learning, there has been no systematic coordination between them, let alone by the Commission, in an attempt to produce a 'European' blueprint for regionalization which the Central and East European states might apply (Christiansen, 1999). Diversity remains the hallmark, leaving the candidates with a bewildering variety of options, the choice among which the Commission experts are in a position to shape. Whether they consciously promote a particular model or not is not the issue here, but rather the way in which national, regional, and ethnic minority political actors in Central and Eastern Europe mobilize diverse understandings of what being or becoming 'European' means for the purposes of state transformation, here with particular reference to regional reform. How does the long-cherished but elusive goal of 'sovereignty' feature in national debates? What vision of 'Europe' – a 'Europe of Nation-States', a 'Europe of Nations (but not states)', or a 'Europe of Regions' – is implicitly or explicitly referred to, by whom, and for what purposes, in the process of territorial-administrative reform?

A further theme pursued in our studies is the impact on regional politics within the Central and East European states of differentiation among them in respect of their access to 'Europe'. All states examined in this volume are members of the Council of Europe, the organization that promotes democratic development at both national and sub-state levels, the latter embodied in the European Charter of Local Self-Government. However, their chances of joining the EU, much more demanding in its entry conditions, are markedly divergent. Poland, Estonia and Hungary, which entered into accession negotiations with the EU in 1998, belong to the so-called 'first wave' of enlargement (which also includes the Czech Republic and Slovenia, not covered in this volume). Slovakia and Romania (along with Latvia, Lithuania and Bulgaria) were left behind, and began accession negotiations only in 2000. While Slovakia has caught up, and hopes to be able to join in the first wave, Romania is lagging behind, deemed to be 'not a functioning market economy' and relegated to the back of the queue of candidates in the European Commission's regular 'Progress Report' on its accession preparations published in November 2000. Finally, our volume also includes Ukraine, the so-called 'outsider' whose membership of the EU, despite its proclaimed commitment to a 'European vocation', is not regarded by the EU's member states or the Commission as a matter for serious discussion in the foreseeable future. Instead of an Association Agreement which opens the way to future membership, Ukraine's relations with the EU are regulated by the 1994 Treaty of Partnership and Cooperation.

It has by now become clear that EU enlargement by stages will have serious repercussions on relations between states within Central and Eastern Europe, thus potentially threatening the stability that has been established in this historically volatile area over the past decade of tumultuous political changes. The key issue has been the likely impact of the adoption by the 'first wave' accession states of the EU's 'Schengen *acquis*': the common visa regime and system of managing the EU's external border now enshrined in the EU Treaty of Amsterdam and therefore a non-negotiable obligation of membership for new entrants (but not for existing member states such as the UK, Ireland and Denmark, whose presence at the Amsterdam negotiating table allowed them to secure 'opt-outs'). This will erect new barriers to free movement into, for example, Hungary and Poland, by citizens of neighbouring states which do not seem likely to join until much later (such as Romania), or not at all (possibly the fate of Ukraine). This prospect creates problems not only at the level of inter-state relations between the 'first wavers' and their eastern neighbours, but it also threatens to generate a new and hitherto overlooked set of tensions at the regional level: within regions on each side of the EU's new eastern external border; between these peripheral regions and their national capitals; and in inter-ethnic relations in what are often ethnically mixed regions. 'Returning to Europe' turns out not only to bring benefits, but costs as well, disproportionately heaped upon these fragile border regions with unpredictable consequences for the stability of states to which they belong, for the enlarged EU and its external border, and for the wider Europe as a whole.

THE CASE STUDIES

This volume comprises case studies covering five Central and East European countries selected to illustrate the multiple political challenges posed by administrative-territorial reform in post-communist states. Three of the states covered are in the 'first wave' of EU accession (Hungary, Poland and Estonia), and a fourth, Slovakia, is likely to catch up shortly. Romania, while a candidate for EU accession, seems likely to remain outside for many years, while Ukraine has yet to see its aspirations for EU membership recognized by the EU. Three of our states (Slovakia, Ukraine, Estonia) are 'new', in the sense that they re-emerged as independent polities only in the early 1990s and therefore faced major challenges in establishing their national identity and state-building. These included the presence of significant, regionally concentrated ethnic minorities that could be expected to have an impact on administrative-territorial reform. Poland and Hungary, while longer-established states, nevertheless experienced major changes in their borders during the twentieth century. In both cases these changes resulted in much greater ethnic homogeneity.

Four of our case studies focus on debates on regional reform at the state centre (Hungary by Fowler, Poland by Kisielowska-Lipman, Slovakia by Bitušíková and Ukraine by Wolczuk). In Hungary, ethnic minorities are today small and territorially dispersed, and the loss of two-thirds of the territory of the Kingdom in 1920 also meant that the distinct regions of historic Hungary now lie beyond the borders of the state. Hungary is therefore exceptional among our cases in its internal homogeneity, and our volume starts with it as the case that shows most clearly the interaction between the 'European' and 'national' elements in the debates over regionalization. In Poland, ethnic and regional identities did re-emerge as a significant issue in the regionalization debates, but Poland's size, national self-confidence, and enthusiastic embrace of the 'European' ideal have meant that these potential centrifugal 'threats' did not prevent wide-ranging political decentralization of the state, which began even before pressure for regionalization was felt from the side of the EU.

In the cases of the new states that follow, Slovakia, Ukraine and Estonia, diverse regional and ethnic minority identities have challenged the 'national' concept pursued by the builders of the new states, and have been a factor inducing the latter to resist political decentralization. But in the cases of Slovakia and Ukraine, the insecurity of their respective national identities has been a further factor inhibiting reform. In all cases, reference to 'European' norms has been deployed, but in contradictory ways, arguing both for decentralization and concessions to ethnic minorities, and for a unitary national state as the 'norm'.

The five regional case studies that follow present the perspective of borderland regions, all of which are multi-ethnic, and all of which face highly significant change in the nature of external state borders with the coming waves of EU enlargement. Narva region (covered by Smith), Upper Silesia (by Bialasiewicz) and the Polish eastern borderlands (by Kisielowska-Lipman) will be on the 'right' side of the new EU borders once Estonia and Poland accede to the EU. While Upper Silesia will eventually find its western border with Germany transformed from an EU external border into an internal one, open for free movement, for Narva region and the Polish eastern borderlands the new EU external border regime will have serious, and potentially damaging, implications not only for the local economies and ethnic minorities, but also for relations with Russia, Belarus and Ukraine. For Ukrainian Transcarpathia and Romanian Banat (both covered by Batt), the exclusion of their respective nation-states from EU enlargement in the medium to long term is seen as a threat to the vital interests of the regions and to their multi-ethnic stability. This fear serves to deepen estrangement from the state capital, whose incompetent and corrupt policies are widely blamed for these regions' difficult predicament.

REFERENCES

Bibó, I. (1946), 'The Distress of the East European Small States', in K. Nagy (ed.), *Democracy, Revolution and Self-determination: Selected Writings of István Bibó*. Boulder, CO: Social Science Monographs, 1991.

Brubaker, R. (1996), 'Nationhood and the National Question in the Soviet Union and its Successor States: An Institutionalist Account', in R. Brubaker, *Nationalism Reframed. Nationhood and the National Question in the New Europe*, Cambridge: Cambridge University Press, pp.23–54.

Camilleri, J. and J. Falk (1992), *The End of Sovereignty? The Politics of a Shrinking and Fragmenting World*. Aldershot: Edward Elgar.

Christiansen, T. (1999), 'Regionalization in Western Europe', in E. Kirchner (ed.), *Decentralization and Transition in the Visegrad*. Basingstoke: Macmillan.

Coulson, A. (ed.) (1995), *Local Government in Eastern Europe: Establishing Democracy at the Grass-Roots*. Aldershot: Edward Elgar.

Fuchs, D. and E. Roller (1998), 'Cultural Conditions of Transition to Liberal Democracies in Central and Eastern Europe', in S. Barnes and J. Simon (eds), *The Post-Communist Citizen*. Budapest: Erasmus Foundation and Hungarian Academy of Sciences.

Geertz, C. (1993), *The Interpretation of Cultures*. London: Harper Collins/Fontana.

Grabbe, H. (2001), 'Europeanizing Public Policy in Central Europe: Asymmetrical Relations and Uncertainty', paper to ECSA Conference, Madison, 30 May–2 June 2001.

Hanson, P. and J. Gibson (eds) (1996), *Transformation from Below: Local Power and the Political Economy of Postcommunism*. Cheltenham: Edward Elgar.

Horsman, M. and A. Marshall (1995), *After the Nation-State. Citizens, Tribalism and the New World Disorder*. London: Harper Collins.

Hughes, J. *et al.* (2001), 'Enlargement and Regionalization: the Europeanization of Local and Regional Governance in CEE States', in H. Wallace (ed.) *One Europe or Several? Interlocking Dimensions of European Integration*. Basingstoke: Palgrave, pp.145–78.

Keens-Soper, M. (1989), 'The Liberal State and Nationalism in Post-War Europe', in *History of European Ideas*, Vol.10, No.6, pp.689–703.

Kirchner, E. (ed.) (1999), *Decentralization and Transition in the Visegrad*. Basingsoke: Macmillan.

Linz, J. and A. Stepan (1996), *Problems of Democratic Transition and Consolidation*. Baltimore, MD: Johns Hopkins University Press.

O'Donnell, G., P. Schmitter and L. Whitehead (eds) (1986), *Transitions from Authoritarian Rule. Prospects for Democracy*. Baltimore, MD: Johns Hopkins University Press.

Romsics, I. and B. Király (eds) (1999), *Geopolitics in the Danube Region*. Budapest: Central European University Press.

Rose, R. and C. Haerpfner (1998), *New Democracies Barometer V. A 12-Nation Survey*. Glasgow: Centre for the Study of Public Policy, University of Strathclyde.

Surazska, W. *et al.* (1997), 'Towards Regional Government in Central Europe: Territorial

Restructuring of Postcommunist Regimes', *Environment and Planning C: Government and Policy*, Vol.15, No.4, pp.437–62.

Zaslavsky, V. (1992), 'Nationalism and Democratic Transition in Postcommunist Societies', *Daedalus*, Vol.121, No.2, pp.97–121.

Hungary:
Patterns of Political Conflict over Territorial-Administrative Reform

BRIGID FOWLER

In the context of the current volume, Hungary represents the case of post-communist regional reform in an ethnically and territorially homogeneous state. Hungarians make up over 90 per cent of the population, with non-Hungarians split among 13 recognized minorities. These are integrated with the majority society – with the exception of the Roma – and are either territorially dispersed, or concentrated only at local level. The territory of present-day Hungary has been divided only twice, both long before living memory: in the Roman era, when the Danube divided the province of Pannonia to the west from the eastern lands ('Hunnia') not formally integrated into the empire; and during the sixteenth and seventeenth centuries, when a swathe of central Hungary came under Ottoman control, the country's north-eastern tip fell within the independent principality of Transylvania and western areas were ruled from Vienna. From the early eighteenth century, all the territory of contemporary Hungary has belonged to the same political entity: the Austrian empire to 1867, the Hungarian state within the Austro-Hungarian Dual Monarchy to 1918, and then independent Hungary. Contemporary Hungary's defining territorial experience has been loss: the country owes its present homogeneity to the 1920 Treaty of Trianon, which, in depriving it of around two-thirds of its former territory, also removed the bulk of its previously substantial non-Hungarian populations and transferred historically distinctive regions, such as Transylvania, Transcarpathia and the Banat, to neighbouring states.

Regional reform in post-communist Hungary has thus not evoked fears of territorial fragmentation or ethnic minority autonomism; the unitary character of the state has not been questioned. Hungary has also not had to grapple with the particular difficulties facing new states, while the elite consensus on reform and the 'return to Europe' has been strong and productive. Reflecting this environment, most accounts of Hungary's post-communist territorial-administrative reforms suggest a comparatively competent, consensual, seamless and technocratic process (Gibson and Hanson, 1996; Surazska *et al.*, 1997; Hughes *et al.*, 2001). However, this impression is not fully borne out by closer examination. In

Hungary as in other post-communist states, territorial-administrative reform has unavoidably raised broad and politically highly contestable questions (Coulson, 1995; Illner, 1998; Horváth, 2000: 36–57) – about the relationship between the state and territorial self-government, the division of powers and responsibilities between territorial tiers, and the drawing of new territorial boundaries. Debate on such questions is fired partly by partisan interests, but also by politicians' understandings of the state, the meanings of its history and traditions, and the implications of Hungary's 'return to Europe'. Politicians' stances on such issues are especially worthy of attention in Hungary because the country established from the outset of its democratic politics a relatively stable system of parliamentary and party government.

This essay examines the ways in which Hungary's national party-political elites have understood and argued about key aspects of the territorial-administrative reform process since 1990. The essay is based on the parliamentary debates on the five main relevant pieces of legislation: the 1990 and 1994 sub-national government reform packages, the 1996 Regional Development Law and its 1999 amendment, and the 1998 National Regional Development Concept.[1] The study falls into five sections. The first sketches the course of Hungary's sub-state reforms in their party-political context. The second, third and fourth discuss in turn the three main forms of political conflict evident in sub-state reform debates: between government and opposition; 'decentralizers' and 'centralizers'; and supporters and detractors of different territorial tiers – the local, the county and the region. A final section discusses the uses of 'Europe' in Hungary's sub-state reform debates.

POST-COMMUNIST SUB-STATE REFORM: AN OVERVIEW

As in other Central and East European states, communist Hungary's sub-state system replicated the Soviet model of fused legislative and executive councils (*tanács* in Hungarian), hierarchically organized and shadowed at all levels by party bodies; in Hungary, these tiers existed at local and county level. Transformation of this system has occurred in three waves: one under each post-communist government. The first, 1990, reform, under the right-wing government of the Hungarian Democratic Forum (MDF), Independent Smallholders' Party (FKGP) and Christian Democratic People's Party (KDNP), awarded a very high degree of self-governing autonomy to the local level (settlements and municipalities). However, the government also sought to retain directly elected government at the county level, and to introduce at that level a representative of the state, to be appointed by the president and endowed with the historical title of *fôispan*, to monitor the operations of sub-national governments. These plans for the county level were opposed by the opposition parties, the liberal Alliance of Free Democrats (SZDSZ) and Federation of Young Democrats (FIDESZ)[2] and the communist successor Hungarian Socialist Party (MSZP). In a compromise, county government was retained, but was to be only indirectly elected by local councils; and state monitoring was to be conducted not at county level but in new regions, by state officials taking the title of Commissioners of the Republic (for the 1990 reform, see Péteri, 1991; Horváth, 1991; Balázs, 1993; Davey, 1995).

By the time of the second post-communist parliamentary elections in 1994, the practical drawbacks of a weak meso level and large-scale local autonomy were widely acknowledged, as in other post-communist states which had decentralized strongly to the local level immediately after 1990. Across Hungary's political spectrum, strengthened county government was seen as one solution to the problem. After a sweeping Socialist election victory, the new MSZP-SZDSZ government restored the direct election of county government and enhanced its responsibilities, although not awarding it financial or legislative autonomy. The Commissioners were replaced with new public administration offices at county level (for the 1994 reform, see Verebélyi, 1993b; Ágh and Kurtán, 1996; Davey, 1996; Navracsics, 1996; Bende-Szabó, 1999; Temesi, 2000). The 1994 reform also foresaw the creation of county-level development councils; this was achieved by the 1996 Regional Development Law. However, the 1996 law also allowed counties to join together voluntarily to form development councils at regional level, although the definition of regional territories had to wait until the 1998 National Regional Development Concept. This designated seven regions by grouping counties together. The mandatory creation of development councils in these regions took place only in a third wave of reform, under the right-wing government of FIDESZ-MPP, the FKGP and the MDF which took office after the 1998 parliamentary elections. The 1999 amendment to the 1996 law also increased the weight of state and central government representatives in the new development councils (for the development of Hungary's regional policy structures, see Horváth, 1998, 1999a, 1999b; Committee of the Regions, 2000; Downes, 2000; Fowler, 2001). Discussion of a general regional tier has moved on to the mainstream political agenda largely in response to the 1999 legislation.

GOVERNMENT/OPPOSITION CONFLICT: THE COMMUNIST LEGACY

All stages of territorial-administrative reform since 1990 have seen parliamentary conflict between government and opposition. The 1990 reforms, which required a two-thirds majority and thus opposition support, were passed only under the pressure of a deadline set by the government in order to be able to hold sub-national elections in September/October that year. The 1994 reforms were passed only because the MSZP-SZDSZ government commanded the necessary two-thirds majority alone, with the opposition walking out of the parliamentary vote. More common ground was found regarding the 1996 Regional Development Law and 1998 National Regional Development Concept, although there was still some sharp debate. However, the 1999 amendment of the Regional Development Law, which like the 1990 and 1994 reforms involved the creation of highly contested mandatory institutions, again saw a sharp government/opposition divide.

This pattern of government/opposition conflict reflects the fact that Hungary has a form of 'normal' democratic politics, in which oppositions oppose, often taking up their positions quite opportunistically. The dominant form of opposition attack on the government, whatever the partisan make-up of the two sides, has been the accusation of centralization. In 1990, the MSZP and liberal opposition saw the retention of county government and the proposed creation of the *fôispán* as the main centralizing measures among the government's plans. In 1994, when the MSZP-SZDSZ government proposed that the Interior Minister appoint the heads of the new county-level public administration offices, the opposition in turn accused it of being centralizing. Debates on the new development councils since 1994 have seen both the MSZP-SZDSZ government and the subsequent right-wing administration accused of centralization, with reference to the county-based mode of regionalization and the inclusion of state and central government representatives in the councils.

The way in which the charge of centralism has been used in government/opposition conflict has been profoundly shaped by the communist experience. Owing to the highly centralized nature of the communist system, decentralization has been strongly associated with the whole notion of democratization and 'returning to Europe'. Already by 1989, there was agreement across the political spectrum that decentralization – establishing autonomous, democratic sub-national self-government – was fundamental to the change of political system. Reaction against communism was the prevailing spirit behind the 1990 debates and reforms, which not only produced a high degree of decentralization in institutional terms but also firmly established in the discursive realm the association between decentralization, autonomous sub-national government and the new post-communist democracy. In particular, a full and wholly revised constitutional chapter on sub-national government (Chapter IX) elevated territorial self-government at local and county level into a constitutional principle.

The mirror image of the link between decentralization and the new democracy has been the association of centralization primarily with communism. Measures perceived as centralizing have typically been more-or-less explicitly cast as 'communist' by their critics, highlighting the continuing power of communism and the *tanács* system as the main negative reference point in sub-state reform debates. This was especially evident in 1990, when the socialist-liberal opposition effectively accused the right-wing government of seeking to maintain elements of the communist system. However, both the MSZP-SZDSZ government's 1996 Regional Development Law and its right-wing successor's 1999 amendment were labelled by opposition politicians as a new 'law on soviets' ('*tanácstörvény*').[3] In these arguments, the 1990 reforms are seen as a benchmark for post-communist decentralization which needs to be defended, with measures seen as centralizing perceived as a threatening and retrograde step back towards communist practices.

The association between decentralization and the new post-communist democracy has had several consequences for the conduct of sub-state reform debates. First, given the consensus among Hungary's mainstream political elites in favour of democracy and against communism, the association instituted a bias in debates about sub-national reform in favour of decentralization and against centralization. The fact that all oppositions have attacked all governments for centralization testifies to the status of the idea of decentralization as a 'good' and centralization as a 'bad' in Hungary's post-communist public sphere. By definition, anything less than maximal decentralization thus becomes open to attack. Debates have typically been conducted along 'valence' lines (see Kitschelt, 1995), with parties competing to be seen as decentralizing, and most feeling a need to present their proposals in terms of the decentralizing principles laid down in 1990.

This pattern of argument has made it difficult to debate what might be a reasonable balance between centralization and decentralization, the central authorities and autonomous sub-national self-government, in a 'normalized' democratic Hungary, once the powerful decentralizing impulse of immediate post-communism had run its course (see also Gorzelak, 1992; Elander, 1997). Already in 1993, Interior Ministry official Imre Verebélyi, one of the architects of the 1990 reform, acknowledged that 'as a negation of the previous dictatorial system, it went too far in the correct direction' (Verebélyi, 1993a: 80). However, rowing back from the 1990 decentralization without being seen to abandon the 'correct direction' in favour of the 'previous dictatorial system' has presented political difficulties. Politically acceptable language with which to argue for some degree of recentralization is not readily available (such language as 'centralizers' have found is discussed in the next section). In Hungary in particular, many of the arguments used elsewhere in Central and Eastern Europe to justify centralizing practices – the demands posed by nation- and state-building, external threat or economic collapse – have not been available. In the debates on the 1996 Regional Development Law, despite Hungary's then-precarious economic balances, MSZP minister Ferenc Baja explicitly rejected economic difficulties as a justification for centralization (21 November 1995). Only the first set of sub-state reform debates, in 1990, found adherents of 'strong central power' arguing in terms of the needs of the country's 'transitional state', and supporters of state 'guardianship' over sub-national governments pointing to the weakness of post-communist civil society.[4]

Second, the tendency to debate territorial-administrative reforms in the large and emotive terms of 'democracy or communism?' has intensified political conflict. This has run directly counter to another implication of the association between decentralization and the new democratic state: the sense that sub-national reforms should enjoy a high degree of political consensus, to reflect the place of the sub-national sector among the foundational structures of the polity. The clearest expression of this idea is the requirement that legislation on sub-national government needs a two-thirds majority in parliament. The 'simple majority' character of the 1996–99 regional development legislation underlines the limited and purely functional nature of the development councils it created; but any move to create elected regional authorities will take the necessary legislation back into the sphere requiring a qualified majority.

Finally, the communist period continues to affect *which* institutional forms are seen as centralizing. 'The centre' is typically assumed to be potentially threatening to sub-national government, whether 'the centre' be the national government or organs of state. Moreover, the involvement of representatives of the state in the sub-national sector has consistently been understood as potentially partisan and likely to enhance the political position of the central government. For example, in 1994 the governing MSZP and SZDSZ stressed that the heads of the proposed new county public administration offices would be civil servants, whereas the Commissioners they would replace had enjoyed the rank of government state secretary. This, they argued, would make for a less politicized, more secure environment for sub-national governments. However, many opposition deputies saw the proposal as designed merely to allow the government to dismiss its predecessor's appointees, and not as achieving a depoliticization of the sub-state sector.

This continuing suspicion of 'the centre', among those not currently in control of it, as hostile and partisan towards sub-national governments, causes particular difficulties in the attempt to institute regional development bodies which conform to the EU model of 'partnership', between national authorities, sub-national government and the 'social partners'. The inclusion of state and central government representatives in the new development councils has been criticized on these grounds from the right under the MSZP-SZDSZ government and from the left-liberal camp under the post-1998 administration. In particular, in 1999, opposition parties claimed that what they perceived as the new regional tier's 'nationalization' (in the sense of state takeover) was designed to ensure government control over the disposition of EU funds, a control which they assumed would be used in partisan fashion (the term 'nationalization' was used by Tibor Kovács, MSZP, 15 June 1999). In short, a decade after the collapse of communism, and without minority ethnic or territorial identities driving sub-national politics, the relationship between 'the centre' and sub-national government is still often understood as inherently conflictual, while the notion of the neutral state seems not yet credible.

'DECENTRALIZERS' AND 'CENTRALIZERS': UNDERSTANDINGS OF THE STATE

Overlaying government/opposition conflict in sub-state reform debates since 1990 has been a less opportunistic, more ideologically driven division between 'decentralizing' liberal parties and a more 'centralizing' political right.[5] Liberals are typically supportive of maximal local government autonomy, while the right is attracted to a stronger central state presence. Right-wing politicians have made arguments in favour of decentralization, but often on functional or opportunistic grounds. For example, some on the right seemed to support local democracy in 1990 mainly as means of dislodging communist-era personnel. In 1994, some right-wing deputies argued for directly elected county government on the grounds that it would yield particular functional benefits, rather than a stronger general counterweight to the state centre. On the whole, the right has looked to the central state to provide order, efficiency and transparency, prevent corruption, and ensure greater socio-economic equality and uniformity of treatment across the country. Large-scale sub-national government autonomy is often suspected of encouraging public sector inefficiency and unreliability, corrupt local politics and the 'unfair' widening of socio-economic disparities (see also Elander, 1997). Many on the right would argue that such apprehensions have been borne out since 1990; but the fear of corrupt local 'fiefdoms' derived also from the incipient disintegration of the late communist era. Already in 1990, some right-wing deputies feared that awarding self-government to all Hungary's settlements would produce over 3,000 'mini-republics' and 'little kingdoms', which would 'throw the state into disorder and make government impossible'.[6] The MDF advocated a strengthening of the Commissioners' role in its 1994 parliamentary election programme (MDF, 1994: 61) and in parliament defended the role of figures able to 'enforce central ideas ... with respect to sub-national governments'.[7] Since the right returned to government in 1998, it has again warned that 'inasmuch as public administration does not work well and effectively, disintegrative processes start' (Stumpf, 1999a).

Indeed, since taking office, FIDESZ-MPP has developed an open critique of the sub-state system established in 1990, based on a particularly robust version of the (pre-devolution) Westminster 'winner-takes-all' conception of government. In this view, as the democratic expression of the popular will, the national administration has both the right and an obligation to ensure the implementation of its policies by all sub-national authorities. In the run-up to the 1998 sub-national elections, Prime Minister Viktor Orbán (1998) suggested that sub-national government should function ideally to further the political goals of its national counterpart. Moreover, this conception seems to blur the distinction between politically derived governmental authority and the state. István Stumpf, Minister in Charge of the Prime Minister's Office, speaks simply of 'the centre' or 'central power' and argues that, with the state now controlled by democratically elected authority, there is no need to see it as hostile to sub-national self-government. Indeed, Stumpf has suggested that the role of the centre can be to defend the interests of citizens even against their own territorial self-governments (Stumpf, 1999b, 2000: 258).[8] FIDESZ-MPP's approach is reflected in its ideas for Hungary's new regional tier. Regionalization is an integral part of the party's plans to achieve a more efficient public administration; on coming to office, it created a Secretariat for Public Administration and Regional Policy within the Prime Minister's Office, bringing the two fields together bureaucratically for the first time. However, the drive for efficiency and the primacy awarded to the state leads the party to conceive the new regional tier (at least initially) as an administrative, statist one, created via the gradual concentration of public administration functions in new regional centres (see Babus, 1998; Government of Hungary, 1999; Juhász, 1999; Népszabadság, 8 May 1999; Stumpf, 1999a; Mikes, 2000a). According to one FIDESZ-MPP deputy, 'it's completely natural that there can be state dominance at the regional level'.[9]

As well as a reaction to the post-communist experience, FIDESZ-MPP's sympathy for the idea of a strong central state reflects the attitude to Hungary's pre-communist past seen across the political right. The foundation of the Hungarian state by King Stephen at the turn of the eleventh century, a positive historical reference point especially important to the right, can be cast as a 'centralizing' move, since the monarch had to impose unitary authority over wayward tribal leaders and their territories. With the exception of the autonomy allowed to Croatia-Slavonia, the Hungarian state crafted after 1867 was also highly centralized. The then-dominant liberal-conservative politicians saw the development of a strong centrally directed administration as a key mechanism of Hungary's national and economic advancement. Highly centralized government continued during the inter-war regime of Miklós Horthy. As right-wing elites tend to see some valuable elements in the pre-1918 and even, sometimes, Horthy periods, they have mobilized pre-communist precedents in support of their ideas for the sub-national sector. The right's historical perspective on sub-state reform was expressed clearly by the MDF-led government's proposals to revive the originally medieval terms *vármegye* ('castle-county'), to replace the simple *megye*; and *fôispán*, a usage which would have cast the proposed post-communist state representatives as the latest incarnations of figures employed by the medieval, post-1867 and Horthy states (see also Ágh and Kurtán, 1996: 256–7).

For liberals, by contrast, the association of a centralized state with Hungary's pre-communist past provides an additional reason to pursue a more decentralized model. While liberals compete with the right to claim the legacy of the early nineteenth-century 'Reform Age' and 1848 Revolution, they typically see little for contemporary emulation in Hungary's subsequent history, with the exception of the short-lived 1946 constitution and 1956 Revolution. Rather, liberals tend to see the post-1989 period as an opportunity to break not only with communism but also with many elements of Hungary's earlier past. Thus in the 1990 sub-state reform debates (which took place against a background of wider government efforts to rehabilitate elements of the pre-communist past), the SZDSZ accused the right-wing administration of being 'stuck in the shackles of … Hungarian history 100 years ago'.[10]

However, liberals have also argued for a decentralized state in abstract, classical terms. In this view, organs of sub-national government are essential elements of a pluralistic state, acting as counterweights to the centre and enjoying legitimacy at least equal to it. Thus the SZDSZ argued in 1990 that the power to sanction sub-national governments should rest not with any central state representative but only with the courts; and that any state figure responsible for monitoring sub-national government activity should answer to parliament, not the national government. This kind of thinking also lay behind the liberals' conversion to the idea of directly elected county government by 1994; and the SZDSZ's call since 2000 for the immediate introduction of directly elected regional government, in opposition to FIDESZ-MPP's purely administrative regional tier (see SZDSZ, 2000: Section II, Paragraph 8; *Népszabadság*, 27 April and 3 May 2000). Both policies reflect a wish to push back an expanding state presence at the relevant territorial tier, and a belief that directly elected territorial self-government is a means of doing so.

Right-wing/liberal differences also rest on wider assumptions about the role of the state in economic and social processes. This was evident in the 1990 debates, when right-wing deputies suggested that the SZDSZ's exclusive trust in self-government was over-ambitious, given the weakness of civil society in immediate post-communism, while the SZDSZ argued that it was precisely the weakness of civil society that made the sustaining of an extensive central state dangerous. While the right tends to be sceptical about the likely results of autonomous action by sub-national governments, the SZDSZ has persistently assumed that such autonomous initiatives would produce the desired institutional and policy outcomes, and it has tended to attribute sub-national governments' failures to their inadequate autonomy, especially in financial terms. While the 1990 decentralization is by now seen by FIDESZ-MPP as due for some rollback, the problem for the SZDSZ is thus that its promise has never been fully realized.

The communist successor MSZP occupies an intermediate position between the right and the SZDSZ on sub-state issues. In much of its language, policy and criticism of right-wing governments, the MSZP has stood closer to the liberals. For example, the MSZP has, like the SZDSZ, come to support directly elected meso government, first at county and now regional level, as a counterweight to the central state. However, the MSZP and SZDSZ also have very different attitudes to the state, attitudes that have affected their approaches to sub-national reform. Owing to its past as the communist-era ruling party, the MSZP is at least comfortable with the exercise of state power, and less inclined than the SZDSZ to be suspicious of the state and its representatives *per se*. Such differences have been evident in SZDSZ and MSZP approaches to the creation of regional development bodies complying with the EU 'partnership' model. The SZDSZ recognizes a role for the state in regional development, but has been the least enthusiastic about this among the major parties, instead seeing greater potential in business sector involvement. Meanwhile, the MSZP has consistently stressed the need for state action and involvement in the regional development field, a stance which finds sympathy among elements of the right. The EU model of statutory regional development bodies, involving regularized consultation between representatives of the state, central government, sub-national governments and the 'social partners', and working on the basis of long-term development plans, fits best with the policy traditions of the MSZP among the main Hungarian parties. The content and tone of the 1996 Regional Development Law, which was drafted by an MSZP-led ministry, suggested a willingness to adopt the EU approach wholesale.

This 'European' model of governance in the regional development field, as instituted by the 1996 Regional Development Law, has provoked two forms of reaction from the right. First, FIDESZ-MPP rejected the new development councils as a form of (post-)communist corporatism. Its 1999 amendment of the 1996 law denied representatives of the economic chambers voting rights in the county-level development councils and excluded them altogether from their regional-level counterparts. Employees' and employers' representatives were also excluded from the county-level bodies.[11] Second, and more broadly, some on the right perceived the MSZP/EU approach as highly bureaucratic, '[bearing] witness to a very narrow, technocratic form of thinking, when they construct all sorts of procedures, this kind of council, that kind of council, some other kind of council, while the legislation does not reflect the real question that we ought to be talking about, that is, how this country can remain a liveable-in, friendly home for all of us'.[12] The 1996 Regional Development Law thus activated a rather different strand of right-wing thought that reacts *against* the modern state, with its bureaucratizing and homogenizing impact, and tendency to obliterate 'authentic', 'natural' and often particularistic identities, at sub-national as much as national level. This strand of thought underpins the free market element of the post-communist right, often at odds with the statist and paternalist elements.

This kind of difference between the post-communist MSZP and elements of the right has even been reflected in an undertone of tension over the terminology to be used as Hungary develops its new EU-compatible regional policy and institutions (see also Navracsics and Oláh, 1997: 149). The MSZP's apparent comfort with the foreign-derived words for 'partnership' (*partnerség*), 'programming' (*programozás*) and 'additionality' (*addíció*), and its preference for the Latin-based '*régió*' over the 'authentic' Hungarian '*táj*' or '*vidék*', aroused instinctive resistance from some on the right.[13]

TERRITORIAL TIERS: LOCAL, COUNTY, REGION

Ideological, historical and institutional factors have generated a further, partly independent, set of conflicts in Hungary's territorial-administrative reform debates, between supporters and opponents of different territorial-administrative tiers. Post-communist debates on the roles of such tiers have turned on the multiple associations of the counties. Most straightforwardly, the counties are associated with both 'communism' and 'centralization'. Unlike their counterparts in several other Central and East European states, Hungary's communist authorities preserved historic meso-level structures, in the shape of the counties, and absorbed them into the structures of the party-state (see Surazska *et al.*, 1997). There, they became the key sub-national channels of communist rule, with the county *tanács* and party secretary enjoying unrestricted authority over the emasculated local level, especially through their control over the distribution of funds. Many post-communist policy-makers therefore saw the counties as inherently opposed to autonomous local government. Indeed, the communist period contributed to the perception of any meso-level institution as a threat to the local tier.

The bias of post-communist debate against the communist period and in favour of decentralization thus disadvantaged the counties and worked in favour of the local tier. This was particularly evident in 1990, when the prevailing political atmosphere was strongly 'anti-county' and 'pro-local'. For example, the government felt obliged to argue for directly elected county government partly by claiming that this would give the local level better representation than under a purely administrative county tier. Nevertheless, the government was forced to concede on this issue, and on its plans to institute the *fôispan* at county level, in the face of the 'anti-county' stance of the opposition liberal parties and MSZP. Later debates about the make-up of development councils, at both county and regional level, have also been shaped by worries about their impact on local government autonomy. Before the 1996 Regional Development Law, parties across the political spectrum backed the creation of dedicated development councils – which would include local government representatives – as an alternative to the handing of regional development authority to the county governments, partly because the latter option was seen as potentially restoring the counties' communist-era hierarchy over the local level (for this debate, see Navracsics and Oláh, 1997: 134–5).

However, because the counties predate the communist period, they have an alternative set of associations, as authentic Hungarian 'national' structures, which can be mobilized by post-communist politicians. Counties were established by King Stephen as part of the foundation of the Hungarian state. For much of Hungary's subsequent history, they acted as loci and symbols of Hungarian national independence against autocratic foreign rule, becoming 'the most stubborn defenders of constitutionalism, self-government and national traditions', in the words of one prominent right-wing figure.[14] When the counties were abolished in Ottoman-controlled Hungary in the sixteenth century, they survived in independent Transylvania. Twice Austrian rulers tried and ultimately failed to abolish the counties, once in 1785 as Joseph II sought to reform the Empire on enlightened, universalist principles, and once in 1850 during the post-1848 reimposition of absolutism (for the history of Hungary's meso level, see Hajdú, 1991; Horváth, 1996: 27–9; Bende-Szabó, 1999). For those on the right who particularly cherish Hungary's pre-communist past, among the MDF, FKGP and Christian Democrats, the counties thus represent proud elements of Hungarian national identity and tradition, to be defended as such. 'The roots of the county are so deep that they cannot be ignored', declared one right-wing deputy in 1990.[15] Moreover, the counties' pre-communist past gives them 'decentralizing' as well as 'centralizing' associations. Albeit dominated by the often reactionary Hungarian nobility, the county assemblies were at least organs of self-government, and as such they resonate with that strand of right-wing thought which is sympathetic to institutions expressing particularistic community identity and autonomy against a uniform central state.

These contradictory aspects of the counties were already evident in the argument which took place in the early 1840s between the 'municipalists' and the 'centralists' among Hungary's liberal reformers. For the 'municipalists', such as the nationalist leader Lajos Kossuth, the counties had value as organs of communal self-government and as specifically Hungarian national institutions, and their reform should wait until Hungary had succeeded in its national struggle against Vienna. For the 'centralists', such as the liberal-national thinker and politician József Eötvös, the counties obstructed the development of the modern, centralized state administration and responsible national and municipal government which were by then characteristic of leading European states; as such, they were an obstacle to Hungary's further progress (for this debate, see Janos, 1982: 76–7; Bödy, 1985: 37–42; Agg, 1994; Schlett, 1999: 181–227). These contradictory associations of the counties were well illustrated by the fact that, in 1990, supporters of county government appealed both to Kossuth, to support the notion of the county as a bastion of democratic self-government[16]; and to Eötvös, when the aim was to legitimate a 'centralist' state conception (albeit with the strong counties Eötvös opposed).[17] Meanwhile, even the MSZP and the liberals have acknowledged that the counties can be 'decentralizing' institutions of self-government. As discussed above, these parties came to support directly elected county government by 1994 as they saw it as capable of countering the central state. However, the MSZP converted wholesale to a 'pro-county' position, apparently reverting to its communist-era traditions. By contrast, the liberals' support reflected a pragmatic prioritizing of the need to roll back the state over their more enduring distaste for the county tier, and they remained in principle 'anti-county' parties.

These multiple associations of the counties have generated complex party alignments since 1994 which do not dovetail either with the distinction between the SZDSZ on the one hand and the 'statist' right and MSZP on the other, or with the divide between left-liberal 'decentralizers' and right-wing 'centralizers'. The disjunction between the 'pro-county'/'anti-county' divide and the main left-liberal/right cleavage in Hungarian elite politics has left both post-1994 governments split between 'pro-' and 'anti-county' parties (see also Navracsics, 1999). The most straightforward position is that of the SZDSZ, which is an 'anti-county', 'pro-local' party, supporting maximal decentralization and rejecting both the communist and pre-communist pasts. The SZDSZ has been the most consistent follower of the idea that post-communist sub-state reform must be based on the local tier, persistently hoping to see both general and functional meso-level bodies – if they must exist at all – emerge from voluntary groupings of local governments. The 'pro-county' camp includes the communist successor MSZP, and the right-wing parties most inclined to defer to pre-communist historical precedent, the MDF, FKGP and Christian Democrats. However, the counties' dual identity as both 'national' and 'communist' creates potential for conflict within this 'pro-county' camp. Right-wing parties which are normally 'pro-county' can turn the principle of self-government by 'natural' communities against the counties and in favour of the local level when the counties are seen to appear in their centralist, (post-)communist incarnation. In this vein, the Catholic principle of subsidiarity, which privileges the lowest possible tier of authority and community, was invoked by right-wing deputies in the 1990 and 1994 debates before it later percolated more widely into Hungary's sub-state discourse via EU sources. For its part, FIDESZ-MPP's position in the 'pro-county'/'anti-county' argument is the anomaly: despite moving into the right-wing camp, the party adheres to its original 'anti-county' position. While this derives in part from anti-communism, by now it seems also to reflect an 'Eötvösian' view of the counties as obstacles to a rationalized, efficient public administration.

The final factor influencing the 'pro-county'/'anti-county' conflict is the partisan linkage between the county governments and the largest party in the national administration evident since the first direct county elections in 1994. After those polls, the MSZP, by then the dominant partner in the national government coalition, also became the largest party in all but one of the 19 county assemblies and held 14 of the county assembly

presidencies (Kurtán *et al.*, 1995: 451; *HVG*, 14 January 1995). Following
the 1998 sub-national elections, FIDESZ-MPP, now the major force in the
national government, held the same number of county presidencies, and
alone or in coalition was the largest party in 15 county assemblies (Kurtán
et al., 1999: 569; Temesi, 2000: 354–7; Interior Ministry). The replication
of national election results at county level gives a natural 'pro-county'
bias to the position of dominant national governing party, thus reinforcing
the perception of the counties as 'centralist'. The local level, however, has
been penetrated only weakly by the national parties, and parties other than
the main government force have much greater opportunity to achieve
office (for the 1990 local election results, see Szabó, 1991; Tóth, 1991;
Bôhm and Szoboszlai, 1992; for 1994, Kurtán *et al.*, 1995: 446–54; for
1998, Kurtán *et al.*, 1999: 563–70; Temesi, 2000: 354–7; Interior
Ministry). Thus, parties' positions in debates over county and local
government seem also to reflect their partisan interests. In backing direct
county elections in 1990, the MDF seemed to expect to repeat its national
victory, whereas a degree of right-wing diffidence when this proposal was
finally implemented by the MSZP in 1994 seemed to reflect expectations
of a repeat Socialist landslide at county level. Such expectations were in
turn presumably a factor in the MSZP's support for the change.
Meanwhile, support for the local level from the SZDSZ and FIDESZ-
MPP (in the latter case, until the party achieved dominance in the national
government) reflected the relative importance to these parties of their
positions in local government.

These patterns of support for and opposition to the local and county
tiers have shaped Hungary's effort to create entities larger than the
counties, to act as the NUTS II regions used in Eurostat statistics and as
the bases for the distribution of Objective 1 EU structural funds.
Potentially, regionalization could involve profound changes in Hungary's
territorial-administrative and political structures. The constitution
recognizes only counties, towns, villages and the capital, and the national
electoral system is tied to the counties. However, in the mid-1990s, the
general notion of creating regions in Hungary was relatively
uncontroversial among national political elites, for several reasons. The
prospect of receiving EU funds played the major role; but, amid much
post-Maastricht talk of a 'Europe of the regions', there was also a sense
among the national elite that regions were a 'European thing to have', a
quintessential feature of 'Europe' in the 1990s, and that having them
would thus boost Hungary's credentials as a modern European state. In
1994, when the KDNP switched to supporting the regional-level
Commissioners after the MSZP-SZDSZ government proposed their
abolition (see Navracsics, 1996: 291–2), one KDNP deputy clutched at

the idea that 'development in the whole of Europe is heading in the direction of regions' to legitimate the u-turn.[18] Later, a FIDESZ-MPP deputy similarly claimed that 'it's difficult to imagine accession to the Europe of the regions with Hungary's current administrative, statistical and other kinds of spatial structures'.[19] Regions were associated with policy goals accepted across the political spectrum – the reduction of inter-territorial socio-economic disparities, the attraction of international investment, and the encouragement of cross-border cooperation, especially with Hungarian-populated areas in neighbouring states.

Initially, these policy objectives were to be met by creating purely functional regional-level institutions, primarily to receive and administer EU structural funds and operating only in the regional development sphere. It is only since the 1999 legislation created mandatory regional development councils, and FIDESZ-MPP began to reveal its plans for the regional tier, that a political debate has got underway about a general regionalization. As noted above, this debate involves a conflict between 'self-governing' and 'administrative' regionalizations; the outcome of that clash will in part determine whether regionalization comes to be seen as a 'centralizing' or 'decentralizing' phenomenon. However, the most politically sensitive issue raised by regionalization, also still to be resolved, is whether regions should exist alongside the counties, or replace them. The 'anti-county' parties, FIDESZ-MPP and the SZDSZ, are also 'regionalizers', who see regions eventually replacing the counties. Although, as of late 2000, their ideas about the immediate nature of regional institutions differed significantly, both FIDESZ-MPP and the SZDSZ see them eventually becoming the upper level in a two-tier sub-national structure, with no counties and only the local level beneath them. 'Neither the country's size nor its resources would stand two meso-tiers, which are anyway unnecessary', according to one key FIDESZ-MPP official in the field (Mikes, 2000b). Meanwhile, 'pro-county' parties of both left and right wish to see any regionalization occur alongside the existing counties. The MSZP wishes to institute directly elected regional authorities on top of the existing directly elected county tier, with a division of responsibilities between them (MSZP, 2000: 52–3). The constraints represented by FIDESZ-MPP's 'pro-county' coalition partners, plus the party's own strong political position in the counties, are reflected in its reassurances that the counties are secure in the immediate future, and that any regionalization replacing them can be only a long-term prospect.

Alongside these questions about the institutional position of the new regional tier, regionalization debates since the mid-1990s have seen argument about how Hungary's new regions were to be delineated territorially. These arguments have elicited different notions of a region. While in some respects the lack of obvious historic regions in post-Trianon Hungary has made the definition of new territorial boundaries less politically controversial than in Poland, Slovakia or Ukraine, it nevertheless left space for much debate, with two possible procedures canvassed. The one implemented has been to constitute regions out of groups of counties, with the new regional boundaries following the existing outer borders of the counties involved. The main argument for county-based regionalization has been that it builds on existing administrative structures and is thus most likely speedily to fulfil the EU demand for 'strong' administrative capacity. '[The] really essential thing [about this kind of region] is that it ... means a checkable statistical and administrative system, bound to public administration', argued Etele Baráth, one of the main MSZP figures in the regional development field. 'Definition by the county borders is what will definitely produce conformity with the European statistical system' (4 March 1996).

However, the question of which groups of counties were to constitute the new regions remained to be resolved. Failure to reach consensus on this issue stymied the MSZP's hopes of designating NUTS II regions in the 1996 law; and the regional division eventually defined in the 1998 National Regional Development Concept remains contested in some respects. As of March 2001, the post-1998 administration seemed to have decided to leave the present division alone, partly to avoid fresh reorganization in the run-up to EU accession, and partly because no alternative is clearly preferable.[20] Argument in the 1998 and 1999 parliamentary debates concerned which counties 'go with' which others; and, relatedly, what size of region Hungary should create – the number of regions posited by various county-based conceptions canvassed over recent years ranges at least from three to eight (see Horváth, 1996: 27–9; *Magyar Hírlap*, 4 September 2000). Criticism of the seven regions defined in 1998, heard mainly from elements within the MSZP and MDF, principally reflects a sense that they are too small to fulfil what is seen as regions' proper role. The wish for strong cross-border cooperation has been a particular rationale for backing larger regions, with links to the former Hungarian territories especially important for some on the right. According to one MDF deputy, referring to two areas transferred in 1920, 'As a result of the Trianon peace treaty, the outskirts of the country were broken off. As a system of institutions, Euroregions are capable of fitting them back. But no one should labour under the naïve illusion that one could fit South Baranya or the Partium onto a current tiny Hungary region.'[21] To suggest historical roots for his proposed three-way regional division within Hungary, however, former MSZP premier Miklós Németh has had to return to the Roman period, suggesting that the two proposed regions outside the Budapest agglomeration might be called 'Hunnia' and 'Pannonia'.[22]

The major difficulty in designating county-based regions has been that the county boundaries often do not coincide with patterns of economic or social development, or with such meso-level identities as exist in Hungary. Although the institution of the county originates with the state itself, county borders have not been stable over time (not least, in the twentieth century, because the post-1920 international borders dissected the pre-1920 counties). The current county boundaries were defined only in 1950, in a rationalization implemented at the height of Hungarian Stalinism (Hajdú, 1991: 105–7; Hajdú, 2000: 99–103). Even elites from 'pro-county' parties recognize that 'some counties in Hungary are unfortunately not economic or geographical units, just administrative units. And if I build the region on a county or group of counties which in themselves are not economic or geographic units, then the region will not be an economic or geographic unit either.'[23]

Such considerations aroused concerns about the fate of local or sub-county areas which might feel cut off from their 'rightful' or 'natural' territorial linkages by the new regional boundaries. On this view, regionalization might threaten local government autonomy in a territorial, as well as institutional, sense. Whether regionalization would be seen as a centralizing phenomenon thus depended not only on the nature of the new regional institutions, but also on the manner in which regional boundaries were to be drawn. The larger the regions were, the fewer localities that were likely to feel themselves to be in the 'wrong' region, and the SZDSZ argued in 1995–96 that, if regionalization must be county-based, counties should be able to belong to more than one region. In 2000, the SZDSZ's Ferenc Wekler was still urging that regional borders be 'porous' until the pattern of development is clearer.[24] However, critics charged that this would produce 'ameboid' regions inadequate to the tasks of EU accession.[25]

To get around the problems posed by county-based regionalization, the governing SZDSZ and its fellow 'anti-county' party, the opposition FIDESZ-MPP, canvassed an entirely different, 'pro-local' regionalization concept in the debates of the mid-1990s.[26] The SZDSZ and FIDESZ-MPP sought a 'bottom-up', 'decentralized' mode of regional delineation, based on emerging voluntary groupings of local governments which often straddled county boundaries. For FIDESZ-MPP, István Balsay argued that associations between these groupings might in turn evolve into regions of the NUTS II scale, bypassing the counties and their borders. This 'bottom-up' regionalization conception appeared more in accord with the pro-local, pro-decentralization bias of post-communist debate than the county-based conception. It also suggested a notion of a region as an 'organic' rather than administrative entity, based on some 'natural' economic or social unity and expressing local community and interest. This notion of a region found sympathy across the political spectrum. In its stress on 'natural' territorial communities and voluntary local action, the 'organic' notion of a region has affinities with both liberal and right-wing thought. However, defining 'organic' regions in Hungary appears to have been seen as too complex and potentially threatening to the counties, and as likely to produce too weak an administrative capacity for EU purposes, for any government seriously to contemplate it.

'EUROPE': UBIQUITOUS BUT VACUOUS?

Amid these multiple conflicts, the appeal to 'Europe' has been one of the most persistent features of Hungary's sub-state reform debates. Sometimes, 'Europe' has featured as a specific institution. In 1990, Interior Minister Balázs Horváth commended the government's sub-national government bill (which referred to the Council of Europe's European Charter of Local Self-Government in its first sentence) partly in terms of its aiding Hungary's bid for Council membership, which was duly won four months later. In regional development policy, the EU has been the key reference point, with the 1996 Regional Development Law presented largely, and its 1999 amendment wholly, in terms of the needs of EU accession.[27] At least as pervasive, however, have been appeals to notions of 'Europe' or 'Europeanness' not tied to any specific 'European' institution. The most striking feature of the use of 'Europe' in Hungary's sub-state reform debates has been that, at each stage in the process and across all three of the conflicts discussed in this essay, both sides in any particular argument have appealed to it. Parties have typically claimed in some way that their position was 'European', while that of their opponents was 'non-' or 'anti-European'.

For example, 'centralizers' have pointed to a number of European countries in justifying central state influence in the sub-national sector, only to be greeted with the riposte that maximal autonomy for sub-national government is the truly 'European' position. In 1990, when the opposition rejected directly elected county government, the administration claimed that a tier of government between the local and the national was a 'European' norm; when the MSZP and SZDSZ in turn proposed directly elected county government in 1994, they appealed to the European Charter of Local Self-Government to support their position. Parties engaging in this kind of argument have included right-wing parties which stress that their preferences, such as that for county government, are in line with Hungarian national traditions; such parties have not seen this as excluding 'Europeanness', instead claiming coincidence between the two. Thus, in Hungary's debates, 'Europeanness' functions as a 'valence' issue, with all mainstream parties keen to be seen as 'European' and assuming that accusations of 'non-' or 'anti-Europeanness' will weigh against their opponents. In this respect, the idea of 'Europe' is similar to 'not-communist' or, in the specific case of sub-state reform, 'decentralization' or 'self-government', in being seen as a post-communist 'good'. This usage of 'Europe' reflects the understanding among Hungarian political elites of the rejection of communism as synonymous with the 'return to Europe', and their far-reaching consensus in support of both.

It is the indeterminacy of 'Europeanness' that has allowed it to be mobilized by all sides in the debates. The range of 'European' models is large, and merely wishing to conform with 'European norms' is little help in selecting detailed options for the sub-state sector. As noted above, the move towards having regions of some sort was triggered largely by 'European' considerations, but these leave plenty of scope for argument – in 'European' terms – about how, where and on what scale regions should be created, the nature of their institutions and their relationship to other tiers of authority. Advocates of county-based regionalization claimed that it fulfilled the 'European' demand for administrative capacity; but for its critics, the regions it created 'did not mean that real economic unit which is generally meant by a region at the European level'.[28] Critics charged the 1999 amendment of the Regional Development Law with violating EU principles of subsidiarity and partnership; but the government claimed to be acting solely in line with EU demands for a 'strengthening' of the regional tier (see European Commission, 1998: 27, 35–6). In turn, advocates of directly elected regional government against FIDESZ-MPP's administrative regionalism also appeal to 'Europe', especially in the shape of the Council of Europe's draft European Charter of Regional Self-Government (SZDSZ, 2000: Section II, Paragraph 8).

The indeterminacy of the idea of 'Europe' reflects the nature of the policy area for 'actually existing', institutional Europe, especially in the form of the EU. Union law does not prescribe uniform regional development institutions, and does not extend into the general sub-national sector at all. This was utilized by a FIDESZ-MPP deputy defending the 1999 changes to the regional tier, who urged his colleagues not to 'kid [themselves] that in the European Union some kind of subsidiarity in this respect is an expectation!'[29] 'As regards the institutional system for regional development, there aren't any norms in the EU to which we have clearly to adjust ...[EU pressure] primarily means that we have to create an effective system of institutions, which guarantees the Union the effective use of the funds it sends'.[30] FIDESZ-MPP deputies cited Portugal, Ireland and the UK to support their view that the EU does not regard a state-dominated regional tier as disbarring a country from the receipt and successful use of structural funds.

Where 'being European' is not formally associated with detailed legal requirements, and a huge variety of institutional arrangements is found among European states, political actors in Hungary have thus sought to 'domesticate Europeanness', trying to marshal 'European' support for widely varying preferences determined on other grounds. This seems to raise two potential difficulties for the EU in particular. First, as in the case of subsidiarity/partnership versus 'strengthening' at the regional level, EU language can be used to support diametrically opposed policy positions. Although 'Brussels' may be sending mixed messages, this also raises the possibility that messages that are not mixed in Brussels might be capable of becoming so in Budapest – in other words, that local understandings change original meanings. Subsidiarity and partnership might not be seen by some EU actors as inimical to the development of a strong regional tier; but for those politicians in the post-communist environment who tend to see autonomous sub-national government and civil society involvement as a recipe for inefficiency, political conflict and the dubious use of public funds, 'strengthening' the regional tier is likely to be interpreted as meaning more central state control.

Second, the EU has not enjoyed a monopoly over 'Europeanness' in the Hungarian debates, being instead only one among several 'European' references. If, as is claimed in one recent study (Hughes et al., 2001; see also Brusis, 1999; Committee of the Regions, 2000: 34), the European Commission is attempting to 'export' to Central and Eastern Europe, through means other than the formal requirements of EU law, a more homogeneous model of regional governance than is found among existing EU members, this raises the prospect of a 'legitimacy gap', through which Hungarian politicians can point to 'European' examples which do not conform to the Commission's 'European' model. Whatever the institutional outcomes directly traceable to EU involvement in the sub-national sector in candidate states, it will be difficult for the Union to claim that they represent the only possible 'European' outcome.

CONCLUSION

Even without the complications of new statehood or historic or ethnic regions, territorial-administrative reform in post-communist Hungary has generated a rich set of debates and political conflicts about ways of arranging the state. Three features of these stand out. First is the continuing importance of the communist period, in shaping interpretations, institutional preferences and political rhetoric. Second, political stances and language now also draw on a decade of post-communist institutional change and experiment (see also Horváth, 2000: 25–6). Much of the Hungarian debate since 1990 has concerned what to do with the legacy not of communism but of the 1990 reforms. Future debate on the regional tier will be shaped by the experiment with the Commissioners in 1990–94 and by the fact that one tier of directly elected meso-level authority, the county, has already been reconstituted in the post-communist period. The third point is the malleability of the ideologies, concepts and historical/institutional associations involved in Hungary's sub-state reform debates. This has allowed parties to 'mix and match' elements to support their particular policy preferences at any point. Among parties' broad political positions, for example, the MSZP's post-communism can back 'decentralizing' self-government but also remains statist in some respects; the right has its own centralist, statist traditions existing alongside an anti-statist strand sympathetic to particularistic community identities, self-government and territorial autonomy. Inasmuch as territorial self-government is seen as a vehicle for the identity and interests of a specific community, it is a principle of the right; but when it is seen as an institutional bulwark against the ambitions of an overweening central state, it has been associated with the liberals. Both left-liberal and right-wing principles of self-government can be realized in either the local level or the county, depending in part on whether the county is in turn seen in its 'communist' or 'national', 'statist' or 'self-governing' guise. Understandings of the county in turn shape responses to the idea of regions, which can also be either administrative or 'organic'. Finally, as we have seen, any of these positions can be cast as 'European'.

ACKNOWLEDGEMENTS

For their help in providing materials drawn on in this article, the author would like to thank András Csite, Barbara Kiss, Gábor Török and Ágota Scharle; Nigel Hardware in the European Resource Centre, University of Birmingham; and interviewees in Budapest in June 2000. Thanks are also due to Judy Batt and Kataryna Wolczuk for commenting on earlier drafts. The final draft was completed in March 2001.

NOTES

1. For the 1990–94 parliament, the debates were read in the hard copy transcript, *Az Országgyûlés ülése*. Transcripts for the 1994–98 and post-1998 parliaments were accessed via the parliamentary website, at www.mkogy.hu. This was also the source for laws and

parliamentary resolutions, and for the post-1994 parliaments, bills and amendments. Quotations or citations in the text followed only by a date in brackets refer to plenary parliamentary sessions. All translations are the author's.

2. In 1995, this party changed its name to FIDESZ-Hungarian Civic Party (FIDESZ-MPP). For simplicity, the party's post-1995 name is used throughout the rest of this essay.
3. István Balsay, FIDESZ-MPP, 12 December 1995; József Torgyán, FKGP, 18 December 1995; Gábor Demszky, SZDSZ Mayor of Budapest, quoted in Mink, 1999.
4. Béla Mizsei, FKGP, 9 July 1990; Sándor Kávássy, FKGP, 16 July 1990.
5. For the purposes of territorial-administrative reform, FIDESZ-MPP is counted as a liberal party until its accession to government in 1998, and thereafter as being on the right. As will become clear in the next section, the right is by no means homogeneous on issues relevant to sub-state reform; this section concentrates on features generalizable across the right.
6. Ferenc Grezsa, MDF, and Sándor Kávássy, FKGP, 16 July 1990; József Baka, MDF, 23 July 1990.
7. Imre Konya, 28 September 1994.
8. Stumpf's comments on the 'over-realization' of the principle of subsidiarity, to the detriment of that of efficiency, echo exactly a passage in the MSZP-SZDSZ government's 1996 public administration reform programme (Prime Minister's Office, 1996). However, as well as a strengthening of state administration, the MSZP-SZDSZ government's plans involved a strengthening of self-government, at the county level, and suggested a lesser suspicion of territorial self-government per se.
9. János Hargitai, 15 June 1999.
10. Ferenc Wekler, 2 July 1990.
11. The government's approach to 'social dialogue' has aroused EU concern, and there are some indications that the exclusion of the economic chambers, at least, might be reversed. See European Commission, 2000: 19, 52–3; Népszabadság, 20 December 2000.
12. Nándor Rott, KDNP, 18 December 1995.
13. For example, a KDNP deputy sought to have the title of the 1996 legislation refer to 'regional development' not as területfejlesztés, which literally means simply 'spatial development', but as vidékfejlesztés, which has the connotation of referring specifically to rural areas. The MSZP minister, Ferenc Baja, responded that he would rather the title of the law referred to 'regional policy', using the straightforward translation regionális politika; 12 December 1995. For some on the right, the fact that the new development councils were to be called tanács, the same word as had been used for 'soviet', appeared a particularly unfortunate but indicative throwback. However, an attempt by one FKGP deputy to have the bodies renamed 'committees' prompted only a debate about which word, 'council' or 'committee', was more polluted by communist-era associations.
14. Sándor Lezsák, MDF, 8 December 1999.
15. Sándor Kávássy, FKGP, 16 July.
16. Miklós Réti, MDF, 16 July; György Szabad, MDF, 23 July.
17. Sándor Kávássy, FKGP, 16 July.
18. Tamás Ispey, 21 September.
19. István Balsay, 23 February 1998.
20. Magyar Hírlap, 4 September 2000 and 23 December 2000. The main open question is the fate of Central Hungary region, which in its original form could fall outside eligibility for Objective 1 funding by the time that Hungary joins the EU.
21. Balázs Horváth, 15 June 1999.
22. Magyar Hírlap, 12 December 2000.
23. Balázs Varga Bernáth, FKGP, 5 February 1996.
24. Népszabadság, 3 May 2000.
25. László Egerszegi, MSZP, 18 December 1995.
26. It is worth noting that the main parliamentarians pressing this approach, Ferenc Wekler for SZDSZ and István Balsay for FIDESZ-MPP, both had experience of the communist sub-state system as members of their respective local tanács in the last years of communist rule. Moreover, in 1990–94 Wekler was a local councillor, and Balsay mayor of the town of Székesfehérvár.

27. Ferenc Baja, MSZP, 12 March 1996; József Torgyán, FKGP, 15 June 1999.
28. Balázs Varga Bernáth, FKGP, 5 February 1999.
29. János Hargitai, 15 June 1999.
30. János Hargitai, 22 June 1999.

REFERENCES

Agg, Zoltán (1994), 'Eötvös József és a megyerendszer', *Comitatus*, June.
Ágh, Attila and Sándor Kurtán (1996), '"Parliaments" and "Organized Interests" in Civil Society: Local Government Legislation and Elections in Hungary (1990–1995)', in Attila Ágh and Gabriella Ilonszki (eds), *Parliaments and Organized Interests: The Second Steps*. Budapest: Hungarian Centre for Democracy Studies.
Babus, Endre (1998), 'Régiók Magyarországon', *HVG*, 26 December.
Balázs, István (1993), 'The Transformation of Hungarian Public Administration', *Public Administration*, Vol.71, No.2, pp.75–88.
Bende-Szabó, Gábor (1999), 'The intermediate administrative level in Hungary', in Martin Brusis and Eric von Breska (eds), *Central and Eastern Europe on the way into the European Union: Reforms of regional administration in Bulgaria, the Czech Republic, Estonia, Hungary, Poland and Slovakia*. Center for Applied Policy Research Working Paper. Geschwister-Scholl-Institute for Political Science, University of Munich.
Bödy, Paul (1985), *Joseph Eötvös and the Modernization of Hungary, 1840–1870*. Boulder, CO: East European Monographs.
Bôhn, Antal and György Szoboszlai (eds) (1992), *Önkormányzati Választások 1990*. Budapest: Magyar Tudományos Akadémia Politikai Tudományok Intézete.
Brusis, Martin (1999), 'Recreating the Regional Level in Central and Eastern Europe: Lessons from Administrative Reforms in Six Countries', in Martin Brusis and Eric von Breska (eds), *Central and Eastern Europe on the way into the European Union: Reforms of regional administration in Bulgaria, the Czech Republic, Estonia, Hungary, Poland and Slovakia*. Center for Applied Policy Research Working Paper. Geschwister-Scholl-Institute for Political Science, University of Munich.
Committee of the Regions (2000), *Preparing for EU enlargement: Devolution in the First Wave Candidate Countries*. COR-studies E-4/99. Luxembourg: Office for Official Publications of the European Communities.
Coulson, Andrew (1995), 'From Democratic Centralism to Local Democracy', in Andrew Coulson (ed.), *Local Government in Eastern Europe*. Aldershot: Edward Elgar.
Davey, Kenneth (1995), 'Local Government in Hungary', in Andrew Coulson (ed.), *Local Government in Eastern Europe*. Aldershot: Edward Elgar.
Davey, Kenneth (1996), 'Hungary: Into the Second Reform Cycle', in John Gibson and Philip Hanson (eds), *Transformation from Below*. Cheltenham: Edward Elgar.
Downes, Ruth (2000), 'Regional Policy Evolution in Hungary', in John Bachtler *et al.* (eds), *Transition, Cohesion and Regional Policy in Central and Eastern Europe*. Aldershot: Ashgate.
Elander, I. (1997), 'Between Centralism and Localism: On the Development of Local Self-government in Postsocialist Europe', *Environment and Planning C: Government and Policy*, Vol.15, No.2, pp.143–59.
European Commission (1998), *Regular Report from the Commission on Hungary's Progress Towards Accession*, via www.europa.eu.int/comm/enlargement/index.htm.
European Commission (2000), *Regular Report from the Commission on Hungary's Progress Towards Accession*, via www.europa.eu.int/comm/enlargement/index.htm.
Fowler, Brigid (2001), *Debating Sub-state Reform on Hungary's 'Road to Europe'*. One Europe or Several? Working Paper 21/01. Brighton: Sussex European Institute, University of Sussex.
Gibson, John and Philip Hanson (1996), 'Decentralization and Change in Post-communist Countries', in John Gibson and Philip Hanson (eds), *Transformation from Below*. Cheltenham: Edward Elgar.
Gorzelak, Grzegorz (1992), 'The Myths of Local Self-government and Administration', in Petr

Dostál *et al.* (eds.), *Changing Territorial Administration in Czechoslovakia: International Viewpoints*. Amsterdam: Instituut voor Sociale Geografie, Faculteit Ruimtelijke Wetenschappen, Universiteit van Amsterdam.

Government of Hungary (1999), Government Resolution 1052/1999, 'A közigazgatás továbbfejlesztésének 1999–2000. évekre szóló kormányzati feladattervéről', *Magyar Közlöny*, No.44, 21 May.

Hajdú, Zoltán (1991), 'Territorial-administrative Reforms in Hungary', in Gyula Horváth (ed.), *Regional Policy and Local Governments*. Pécs, Hungary: Centre for Regional Studies of the Hungarian Academy of Sciences.

Hajdú, Zoltán (2000), 'A magyar közigazgatási régiók tértörténeti problematikája', in Ferenc Glatz (ed.), *Területfejlesztés és közigazgatás-szervezés (Megye, régió, kistérség)*. Budapest: Magyar Tudományos Akadémia.

Horváth, Gyula (1996), *Transition and Regionalism in East-Central Europe*. Europäisches Zentrum für Föderalismus-Forschung Occasional Papers No. 7. Tübingen: Europäisches Zentrum für Föderalismus-Forschung.

Horváth, Gyula (1998), *Regional and Cohesion Policy in Hungary*. Centre for Regional Studies of the Hungarian Academy of Sciences Discussion Paper No.23. Pécs, Hungary: Centre for Regional Studies of the Hungarian Academy of Sciences.

Horváth, Gyula (1999a), 'Changing Hungarian Regional Policy and Accession to the European Union', *European Urban and Regional Studies*, Vol.6, No.2, pp.166–77.

Horváth, Gyula (1999b) 'European Access and Changing Hungarian Regional Policy', in Annamária Duró (ed.), *Spatial Research in Support of the European Integration*. Centre for Regional Studies of the Hungarian Academy of Sciences Special Discussion Paper. Pécs, Hungary: Centre for Regional Studies of the Hungarian Academy of Sciences.

Horváth, Tamás M. (1991), 'The Structure of the Hungarian Local Government (Past and Present)', in Klára Takács (ed.), *The Reform of Hungarian Public Administration*. Budapest: Hungarian Institute of Public Administration.

Horváth, Tamás M. (2000), 'Directions and Differences of Local Changes', in Tamás M. Horváth (ed.), *Decentralization: Experiments and Reforms*. Budapest: Local Government and Public Service Reform Initiative.

Hughes, James *et al.* (2001), 'Enlargement and Regionalisation: the Europeanisation of Local and Regional Governance in CEE States', in Helen Wallace (ed.), *Interlocking Dimensions of European Integration*. Basingstoke: Palgrave.

Illner, Michal (1998), 'Territorial Decentralization: An Obstacle to Democratic Reform in Central and Eastern Europe?', in Jonathan Kimball (ed.), *The Transfer of Power: Decentralization in Central and Eastern Europe*. Budapest: Local Government and Public Service Reform Initiative.

Interior Ministry, Central Data Processing, Registration and Election Office, at www.valasztas.hu

Janos, Andrew (1982), *The Politics of Backwardness in Hungary 1825–1945*. Princeton, NJ: Princeton University Press.

Juhász, Gábor (1999), 'Közigazgatás-átszervezés régióvitákkal', *HVG*, 22 May.

Kitschelt, Herbert (1995), *Party Systems in East Central Europe: Consolidation or Fluidity?* Studies in Public Policy No.241. Glasgow: Centre for the Study of Public Policy, University of Strathclyde.

Kurtán, Sándor *et al.* (eds) (1995), *Magyarország politikai évkönye 1995*. Budapest: Demokrácia Kutatások Magyar Központja Alapítvány.

Kurtán, Sándor *et al.* (eds) (1999), *Magyarország politikai évkönye 1998-ról*. Budapest: Demokrácia Kutatások Magyar Központja Alapítvány.

MDF (1994), *Biztos Lépések, Nyugodt Jövô! Magyar Demokrata Fórum Program 1994*. Budapest.

Mikes, Éva (2000a), Speech to a conference of the Network of Institutes and Schools of Public Administration in Central and Eastern Europe, 13 April, available via the website of the Prime Minister's Office, at www.kancellaria.gov.hu.

Mikes, Éva (2000b), Speech to Somogy county notaries, 11 November, as reported on the website of the Prime Minister's Office, at www.kancellaria.gov.hu.

Mink, Mária (1999), 'Módosuló területfejlesztési törvény', *HVG*, 5 June.

MSZP (2000), *Magyarország Mindannyiunké! Az Esélyegyenlôség Programja*, via www.mszp. hu.

Navracsics, Tibor (1996), 'Public Sector Reform in Hungary: Changes in Intergovernmental Relations (1990–1995)', in Attila Ágh and Gabriella Ilonszki (eds), *Parliaments and Organized Interests: The Second Steps*. Budapest: Hungarian Centre for Democracy Studies.

Navracsics, Tibor and Miklós Oláh (1997), 'A parlamenti pártok és a területi politika', in *Parlamenti pártok és szakpolitikák 1994–1997*. Budapest: Magyar Politikai Intézet.

Navracsics, Tibor (1999), 'Az országos területfejlesztési koncepció országgyûlési vitája', in András Lánczi (ed.), *Parlamenti pártok es törvényhozás 1997–1998*. Budapest: Magyar Politikai Intézet.

Orbán, Viktor (1998), Speeches on 26 September (to FIDESZ-MPP mayors, Budapest) and 27 September (to the organization Hungarian Civic Cooperation), as reported on the government website, at www.meh.hu/defhu.htm.

Péteri, Gábor (1991), 'Changes of Concepts: Legislation on Local Governments 1987–1990', in Klára Takács (ed.), *The Reform of Hungarian Public Administration*. Budapest: Hungarian Institute of Public Administration.

Prime Minister's Office (1996), *A közigazgatás reformjának programja*, Section 13.

Schlett, István (1999), *A magyar politikai gondolkodás története*. II/1 kötet. Budapest: Korona Kiadó.

Stumpf, István (1999a), Speech to public notaries, Siófok, 23 September 1999, available via the website of the Prime Minister's Office, at www.kancellaria.gov.hu.

Stumpf, István (1999b), Speech to the National Self-government Conference, 8 October 1999, available via the website of the Prime Minister's Office, at www.kancellaria.gov.hu.

Stumpf, István (2000), 'Az önkormányzatiság egy évtizede és a jövô', *Magyar Közigazgatás*, Vol.50, No.5, pp.257–9.

Surazska, Wisla *et al.* (1997), 'Towards regional government in Central Europe: territorial restructuring of postcommunist regimes', *Environment and Planning C: Government and Policy*, Vol.15, No.4, pp.437–62.

Szabó, Gábor (1991), 'Local Elections in Hungary 1990: Some Facts and Consequences Based on Statistical Data', in Klára Takács (ed.), *The Reform of Hungarian Public Administration*. Budapest: Hungarian Institute of Public Administration.

SZDSZ (2000), *A Korszakváltás Programja*, via www.szdsz.hu

Temesi, István (2000), 'Local Government in Hungary', in Tamás M. Horváth (ed.), *Decentralization: Experiments and Reforms*. Budapest: Local Government and Public Service Reform Initiative.

Tóth, Zoltán (1991), 'Önkormányzati választások 1990', in Sándor Kurtán *et al.* (eds), *Magyarország politikai évkönye 1991*. Budapest: Ökonómia Alapítvány – Economix.

Verebélyi, Imre (1993a), 'A magyar közigazgatás modernizációja', in Sándor Kurtán *et al.* (eds), *Magyarország politikai évkönye 1993*. Budapest: Demokrácia Kutatások Magyar Központja Alapítvány.

Verebélyi, Imre (1993b), 'Options for Administrative Reform in Hungary', *Public Administration*, Vol.71, No.2, pp.105–20.

Slovakia:
An Anthropological Perspective
on Regional Reform

ALEXANDRA BITUŠÍKOVÁ

The Slovak Republic is a new state that came into existence on 1 January 1993, as a result of agreement between the parliaments and governments of the Czech and the Slovak Republics to dismantle the Czecho-Slovak Federal Republic. For the first time in their history, the Slovaks have their own state (with the exception of the short period of the Nazi-sponsored Slovak Republic in 1939–45). For almost 1,000 years Slovakia was part of the multi-ethnic Hungarian Kingdom, known as 'Upper Hungary'. From 1918 to 1992 (excepting the 1939–45 period), it was a part of Czechoslovakia. After the 'Velvet Revolution' in Czechoslovakia in November 1989 and the 'Velvet Divorce' of 1993, enormous transformations in political, economic, social and cultural development took place. With the break-up of the common state, democratization in Slovakia has been accompanied by two rather conflicting challenges: on the one hand, the formation of a new, independent state, and on the other, 'returning to Europe'. Each has its own emphasis, but they revolve around a common set of goals: to redefine the place and interrelationship of the state and nation, and to redefine people's identities, which were suppressed and distorted over the past fifty years. Struggling for national identity, while at the same time seeking to 'return to Europe' places the state, especially in terms of its 'national' identity, at the heart of process of redefining identities. For Slovakia (as for Ukraine: see Wolczuk's contribution), the task was to establish the new state, with its new institutions and national symbols (flag and emblem), and to implement the new political rules governing its functioning. It also meant coming to terms with the fact that the Slovak majority had to coexist in the new state with significant ethnic minorities. Moreover, the Slovaks had rather limited political experience, in contrast to the Czechs, who inherited a fully functioning state, with the institutions and political know-how of the former Czechoslovakia (Szomolányi and Gould, 1997).

The Slovak Republic is among the smallest European states in terms of area and number of inhabitants. It has roughly the same area as Austria or Hungary, and a population of 5.3 million. Despite its small size, the country shows deep regional, ethnic, religious, economic, social and cultural differentiation. By ethnicity, about 85 per cent of the inhabitants declare themselves Slovak, and 11 per cent Hungarian. Other minority groups include Czechs (1.1 per cent), Rusyns/Ukrainians (among whom there are the same disagreements over identity as found in Transcarpathia: see Batt's contribution) account for 0.6 per cent, and Germans for 0.1 per cent. The Roma, according to the last census in 1991, account for 1.6 per cent of the total, but more reliable unofficial estimates indicate that the real number of Roma in Slovakia could be between 400,000 and 600,000, or 7–11 per cent of the total population. A significant part of them, however, for various reasons declare either Slovak or Hungarian nationality. By religion, 69 per cent of the inhabitants are Catholic and 10 per cent Protestant (including Evangelical, Lutheran and other denominations). Smaller minorities of Greek Catholics (Uniates), Orthodox and Jews are also present.

REGIONAL DIFFERENCES: THE LEGACY OF SOCIO-ECONOMIC BACKWARDNESS

Slovakia has among the biggest regional differences to be found in any of the Central European countries. These result from its historical, political, social and cultural development in Central Europe, on the border between West and East. Regionalism and localism have always had strong roots in Slovakia, and persist up to the present. One of the reasons for this is the fact that until the 1950s, Slovakia was a pre-industrial country with a traditional social structure and rural way of life. Industrialization and urbanization began about 50 years later than in the more westerly European countries. In spite of the urbanization and modernization that took place in the second half of the twentieth century, there are still large numbers of villages and small towns in Slovakia. The share of the urban population (defined as inhabitants of towns with a population of over 5,000)1 is 56 per cent, by comparison with the European average of over 80 per cent (Gajdoš and Pašiak, 1995; Slovensko-Ľud, 1974: 522–3). Living in small villages and towns means a different lifestyle, a different way of thinking, acting and communicating, different values and norms. Although most of the Slovak countryside is still culturally rural, the development of the regions is uneven. There are wide differences between regions along several divisions: east to west, mountainous and lowland areas, urban and rural areas, and areas with diverse religious and ethnic composition.

The traditional conservatism of the majority rural peasant society accounts for the aversion to change and to modernizing reforms that is characteristic of Slovak society as a whole. The system of traditional values, norms, customs and rituals established over centuries has strongly influenced the mentality of the people. Peasants have always had to rely on their own labour and self-sufficiency; and external conditions, especially natural conditions, have differed from one region to another. In mountainous regions, where life was harder than in the lowlands, solidarity within the local society, mutual assistance among neighbours and family, and low social differentiation were characteristic. This contributed to the feeling of equality, and to egalitarian attitudes. Poverty was considered normal and natural, while wealth was regarded with suspicion, even as immoral and dishonest. These negative attitudes towards wealth and wealthy people, and envy of them, have remained visible up to now. Private shopkeepers, doctors, entrepreneurs, and so on are less readily accepted in the mountainous and marginal regions than in the south-western regions of Slovakia. This attitude was reinforced by the ideology of the former communist regime, which propagated the image of the 'capitalist enemy', the private entrepreneur and businessman who exploit their employees.

In the lowland parts of southern and western Slovakia, natural conditions have always been better, social differentiation deeper, the tendency to egalitarianism less strong, with fewer social constraints on the display of wealth and social status. The people living here were used to trading the products of their gardens and fields, and regularly visited markets and fairs far away from their homes – in Bohemia-Moravia, Austria and Hungary. Trading in various products fostered better organizational abilities, an economic and entrepreneurial spirit, and an energetic inventiveness that are very useful in the current period of economic transition. When compared with the inhabitants of the poorer mountainous regions, the attitudes and life-strategies of lowlanders seem more active and adaptable to the new conditions of the market economy. In addition, their economic starting-point has been more favourable (Feglová, 1996).

Life-strategies in marginal regions and regions with high levels of religiosity tend to be passive, negative and submissive as a result of long years of submission to political and clerical power, bureaucracy, higher social strata or the Christian obligation to accept what was given by God. However, submission, relying on state protection and superior authorities to resolve all problems is evident in the current situation throughout Slovakia in a period when people have lost their social certainties and their economic situation has deteriorated.

Ethnic and religious differentiation among the population of Slovakia has also had a significant impact on the transition. Ethnic differentiation is most marked between the Slovaks and the Hungarians, who are the biggest minority in Slovakia according to the last census. In popular

Slovak stereotypes, the Hungarians are considered superior, high-handed, megalomaniac, proud, successful and immodest. Comparing themselves with Hungarians, the Slovaks see themselves as modest, lacking independence and self-confidence, passive and conservative. Strong negative stereotypes towards the Hungarians, Jews and Roma/Gypsies are accompanied by a more general insecurity and xenophobic fear of any 'others' in Slovak society.

Religious differentiation is most visible between the Catholics and the Protestants. The Protestants display tendencies and, at the same time, tolerance, of difference; higher ambitions and a positive approach to education. The Catholics are more conservative and traditional, passive, modest, lacking in self-esteem, mistrustful of change, and submissive. They display a tendency to strong family and neighbourhood solidarity and cooperation, and are less tolerant towards other groups. The Calvinists of southern Slovakia, who belong mostly to the Hungarian minority, present specific features, including a high level of ethnic and religious endogamy, elitism and a sense of exceptionality (Feglová, 1996).

All these regional differences – the result of discontinuous historical development in a geographically varied and, until recently, poorly integrated country – have their impact on the current transformation and modernization processes. Various administrative reforms have also had a significant impact on the fixation of these regional differences.

INSTITUTIONAL LEGACIES

The institutionalization of regional difference in Slovakia began under the old Hungarian Kingdom, and dates back to the tenth century, when the division of the country into counties (*comitatus*) and districts (*districtus*) began. These were stabilized in cartographic representations in the fourteenth century. The old districts respected the more or less natural boundaries of mountain ranges, rivers and lowlands, resulting in the strong local identities that can still be perceived today.

These administrative units functioned in a more or less stable form until 1923, when the first administrative reform took place under the new Czechoslovak Republic. Slovakia was first divided into 79 districts (*okresy*) and six larger regions (*kraje*). Then in 1928 all districts were replaced by a single Slovak 'country' (*krajina*). After a few changes during and after the Second World War, a new model of regionalization was introduced in 1948 that followed a three-tier model, with, at the lowest level, the municipality (*obec*), the middle tier district (*okres*), and three regions (*kraje*) – Western, Central and Eastern Slovakia – as the biggest administrative units.

Regional development in the communist Czechoslovak Socialist Republic was constrained by strict centralization and the hierarchization of the towns and regions, supported by state paternalism. This pattern persisted despite the formal federalization of the state in October 1968, which gave greater recognition to the distinct Slovak national identity but ignored its internal heterogeneity. The main feature of the communist reform was its tendency, justified ostensibly by the principle of universalism, to deliberately destroy local and regional specificities, denouncing localism, local patriotism, regionalism or ethnic diversity as alien to the aims of socialist society (Gajdoš and Pašiak, 1995: 225). Regional specificities were seen as a dangerous source of pluralism that did not correspond with the idea of socialist universalism and uniformity.

This system disrupted the continuity of local and regional development by introducing new centralized localities, undermining traditional social and cultural networks and favouring the development of selected areas, especially at the expense of small localities. These changes weakened local and regional identities although the consciousness of regional solidarity, based on the natural boundaries of the old districts, did not disappear completely. The abrupt social and economic changes driven forward by an ideologically motivated socialist development programme in fact reinforced attitudes and life-strategies carried over by the people from their recent, rural past: their aversion to change, modernization and reforms; their lack of interest in public life; tendencies to egalitarianism, passivity, paternalism, dependence on the state; their lack of self-esteem and self-confidence; collectivism, familiarism and conservativism (Danglová, 1995: 38–9; Bitušíková, 1999). This relatively traditional rural culture and behaviour, permeated by communist ideology, has favoured the emergence of populist and nationalistic politicians in the development of Slovakia since 1989 (Szomolányi and Gould, 1997).

SEARCHING FOR IDENTITIES

Having been deprived of the attentions of the paternalistic, authoritarian 'nanny-state', to use Richard Hill's term (Hill, 1996: 25), the people of Slovakia started to look for new security and reassurance in various identities. 'Transition' has been accompanied by the formation of a 'nation-state' in which at least 15 per cent of the population belongs to ethnic minorities. At the same time, it has meant adjusting to the demands of 'returning to Europe', in the sense of seeking membership in the EU and NATO. In the process of building a nation-state, which the Slovaks must share with the minorities, old ghosts of nationalistic tensions have reawakened. The nationalistic ideology of some political parties, especially the Slovak National Party (*Slovenská národná strana* – SNS) and the Movement for Democratic Slovakia (*Hnutie za demokratické Slovensko* – HZDS), which play on appeals to Slovak ethnic identity, has exploited historical and cultural traditions, myths and symbols in order to revive feelings of historical continuity and bonds of loyalty. As Václav Havel has noted,

> the desire to renew and emphasize one's identity, one's uniqueness, is ... behind the emergence of many new countries. Nations that have never had states of their own feel an understandable need to experience independence. It is no fault of theirs that the opportunity has come up decades or even centuries after it came to other nations (Havel, 1996: 131).

The construction of national identity has been based upon two mechanisms: firstly, the reinterpretation, glorification and mythologization of Slovak history and culture, and the manipulation of national symbols (the national flag, emblem, 'national' mountain peak, etc.) and rituals ('national' pilgrimages and ceremonies celebrating Slovak sovereignty); and as a concomitant, the creation of ethnocentric myths and stereotypes, fostering xenophobia, racism, and a defensive ideology against 'the others', internal and external 'enemies'.

Such a national identity based on irrational ethnocentric feelings collides with the aspiration to 'return to Europe', where this is interpreted as a threat to national identity, national interests and sovereignty and evokes fear of losing national roots, the disintegration of 'home' and the homogenization of culture. This mind-set has been well expressed by the HZDS ideologist, Augustín Marián Húska:

> These small nations have the right ... to defend their own face, their own identity, and their uniqueness, spiritual-religious and national culture ... Therefore we have to take care otherwise the whole integration process will be only a melting pot where uniqueness, all the specific features of different nations dissolve (Húska, 1998).

Similar nationalistic statements have been made by representatives of the *Matica slovenská*,[2] a cultural organization of the Slovaks which played an important role in the Slovak national awakening in the nineteenth century, and which, since 1989, has taken on a highly visible role in nationalist political activities linked closely with the SNS and HZDS. The emphasis on state sovereignty in the following statement by its chairman, Jozef Markuš, is characteristic:

> Slovakia has gone through the development from a totalitarian

regime to parliamentary democracy. Another change, and from *Matica Slovenská's* point of view, even more important, is obtaining the state sovereignty of the Slovak Republic (cited by Harmádyova and Bunčák, 1998: 16).

Myths of ancient historical roots and cultural uniqueness, as well as various notions of 'threat' and 'enemies', are not only a Slovak peculiarity; they are present in all the small Central European nations who have suffered chronically from the fear of oppression and obliteration. Today, the threat reappears in the shape of 'Europe as a melting-pot'. For these nations, struggle for national emancipation and for their very survival has been the *Leitmotif* of their history. The 'national question', the quest for national sovereignty and self-determination, has been, to use Milan Kundera's phrase, an 'eternal uncertainty', which is often difficult for the older nations of long-established states in Western Europe to understand.

Living under different empires and states has disrupted the continuity of national identity-formation in the past. Representatives of the older generation have lived their lives under several regimes and state-formations: the Austro-Hungarian Empire, the democratic state of the first Czechoslovak Republic, the fascist Slovak State, the federal Czechoslovak Socialist Republic, the post-communist Czecho-Slovak Republic, and now the new Slovak Republic. The confusing impact of this, characteristic of the whole of Central Europe, has been well described by Lajos Grendel:

> The Schmidt family [who lived in the Slovak city of Košice] were real Central Europeans. During their lives they were twice Hungarian citizens, twice Czechoslovak citizens, and recently they died as citizens of the Slovak Republic. They experienced democracy, fascism and communism. Their forebears were Germans, but they felt themselves Hungarians although they were proud of their German roots. When communism came, they had to forget both. At each census they were asked about their nationality. One day uncle Schmidt became fed up with it. 'So tell us who you are – Slovak or Hungarian?' an official asked. 'Betwixt and between. I am of Košician nationality' (Grendel, 1996: 2).

Ambiguous national identity in the past has contributed to strengthening the local and regional identities of the people. Numerous anthropological studies have brought out the strong sense of attachment to locality or region. It seems that people identify most strongly with their local community, then with the nation or state, and finally with transnational regions – Europe or the world. According to the findings of sociological and anthropological surveys (Ivantyšyn *et al.*, 1998; Krivý, 1998; Bitušíková, 2000b), the older generation is more oriented towards the nation, and more anti-European. The younger generation is characterized by lower levels of authoritarianism, paternalism and anti-westernism than their parents, and firmly support Slovakia's integration into the EU (80 per cent). Surprisingly, however, they also claim stronger local or regional identity than either national or European identities.

Results from interviews with university students demonstrate interesting relations between local, national and European identities.[3] Students with strong local identities were more open to identification with Europe than students who felt more 'national'. Students who claimed strong pro-Slovak feelings expressed their negative feelings about Slovakia's integration into the EU. They expressed fears of losing national features, national uniqueness, independence and sovereignty; also of the commercialization of culture and the way of life, and of influence by other cultures. They often defined themselves in opposition to the idea of a United Europe, seen as a forced construct of different European states with insurmountable cultural barriers between them. In contrast, the students who expressed strong local and European identities perceived European diversity as one of the main positive characteristics of Europe.

The anthropological focus on identity can contribute to a deeper understanding of the transformation processes in post-communist Slovakia. Identity is not stable and fixed; it develops and changes in time and space, and is influenced by knowledge, experience, and internal and external conditions. Debates on identity usually appear in periods of great transformations. The current programme of regionalization of Slovakia and reform of its public administration belongs to the most significant changes of recent years.

REFORM OF THE REFORM

The establishment of the Slovak Republic in 1993 opened up new conditions for the idea of the citizen as key actor in the social, political and economic transformation. New opportunities were provided by tendencies to strengthen decentralization, to renew localism and regionalism, to bolster the authority and independence of local and regional communities, and to revitalize traditional relations and networks in order to activate individual and group interests.

Slovakia's transformation was complicated by the four years of Vladimír Mečiar's government (1994–98) that led Slovakia into international isolation. Only after the 1998 election did a new Slovak government begin to reverse this situation and open negotiations on accession to the European Union. The latest *Regular Report of the European Commission on Slovakia's Progress Towards Accession* (see European Commission, 2000) recognizes the achievements, but is very critical of delays in the reform of public administration and the civil service, as well as of the problems concerning minorities, especially the Roma.

Reform of public administration started shortly after 1989 with the renewal of the municipal level (*obec*) that has become a stable element of democracy in Slovakia. However, the process of decentralization – handing over political and economic power from the central state level to the local and regional level – has been attended by a number of difficulties. Some of these are comparable to those described by Fowler in this volume. But the main difficulties have been specific to Slovakia's unstable and polarized political development. The current state of public administration is the result of the incoherent and over-politicized approach taken by the previous governments. The absence of professional and public debate on the reform brought about a situation where all decisions were made on the basis of short-term party-political advantage. There was no coherent vision of how the state might best function.

This approach characterized the reform of public administration and the new territorial-administrative division introduced by Vladimír Mečiar's government in 1996, when eight new regions and 79 districts were established, each hosting corresponding offices of the state.[4] (Korec *et al.*, 1997). This reform was a model with a hierarchic organization of the increasing state administration: centre – regions – districts (*centrum – kraje – okresy*). The implementation of the change was not followed by other important steps – decentralization, the transfer of competences and properties, tax reform, healthcare reform, etc. The reform served the political parties of the then coalition (HZDS, SNS and the Association of Workers in Slovakia – *Združenie robotníkov Slovenska* – ZRS) as a means of strengthening their power, and led to an uncontrolled expansion of the state administration at all levels, which remained under strong central control. The restricted competences and authority of municipal self-governments meant that their political power was undermined. The reform remained structurally unfinished, leaving the hierarchically organized state administration in a dominant position.

Public administration characterized by strong state centralism and paternalism contributed to the growth of regional differences, with enormous variations in the standard of living and unemployment rates. Unemployment fluctuates between two and five per cent in the regions of Bratislava, Trenčín and Banská Bystrica, while reaching up to 30 per cent in some marginalized regions of central and eastern Slovakia. According to EUROSTAT, in the second half of the 1990s GDP in Bratislava reached 117 per cent of the EU average, but in other Slovak regions it was only 34–38 per cent of the EU average (Lipták, 2000: 6). The centralized, politicized system also aggravated the problem of political exclusion of the minorities. Centralism did not allow any scope for popular initiative in the regions, towns and villages, but gave excellent opportunities for central institutions, controlled by the governing political parties, to intervene and make important decisions in the name of citizens.

It is clear that consistent reform of the public administration cannot be realized without wide-ranging decentralization to strengthen the power of citizens through their elected representatives at the local or regional level. The vertical redistribution of power is necessary to transform the ethos of public administration into that of service to the public. Indirectly, it should also contribute to the transformation of political parties, strengthening their local roots. The issue of decentralization separates out those politicians and political parties who really take the citizen seriously as the basis of the democratic state from those who exploit parliamentary democracy for personal or short-term party-political gain. The slow progress of decentralization in Slovakia indicates that most politicians and political parties are still mainly concerned with the latter. In addition, public administration reform does not meet with much interest or understanding on the part of the general public. People have been used to relying on the strong, paternalistic hand of the state, and are still all too ready to bow to the dictates of unelected state officials. Decentralization means redefining the state. Whether the citizens of Slovakia are ready for it seems open to question.

The present government of Mikuláš Dzurinda, which came to power after the 1998 election, made public administration reform one of the priorities of its programme. The government appointed a plenipotentiary for the reform of public administration in the person of Viktor Nižňanský, a founding member and former chairman of the Union of Cities and Towns in Slovakia (*Únia miest a obcí Slovenska*), a non-governmental organization associating villages, towns and cities represented by their mayors. He was tasked to work out the strategy and conception of the public administration reform. After a number of discussions with representatives of the government, central state institutions, local and regional governments, NGOs and professionals, Nižňanský drew up the *Conception of Decentralization and Modernization of Public Administration* (*Koncepcia decentralizácie a modernizácie verejnej správy*), which was accepted by the Slovak Government in April 2000 and recommended for further parliamentary and legislative procedures.[5]

Nižňanský's proposal centred on far-reaching decentralization of competences, and administrative-territorial division of responsibilities between three levels (municipality – region – state). The aim was to achieve increased efficiency and to adjust the state to the requirements for Slovakia's accession to the European Union. The reform had to be compatible with European standards as a precondition for satisfactory management of transfers from the European Union's Structural Funds. It also aimed to promote cross-border regional cooperation. The changes were to lead to flexible, effective, transparent and de-politicized administration, better cooperation between the public and non-governmental sectors, and a satisfactory framework for the solution of minority problems. Public administration reform was supposed to be a starting point for further reforms in education, healthcare, social welfare and culture, and to provide the basis for new legislation to promote regional development in the framework of the EU regional policy.

A three-fold decentralization was envisaged: of competences; of finances; and of political power. The stated objectives of the proposal were:

- to strengthen the institutions of democracy and empower citizen participation in decision-making;
- to strengthen local governments in line with Slovakia's commitments to European norms (mainly European Charter of the Local Self-Government and European Charter of Regional Planning);
- to strengthen the protection of minority rights;
- to enhance transparency and fight all kinds of corruption;
- to increase the efficiency of public administration;
- to open up opportunities for inter-regional and cross-border cooperation;
- to diminish inequalities in local and regional development.

The proposal suggested three levels of public administration, with territorial divisions at (1) the local level – the municipality (*obec*), based on that already in existence in villages and towns; (2) a new middle level of 'higher territorial units' (*vyšší územný celok* – VUC – region); and (3) the top level, comprising the central state institutions. Thus territorially, public administration at the local government level (already comprising the municipal local offices and their elected councils) will be complemented by similar institutions at the regional level, the VUC offices and elected VUC councils. The regional–territorial self-government (VUC) will act as a legal entity in respective areas and will be independent of the state administration. Both representatives of local and regional self-governments, elected by citizens, will have a final word in decision-making.

State administration will be provided and secured by ministries, central authorities of the state administration with local offices and regional offices (compatible with former *krajské úrady*), institutions and agencies charged by the state, and the National Council of the Slovak Republic. The exclusive competences of the state administration on the local level will cover institutions like police corps, military administration, state veterinary office, state hygienist office, environmental office, cadaster office, land and forest office, social office and tax office. State administration on the regional level will include areas like defence, general internal administration, protection of civil rights and freedoms, issues related to state citizenship, issuing of state documents, tax policy, trade licence enterprise, currency policy, execution of state control, economic policy, infrastructure and cross-border cooperation. The responsibilities and competences of municipal and VUC self-government are to increase *vis-à-vis* the state administration, and the role of the new VUC elected councils should rectify the most glaring shortcoming of the previous, incomplete reform. The proposal suggested dissolving or merging the 79 state administration districts (*okresy*) and district state administration offices (*okresné úrady*) set up by the previous reform, to match the new territorial division into fewer and larger VUC regions. State administration at the regional level will function alongside and in coordination with the new VUC institutions of self-government. The latter would be independent legal and economic entities, acting as associations of municipalities and taking responsibility for the socio-economic development of the regions.

This new territorial organization of public administration means a new regionalization of Slovakia, based on criteria of homogeneity, transparency, subsidiarity, flexibility and effectiveness. The suggested model proposed therefore the formation of 11 +1 (11 VUC + Bratislava VUC) state administration regions in parallel with the 11+1 VUC self-governing regions. The proposed regions more or less followed the territories and borders of historical counties and regions (*comitati, counties, župy, okresy*), which at one time or another had self-governing power. To that extent they took account of specific ethno-cultural, historical, demographic and socio-economic features, and reflected strong regional identities. The internal homogeneity and solidarity of the regions, their natural structures and patterns of population mobility were respected with a view to unleashing the socio-economic potential of the given territory. The proposal also supported development of several strong urban centres as a counterweight to the much-criticized 'Bratislava-centrism', on which more below.

Given that it was one of the main points of the governmental programme after the 1998 election, all the coalition political parties supported the reform strategy. However, problems appeared after Nižňanský's programme was unveiled and the government sent it for further consideration in the National Council, the Slovak parliament. The reform then became a political football, and the passage of the necessary legislation has been much delayed. Several deadlines passed, raising fears for the consequences for Slovakia's progress towards accession in the EU. In the final months of 2000 and early 2001, debates on the reform of public administration and new regionalization intensified. Representatives of different political parties, trade unions, the academic community, independent regional associations, ethnic minorities and NGOs introduced divergent views on the reform. The most common arguments in these discussions revolved around, firstly, the question of dissolving the existing district state administration offices (*okresné úrady*); secondly, the proposed number of higher territorial units (VUCs and urban centres) to be established and their borders, including finally the demand raised by the Hungarian Coalition Party's for an additional Komárno VUC, in which Hungarians would comprise more than 50 per cent of the population.

The argument against the dissolution of the 79 district state administration offices came from the Democratic Left Party (*Strana demokratickej l'avice* – SDL), which was mostly in favour of keeping a centralized power structure. But its representatives also argued that dissolution of the district offices would increase unemployment among state employees. It was the only party to put this argument openly. On the other hand, the Democratic Party (*Demokratická strana* – DS) was the only one to agree with the outright abolition of district state administration. The other parties did not express their opinions: dissolution of the district state offices is an unpopular decision that will have an impact on a large number of people working in these institutions, and those who openly support it recognize that they could lose a lot of votes in the next elections. Nižňanský, the author of the reform, argued logically that if the reform was to transfer more competences to the self-governments, the district state offices were redundant and expensive. The qualified employees from these offices (over 17,000) would have to apply for jobs in the offices of the local and VUC self-governments or state administration. Nižňanský's argument was supported by most municipal politicians, the academic community, NGOs and professional associations.

Another set of arguments in the debates on the reform came from the regions, reflecting regional differences and rivalries and an old regional aversion to Bratislava and its centralism. In these discussions regional identities were invoked as a means of mobilizing popular support. People feel more secure in their local and regional identities. Alongside the idea of 'returning to Europe' we also witness a 'return' to locality, village, town or region. Revitalizing local and regional identities has been strongly connected with the processes of democratization and decentralization, which make citizens more responsible for local and regional problems. This strategy is often identified with a broader European tendency towards community and region. Regional ethno-cultural and identity factors are highlighted also in *The European Charter of Regional Planning* and *The European Charter of Regional Self-Government*. As the former mayor of Bratislava, Peter Kresánek, asserted:

> Locality and region mean more than the state in Europe. The future of Europe lies in its regions. People have regional identities, which should be supported. Slovakia is a country with 16–17 regions and each has a unique identity. If de-centralization in Slovakia followed historical regions, people would be involved in regional life, and not in problems of ethnicity, economy etc. (Harmádyová and Bunčák, 1998: 36).[6]

The new regionalization thus meant new regional borders and new regional centres. The question of how many regions, and where their borders and capitals should be, naturally generated much controversy, which culminated in the spring months of 2001. Nižňanský's expert group, professionals, NGOs and regional associations represented by the Union of Cities and Towns in Slovakia (*Únia miest a obcí Slovenska* – UMO) and the Association of Towns and Villages of Slovakia (*Združenie miest a obcí Slovenska* – ZMOS), supported the model of 12 (11+1) regions (VUCs).[7] Their arguments issued from the idea of regions as natural ethno-cultural and socio-economic entities with strong internal integrity and identity leading to the mobilizing and revitalizing of the regions and seats. The proposed 11+1 model respected regionalization criteria, helped to minimalize handicaps of marginalized regions, created better conditions for cross-border cooperation and was compatible with other European models (in terms of the size of the country and the number of regions). The advocates of fewer regions – VUCs (eight regions – the present variant or 3+1 regions – the variant before 1989), mainly representatives of the opposition (HZDS, SNS), left-wing coalition political parties (SDL and SOP – Civic Understanding Party, *Strana občianskeho porozumenia*), trade unions (*Konfederácia odborových zväzov Slovenskej republiky*) and the President of the Slovak Republic Rudolf Schuster argued that forming 12 new regions and dissolving of 79 districts (*okresy*) would be too expensive and would increase unemployment. These arguments did not recognize natural ethno-cultural and socio-economic criteria for regionalization, but followed political criteria, supporting the model of the reform that could strengthen political power in the regions.

Another argument concerned proposed regional centres. Where the creation of new higher territorial units followed natural and/or historical regions with an obvious regional urban centre (e.g. Trenčín in VUC Trenčiansky kraj, Žilina in VUC Žilinský kraj or Nitra in VUC Nitriansky kraj), the changes did not run up against resistance from regional or local sensitivities about identity. However, there were a few problem cases, firstly, where regional representatives did not agree either with the proposed borders or with the proposed regional centres; secondly, over the question of Bratislava; and finally, over the specific demands of the Hungarian ethnic minority.

A notable example of the former problem was the proposed Gemer-Novohrad VUC where two towns – Lučenec and Rimavská Sobota – fought for designation as the regional centre. The dispute acquired the character of a tragicomedy when demonstrators led by Tibor Papp, an American lobbyist for Lučenec, protested against Rimavská Sobota in front of the government office in September 2000. They chose a rather original way to attract popular and media attention to the 'dim-wit' state officials who supported Lučenec: they brought 87 hens as symbols of stupidity with them and started to throw them through the fence. Eleven hens did not survive and most of others were injured. The case, now known as the 'hen demonstration', attracted especially the attention of the NGO Freedom for Animals, who took legal steps against the organizers of the protest. After this incident, Nižňanský and various experts suggested a regional referendum in which the citizens will decide on the regional centre (it has not yet been organized). This case is just one example of the local and regional politicians' approach. It is not decentralization and rational organization of public administration that absorbs local representatives' attention, but 'cat-and-mouse wars' over positions in the new regional centres, rivalry between small and smaller towns, local and partial interests and quarrels.

The variant of the reform of 1996 disrupted the natural borders of some regions (Spiš, Zemplín, Gemer, Novohrad); therefore their representatives and citizens were expecting the new reform to create new, separate regions that would revitalize natural ethno-cultural, identity and socio-economic ties.

Bratislava-Centrism

Intellectual debates on decentralization and regionalization often attack the problem of 'Bratislava-centrism' and the position of the Slovak capital at the far south-western end of Slovakia. Juraj Mesík (NGO Ekopolis) asked:

> Can this country afford to have its capital in Bratislava, on the geographical periphery? Doubts about acceptability of Bratislava as the capital of Slovakia do not arise from historical concerns [Bratislava was once the capital of Hungary], but from practical ones. Bratislava, partly because of its extremely asymmetrical position near Vienna, functions as a thick filter stopping progress and investment trickling through into the country ... There is no other capital that is situated on the far pole of a rhomboid-shaped country, on the sharp border between two worlds – 'Western' and post-communist, and no other capital serves as a satellite of another country's capital (Vienna) (Mesík, 2000: 52).

The asymmetrical geographical position of the Slovak capital contributes to a simplified opposition between 'advanced west' and 'backward east', which is alive not only in mental maps of the inhabitants and representatives of Bratislava, but also affects the image of Slovakia abroad. Most visitors to Slovakia or foreign investors start and finish their visit to Slovakia in Bratislava, as a number of surveys demonstrate. The position of the Slovak capital on the 'Western' border results in the positive index of economic development of the city, its having the lowest rate of unemployment and highest foreign investment, which deepens the gap between the capital and the regions. Discussions on removing the capital either to the eastern part of Slovakia (Košice) or to central Slovakia (Banská Bystrica – Zvolen) face strong criticism from politicians and central institutions based in Bratislava. Nevertheless, the fact is that Bratislava does not play an important role in the identity of Slovak citizens. More than 92 per cent of the inhabitants of Slovakia live outside Bratislava in regions with strong identities and cultures. The capital is not the source of their pride. It has not been a capital since the seventeenth and eighteenth centuries, when it became the Hungarian capital and coronation site of Hungarian kings during the Turkish occupation of Buda. Under communism, it was a centre of a centralized political system and it has preserved this centralism up to the present. In recent years, since European integration has come on to the agenda, a number of European institutions and agencies have opened in Bratislava. Regional representatives from the political, public and non-governmental sectors all report their experience of Bratislava as a barrier between Brussels and the rest of Slovakia. One of the reasons why they call for decentralization is the lack of information and difficulty of direct access to European institutions, and they expect decentralization and the new regionalization to bring more responsibility and decision-making power to the regions, and greater balance in the development of regional centres.[8]

An important and unique phenomenon of Bratislava is its impact, or rather, lack of impact on political life and political development in Slovakia. In contrast to other Central European capitals, especially Prague and Budapest, Bratislava represents a weaker political stream in the country. It is in the countryside that electoral outcomes are decided. Mečiar's victory in the 1994 elections was the result of rural voters' choice, and the victory of the democratic opposition in 1998 was a result of a massive campaign orchestrated by Slovakia's lively NGO community to mobilize voters in the country, especially in the urban regional centres.

Although there was a lot of debate for and against Bratislava as a capital of Slovakia, the reform did not change its position, which is enshrined in the Constitution of the Slovak Republic. Bratislava will obtain a status as a higher territorial unit with both levels of self-government (self-government of VUC and municipal self-governments in different city quarters) and the status of the capital defined in a separate law on Bratislava.

Minority Claims

One of the significant issues that the new regionalization was supposed to take into account was ethnicity. According to the law No. 184 Coll. from 10 July 1999 on minority languages,[9] all minority languages in Slovakia have equal status with Slovak in those towns and villages where the minority population exceeds 20 per cent. Here, minorities can use their native tongue in all transactions with state and local government officials, and official documents are to be made available in translation. When it came to the new regions, the question of where the borders were drawn could have a big impact on the status of minority languages. One of the Hungarian minority's main objections to the eight regions defined by Mečiar's earlier reform was that the borders were gerrymandered deliberately to prevent the Hungarians reaching 20 per cent in any of them. Nižňanský's proposed regions followed historical regional structures and were based explicitly on a 'civic', not an ethnic, principle. The percentage of Hungarian population in his proposed regions varied between 15 and 37 per cent on average, resulting in three regions with a Hungarian population of over 20 per cent. Therefore most Slovak politicians, as well as representatives of the non-governmental sector, were taken by surprise when the Hungarian Coalition Party (*Strana maďarskej koalície* – SMK) demanded the creation of an additional, thirteenth, higher territorial unit, Komárno VUC, which would have more

than 50 per cent Hungarian population. This demand was introduced at the
end of August 2000, after most of the sticking points of the reform had
been resolved, and it further delayed the process of legislating on the
reform. While SMK, as a coalition partner, had won respect from its
Slovak partners as a cornerstone of democracy, responsibility and
constitutionalism in Slovakia, the SMK political representatives'
declaration they would not support the reform in parliament if their
demand were not accepted, caused some dismay. Experts from
Nižňanský's professional team argued that this demand elevated the ethnic
principle above the 'civic' principle, and did not follow natural regional
networks and economic structures. The coalition partners of SMK also
disagreed with the creation of the thirteenth VUC. Some of them, for
example Ladislav Pittner, the former Minister of Interior from the
Christian Democratic Party (KDH), used the same terminology as that of
the opposition, especially the Slovak National Party (SNS), to denounce
the SMK claim as the first step to 'ethnic autonomy', thus suggesting it
was a threat to the territorial integrity of the state. The leader of SMK,
Béla Bugár, on the other hand, justified the claim by pointing to the
marginality and poverty of the southern Slovak regions, where the
Hungarian minority is concentrated, and argued that this was the result of
centralistic state decisions against the ethnic minorities. However, ethnic
bias is probably not the main reason (if at all) for the marginalization of
the southern regions. The main reasons for big regional differences lie in
the west–east gradient (the further to the east, the more poverty and
unemployment), and in the gradient from regional centres to regional
peripheries. The poorest and most problematic regions of Slovakia are not
those with the highest percentage of minorities, but areas where these
gradients meet (the regions of Zemplín, Šariš, Spiš, Gemer, Malohont and
Novohrad).

The most interesting argument against the creation of Komárno VUC
came in fact from the inhabitants and mayors of the towns in the proposed
Komárno region. According to a survey organized by the Hungarian
minority daily *Új Szó* in October 2000,[10] only two mayors from six urban
centres openly agreed with the creation of a Komárno VUC. Most
respondents were more interested in the distribution of competences to the
municipal self-governments than in the borders of the new regions, and
for many of them it was not Komárno, but rather Bratislava, Trnava or
Nitra to which they looked as the centre of political, economic, social and
cultural life. The mayor of Galanta admitted: 'I would like to see the
creation of a Komárno VUC, but I represent not only Hungarians in the
city, but also 53 per cent of the Slovaks who elected me and who wish to
stay in Trnava VUC. I am obliged also to represent their interests.'[11]

After hectic debates during spring 2001 on the number of regions, SMK, which has insisted on the organization of southern Slovakia along ethnic lines with the thirteenth Komarno VUC, left coalition negotiations. This act delayed and endangered the reform legislation because without SMK there was not enough support for the reform with 12 regions in the Parliament.

The most problematic minority in Slovakia, the Roma, have remained marginal and neglected in the debates on the reform. The Romani population is dispersed in all regions, with the highest percentage in the south-eastern and north-eastern regions, where there are villages with almost 80 per cent Roma population. The bad living conditions of the Roma communities, high unemployment, poor health, low education and Slovakia's inability to solve these problems quickly, has damaged the country's image and international reputation. The government approved the Strategy for the Solution of the Problems of the Roma National Minority in 1999, but its implementation has been slower than expected, which has resulted in criticism of the Roma minority situation by the European Commission in its Progress Report 2000 on Slovakia. The regional reform is supposed to help improve the Roma situation in the regions, especially through decentralization, which gives more opportunities to local and regional politicians to manage the problems. Recent Slovak experience demonstrates that the most effective way of tackling the problems of the Roma is by starting not in governmental offices, but at the local or regional level. In the 1998 local elections, six mayors and 86 council members were elected from Roma political parties. The Roma activists are now trying to mobilize the Roma electorate for the next local and parliamentary elections. This requires not only unifying the political strategies of different Roma representatives, but also reviving the Roma identity. While the reform of public administration, decentralization, and regionalization may indeed help, the deep and complex problems of the Roma will not be resolved by this alone.

FINAL ACT: GOOD NEWS FOR SLOVAKIA?

All representatives of the Slovak Government, Slovak National Council and political parties were aware that if the public administration reforms were not passed by parliament by the beginning of summer 2001, it would be impossible to implement them within the government's term of office. The transfer of properties and competences to local and VUC self-governments had to be complete by late autumn 2001, when local elections were due in Slovakia. The system was supposed to start operating in 2002.

The last chance for the parliament to make its decision came on 4 July 2001 when the parliament overturned the 12-region variant previously favoured by the Slovak government as well as all independent regional associations, and voted by a solid majority for the variant with eight self-governing regions. The SDL and SOP, both members of the government coalition, joined with the opposition to back many of the 70 amendments submitted, with the result that the powers of the state and centralism were significantly reinforced. The question of the dissolution of the 79 districts and district offices (*okresy* and *okresné úrady*) was not even discussed. Almost all MPs from the SDL and SOP voted with the opposition for eight regions. In the final vote on the Law on Higher Territorial Units, the representatives of the Slovak Democratic Coalition also decided to support the changed version, and voted for it. Thus the parliament voted to keep the existing regions, but with new, decentralized self-governing powers. The question of the districts (*okresy*) remained open.

The reform was supported by 112 MPs in the 150-seat legislature. The Prime Minister Mikuláš Dzurinda expressed his relief, saying: 'I am very happy today. We have taken an irreversible step towards decentralization in Slovakia.'[12] However, not everyone shared his satisfaction. Viktor Nižňanský, the architect of the reform and the government plenipotentiary, resigned from his post. Deputy Prime Minister Ivan Mikloš also resigned as the government coordinator of the reform programme. After the final vote, Nižňanský suggested that the pressure to meet EU requirements had overridden principle and rational debate about Slovakia's needs:

> It is good news for the European Union, and secondarily for Slovakia as well. From the EU's point of view it does not matter whether there will be eight or twelve regions. The European Union will be satisfied with this decision. But we did not use the chance that this government coalition had. Under previous governments, all the present coalition parties wanted to change the bad territorial administration. Now they have approved it in parliament.[13]

The decision of the two government parties, SDL and SOP, to side with the opposition against their coalition partners drew protests from some coalition politicians and parties. The Christian Democrats (KDH) rejected the Prime Minister's approach of compromising in order to get the law passed at any cost. The Hungarian Coalition Party (SMK), not surprisingly, were bitterly disappointed in the result, and threatened to leave the government. The SMK strongly criticized the behaviour of their coalition partners, and had fundamental objections to the eight-region territorial division, which they had consistently attacked for ignoring the interests of the Hungarian minority, who would now have reduced chances to win posts in the regional councils. However, meeting in August, the SMK decided to postpone its decision on withdrawal from government until the next parliamentary session, beginning in September 2001, when the important succeeding reform law ceding central powers to newly created regions (transfer of properties, finances and competences at the municipal and regional level) should be approved.

The biggest disappointment was expressed by regional associations, NGOs and mayors in those regions that were expecting new territorial borders to revitalize cultural identities and socio-economic development: Spiš, Zemplín, Liptov and Novohrad. For example, Karol Mitrik from the Spiš Association of Towns and Villages complained, 'Parliament by its decision has harmed Spiš region more than King Zigmund in the fifteenth century when he lent sixteen Spiš towns to the Polish king. But then that was feudalism, while today we enjoy democracy.'[14]

The process of decentralization and regionalization in Slovakia has been a long and difficult one. The main source of delay in the reform came not from the public and non-governmental sphere, but from political parties that were unwilling to relinquish power. The Slovak media regularly criticized the slow progress and problems of the reform, as indicated by a characteristic selection of newspaper subtitles: *Slovak roulette; Reform has stopped, nervousness grows; Postponing of the reform threatens our credibility; Enough alternatives; The public administration reform is point of honour for each MP; Komarno VUC versus the reform; Counterproductive coalition czardas; SMK to block the reform; Minorities want to be majorities,* etc. The low level of interest in the reform among most local and communal politicians and the general public was also alarming. The national coordinating committee of NGOs (*Grémium tretieho sektora*), meeting on 9 March 2001 to discuss the reform of public administration, had already warned: 'Politicians are still following their individual interests with the aim of transferring centralism to big districts and preserving their own party influence over as much territory as possible.'[15]

Future developments will show whether this prediction is borne out in practice. Domestic and external assessments may, of course, differ. From the EU's point of view, Slovakia made an important step towards European standards of regionalization and decentralization. The parliamentary decision opened the door to negotiations about regional planning and structural funds, which should positively influence the development of the Slovak regions and improve the quality of life of their citizens. Nevertheless, the process of passing the law opened up deep rifts within the government, damaging its credibility as it approached an election year. Thus the spectre of renewed political instability in Slovakia looms, somewhat overshadowing the favourable impact that Slovakia's parliamentarians seem to have expected to make on their country's prospects for EU accession.

ACKNOWLEDGEMENTS

Sections of this paper were presented at the 4th International Anthropological Congress of Ales Hrdlička in Prague, Czech Republic, 30 August–4 September 1999, and the conference 'Between the Block and the Hard Place', School of Slavonic and East European Studies, London, 5–7 November 1999.

NOTES

1. Size of population is most often used as a criterion for defining what is urban and what is not. According to the United Nations definition, an urban locality is one with more than 20,000 inhabitants, but most countries use their own national criteria, e.g. only 250 persons are needed to qualify an area urban in Denmark; 2,500 in the USA; 10,000 in Greece (Palen, 1987: 8). In Slovakia, 5,000 inhabitants are necessary to define an area as urban (Slovensko-Ľud, 1974: 223). In addition to the number of inhabitants, other criteria are also used in different countries to define an urban locality (administrative, economic, social and cultural criteria).
2. *Matica slovenská* (MS) is a national cultural institution of the Slovaks, which played an important role in the period of Enlightenment in the nineteenth century. After 1989 leading representatives of MS adopted a nationalistic ideology and politicized the activities of MS, which placed it among the opposition together with the Slovak National Party and the Movement for Democratic Slovakia.
3. The survey was carried out among 74 students (18–24 years old), using face-to-face interviews and questionnaires. Given the small number of respondents and their social status (students) we cannot consider the sample representative – the results demonstrate only trends among young people.
4. *Zákon NR SR c. 221/1996 Z. z. o novom územnom a správnom usporiadaní SR*, Law 221/96 Coll.
5. *Resolution of the Slovak Government No. 230 from April 11, 2000*, www.government.gov.sk
6. Peter Kresánek mentions 16–17 regions. Historically, the number of natural geographical and ethno-cultural regions and sub-regions in Slovakia fluctuated between 12 and 17 regions. Nižňanský's proposal suggested 12 regions following the criteria of the EU statistical units – NUTS (mainly the relation between the size of the country and the number of regions).
7. According to a survey organized in 2001, from 57 regional associations, 40 supported the model of 12 VUCs, six supported the model of eight 8 VUCs, eight supported the model of six or 3+1 VUC and three did not have any opinion (*Koncepcia decentralizácie a modernizácie verejnej správy*, www.government.gov.sk).
8. Articles on Bratislava have appeared in the national press in terms of debates on the reform of public administration, and their authors come mainly from NGOs or academic community (J. Mesík, V. Krivý, Z. Hochmut, etc.). No official representatives of the state paid attention to this problem.
9. *Zákon NR SR c. 184 z 10. júla 1999 o používaní jazykov národnostných menäín*, www.government.gov.sk/mensiny/zakon184/html).
10. *Új Szó* 10 October 2000.
11. SME, 14 October 2000, Vol.8, p.2.
12. SME, 6 July 2001, Vol.9, p.1.
13. Ibid., p.3.
14. Ibid.
15. SME, 12 March 2001, Vol.9, p.3.

REFERENCES

Amato, G. and J. Batt (1999), 'The Long-Term Implications of EU Enlargement: Culture and National Identity', *Policy Paper*, No.99/1, San Domenico di Fiesole: European University Institute, The Robert Schuman Centre.

Benža, M. (1998), *Status of Persons Belonging to Ethnic Minorities in the States of Europe*. Bratislava: BB Print.

Bitušíková, A. (1999), 'Socio-Cultural Aspects of Transformation in Slovakia', in R. Muršič and B. Brumen (eds), *Cultural Processes and Transformations in Transition of the Central and Eastern European Post-Communist Countries*, Ethnological Contacts 9. Ljubljana: University of Ljubljana.

Bitušíková, A. (2000a), 'Contrasting Symbols and Rituals', in T. Dekker, J. Helsloot and C. Wijers (eds), *Roots and Rituals. The Construction of Ethnic Identities*, pp.219–28. Amsterdam: Het Spinhuis.

Bitušíková, A. (2000b), 'The Global vs. the Local – European vs. National: Paradoxes of New Identities', in P. Skalník (ed.) *Voices from the Periphery. Prague Studies in Sociocultural Anthropology I*, pp.51–61. Prague: Set Out.

Bútorová, Z. (ed.) (1998), *Democracy and Discontent in Slovakia: A Public Opinion Profile of a Country in Transition*. Bratislava: Institute for Public Affairs.

Carmichael, C. (1999), 'Old Ties and New Identities: Language and National Identity in a Changing Europe', in R. Muršič and B. Brumen (eds) *Cultural Processes and Transformations in Transition of the Central and Eastern European Post-Communist Countries*, Ethnological Contacts 9, Ljubljana: University of Ljubljana.

Danglová, O. (1995), 'Kultúrna rezistencia slovenského vidieka', *Text – Revue pre humanitné vedy*, 1–2, pp.38–46.

European Commission, (2000), *Report on the Slovak Republic's Progress in its Integration into the EU 2000*, www.europa.eu.int/comm.enlargement/slovakia

Falťan, L., P. Gajdoš and J. Pašiak (1995), 'Lokálne aspekty transformácie. Marginálne územia na Slovensku – história a súčasnosť', *Sociológia* Vol.27, No.1–2, pp.31–8.

Feglová, V. (1996), 'Charakter jednotlivych regiónov', in V. Krivý, V. Felová, D. Balko, Slovensko a jeho regióny. Sociokultúrne súvislosti volebnej správania. Bratislava: Media.

Gajdoš, P. and J. Pašiak (1995), *Vývoj sociálno-ekologickej situácie slovenskej spoločnosti*. Bratislava: Veda SAV.

Grendel, L. (1996), 'Stredná Európa a jej prízraky', *Sme – Fórum*, Vol.4, 13 June, p.2.

Hann, Ch. M. (1995), *The Skeleton at the Feast. Contributions to East European Anthropology*. Canterbury Kent: Centre for Social Anthropology and Computing, University of Kent at Canterbury.

Harmádyová, V. and J. Bunčák (1998), 'Transformácia v hodnoteniach slovenskej elity', *Sociológia*, Vol.30, No.1, pp.9–46.

Havel, V. (1996), 'Dilemmas of Post-Communist Developments', in G. Augustinos (ed.), *The National Idea in Eastern Europe. The Politics of Ethnic and Civic Community*. Lexington, MA: D.C. Heath and Company, pp.127–34.

Hill, R. (1996), *Us & Them*. Brussels, A Division of Europublic SA/NV.

Húska, A. M. (1998), 'Odznelo na mítingu HZDS', *Sme – Fórum*, Vol.6, 16 May, p.2.

Hyde-Price, A. (1996), *The International Politics of East Central Europe*. Manchester and New York: Manchester University Press.

Ivantyšyn, M., M. Velšic and Z. Bútorová (1998), 'First-Time Voters', in Z. Bútorová (ed.), *Democracy and Discontent in Slovakia: A Public Opinion Profile of a Country Transition*. Bratislava: Institute for Public Affairs, pp.135–50.

Kanovský, M. (1997), 'Európa ako úloha', *OS*, Vol.1, No.3, July, pp.9–10.

Kol. 1974. *Slovensko – L'ud 3*, Part 2. 1st Edition, Bratislava: Veda.

Korec, P., V. Lauko, L. Tolmáči and G. Zubriczký (1997), Kraje a okresy Slovenska. Nové administratívne členenie. 1st Edition, Bratislava: Q111.

Krivý, V. (1993), 'Sociokultúrne pozadie problémov transformácie na Slovensku', *Sociológia*, Vol.25, No.4–5, pp.311–26.

Krivý, V. (1998), 'Citizens' Values Orientations', in Z. Bútorová (ed.), *Democracy and*

Discontent in Slovakia: A Public Opinion Profile of a Country Transition, pp.37–49. Bratislava: Institute for Public Affairs.

Lipták, L. (2000), 'Hlavné – nehlavné mesto', *OS*, Vol.4., No.8, pp.3–7.

Löfgren, O. (1996), 'Linking the Local, the National and the Global. Past and Present Trends in European Ethnology', *Ethnologia Europea*, Vol.26, No.2, pp.157–68.

Luthzeler, P.M. (1998), 'Contemporary Intellectuals and Writers on a Multicultural European Identity', in L. Passerini (ed.), *The Question of European Identity: A Cultural Historical Approach.* Working Papers HEC No.98/1, San Domenico di Fiesole: European University Institute, pp.1–21.

Mesík, J. (2000), 'Reforma videná "z vidieka"', *OS*, Vol.4, No.5, pp.51–3.

Muršic, R. and B. Brumen (eds) (1999), *Cultural Processes and Transformations in Transition of the Central and Eastern European Post-Communist Countries*, Ethnological Contacts 9, Ljubljana: University of Ljubljana.

Nižňanský, V. (2000), *Koncepcia decentralizácie a modernizácie verejnej správy.* www.government.gov.sk.

Nižňanský, V. (2000), 'Decentralizácia moci', *OS*,Vol.4, No.5, pp.42–3.

Palen, J. J. (1987), *The Urban World.* 3rd Edition. New York: McGraw-Hill, Inc.

Rutland, P. (1999), 'The Meaning of 1989', *Transitions*, Vol.6, No.1, pp.24–8.

Szomolányi, S. and J. A. Gould (1997), *Slovakia – Problems of Democratic Consolidation. The Struggle for the Rules of the Game.* Bratislava: Slovak Political Science Association.

Vermeersch, P. (2000), 'Bad Reputation: Vying for Position', *Central Europe Review* (ce-review.org). Vol.2, No.41, 27 November 2000.

Zákon NR SR c. 184 z 10. júla 1999 o používaní jazykov národnostných menšín: www. government.gov.sk/mensiny/zakon184/html

Zetterholm, S. (1994), *National Cultures and European Integration.* Oxford and Providence, RI: Berg Publishers.

Catching Up with 'Europe'?
Constitutional Debates on
the Territorial-Administrative Model
in Independent Ukraine

KATARYNA WOLCZUK

At first sight, Ukraine is custom-made for far-reaching regionalization or even federalism. Endowed by history with well-accentuated regional divisions, it also has an indigenous reservoir of political ideas on federalism and decentralization dating back to the late nineteenth and early twentieth centuries. Yet upon emerging as an independent state from the break-up of the Soviet federation in 1991, Ukraine became haunted by the spectre of centrifugal forces. This experience was formative for the new polity, putting a premium on unity and territorial cohesion.

After several years of debate on Ukraine's geopolitical orientation and model of statehood, the 1996 constitution marked a victory for the proponents of the 'return to Europe'. However, being European entailed, first of all, forging a sovereign nation-state out of the disparate regions. As far as the Ukrainian elites were concerned, 'returning to Europe' did not imply any shortcuts. Ukraine still needed to replicate the Western trajectory of state-building to achieve integration and unification by means of a centralized, unitary territorial-administrative model that would impose uniform policies across the territory, and subordinate sub-state, regional interests to those of the centre. This meant that Ukraine did not draw from the reservoir of its own indigenous, pre-Soviet traditions.

This essay examines the constitutional deliberations on models of statehood. We begin with an outline of the historical, political and regional context. The next section traces the constitutional debates over the choice between the unitary or federal models of the state, the position of Crimea, and the form and competences of local and regional self-governing bodies. The final section analyses the outcome, that is the territorial-administrative model that Ukraine adopted in the constitution and post-constitutional legislation.

THE CONTEXT

Regionalism

That regionalism should figure so prominently in today's Ukraine is hardly a surprise in light of the fact that the country is essentially an amalgam of regions with different ethno-linguistic, economic, cultural and political profiles. During the centuries of Ukraine's statelessness, these regions belonged to different states whose boundaries shifted over time. Ukraine was a 'battleground' over which the surrounding states, such as the Grand Duchy of Lithuania, the Ottoman Empire, the Polish-Lithuanian Commonwealth, the Crimean Tatar Khanate, Moscovy, the Russian empire, the Habsburg empire, Poland, Romania and Hungary fought for domination.

The bulk of ethnographic Ukrainian territories were unified for the first time in history within the boundaries of the Ukrainian Soviet Socialist Republic, initially made up of nine *gubernias* of the Russian empire.[1] In September 1939 Western Ukraine (Galicia and Volynia), which had been part of Poland in the inter-war period, was annexed by the USSR and incorporated in the Ukrainian Soviet Socialist Republic (UkrSSR). In 1940 Romania lost Northern Bukovina to the UkrSSR, and in 1945 Transcarpathia (then known as Subcarpathian Ruthenia) was ceded to the USSR by Czechoslovakia.[2] The formation of present-day Ukraine was completed with the transfer of the Crimean Oblast (which until 1945 was the Crimean Autonomous Socialist Republic) in 1954. Thereafter, the UkrSSR consisted of 25 *oblasti* and two city authorities, Kiev and Sevastopol.

Soviet *oblasti* were purely territorial-administrative units and did not correspond to historical regions. Yet several decades of Soviet rule did not annihilate memories or the legacies of pre-Soviet divisions. The territorial division that Ukraine inherited from the Soviet Union was haunted by a lack of historical legitimacy, evident in the persistence of traditional names for historical and geographical regions that comprise several *oblasti* and/or cut across *oblast'* boundaries, such as Galicia, Slovodska Ukraine, Volynia, Donbas, Transcarpathia, Bukovina, Novorossiya, or Podila. Yet despite the lack of congruence between historical regions and Soviet *oblasti*, the terms *oblast'* and region tend to be used interchangeably. The confusion about what constitutes a region in Ukraine is further compounded by macro-regional divisions of the territory with distinct socio-demographic, economic, cultural and political characteristics, such as Eastern Ukraine, South Ukraine, Western Ukraine, and Left Bank, often used in everyday life and the media in Ukraine, although their physical boundaries are far from clear-cut. For example, Western Ukraine in the narrowest ('political') sense means Galicia (Halychyna), that is the three *oblasti* of Lviv, Ternopil, and Ivano-Frankivsk. In a wider sense it includes also Volynia (Volynia and Rivno *oblasti*), and geographically Chernivtsi and Transcarpathia as well. Apart from administrative *oblasti*, historical regions, and macro-regions, social scientists and geographers have endeavoured to delineate regions 'objectively' on the basis of various characteristics, without reaching consensus.

Nevertheless, even if regional boundaries cannot be easily drawn, there is little disagreement that regional diversity is one of the most salient features of the Ukrainian state and society (see Solchanyk, 1994; Liber, 1998; Birch and Zinko, 1996; Hesli, 1995; Kubicek, 2000; Birch, 2000). Broadly speaking, regionalism in Ukraine can be characterized as a graduation between two opposing poles centred on Donetsk in the east of the country and Lviv in the west (see Nemiria, 1996). Ideal-type profiles of the 'East' and 'West' can be presented in terms of the dichotomy shown in Table 1.

This bi-polarity is regularly highlighted in most studies of Ukraine, not least because it was confirmed by the striking East–West divide in the population's voting pattern during the parliamentary and presidential elections in 1994 (see Arel and Wilson, 1994). In reality, however, regional differences are much more nuanced between the two poles. For example, while the Left Bank (east) is more industrialized than the Right Bank (west), it contains some agricultural *oblasti*, such as Sumy; on the Right Bank, Volynia is less nationalistic than Galicia; similarly,

TABLE 1

Characteristics	'West'	'East'
Density of population	Low	High
Urbanization	Low	High
Ethnic composition	Ukrainian	Ukrainian and Russian
Language spoken	Ukrainian	Russian
Religion	Catholicism	Orthodoxy
Economic profile	Agricultural	Industrial
Political orientation	Moderate or radical nationalism, and liberal	Communist or liberal
Geopolitical preferences	Pro-European	Pro-Russian/CIS
Historical memories	Soviet Union as 'invader', Russians as enemies	Soviet Union as a legitimate state, Russians as the 'Slavic brothers'

Orthodoxy co-exists with Catholicism in Western Ukraine, and so forth. Overall, there is not a single regional divide in Ukraine but many that overlap. Some differences reinforce regional distinctiveness, whereas others weaken it.

In Search of an Indigenous Model

The task of hammering out a suitable territorial-administrative system was compounded by disputes over what could be legitimately defined as the indigenous tradition of statehood. The positive or negative evaluation of the Soviet period in Ukraine's history is not the only thorny issue; disputes also linger over the interpretations of the pre-Soviet tradition.

Federalism was espoused by the intellectuals of the Ukrainian national movement in nineteenth-century tsarist Ukraine (Rudnytsky, 1952, 1977; Lindheim and Luckyi, 1996: 171–83), but these ideas came to nought in 1917 because the Russian elites refused to recognize Ukraine's right to autonomy, let alone to federalize the remnants of the tsarist empire; while the legacy of the short-lived Ukrainian National Republic of 1917–21 is ambiguous, its draft constitution of April 1918 put forward a unitary, decentralized model, vaguely referring to 'extensive self-government' and 'decentralization' (see Sliusarenko and Tomenko, 1997: 105). Federalist elements reappeared when the UNR united with its Galician counterpart, the Western Ukrainian People's Republic in January 1919 in a quasi-federal arrangement allowing for Galician autonomy as the Western Ukrainian Oblast of the UNR (see Bruski, 1997). Nevertheless, due to the profound political instability and military struggle which by early 1919 engulfed the territory of Ukraine, the institutional arrangements made between 1917 and1921 were essentially provisional and ill-defined, and were never properly tested in practice.

While the UNR constitutes the key element in the non-Soviet tradition of Ukrainian statehood, the extent to which the Soviet system can be regarded as part of the indigenous state tradition remains intensely contested among ideological camps in Ukraine. Nevertheless, it was the Soviet model that left the greater imprint on Ukraine as it lasted for longer and became the institutional baseline from which the territorial-administrative reform started in 1991. As was pointed out, between 1954 and 1991, the UkrSSR comprised 25 *oblasti* and two cities of 'republican subordination' (Kiev and Sevastopol). *Oblasti* were further divided into districts (*raion*), cities (which were further divided into *raiony*), and rural settlements. Each of these units was represented by a council of people's deputies (*rada narodnykh deputativ* – the so-called *soviets* in Russian, or *rady* in Ukrainian). The *rady* formed 'a single system of organs of state power', a hierarchy of layers of government topped by the Supreme

Soviet – the highest state body in the republic. The councils, which provided an institutional locus for mass participation in politics, combined state power and self-government at the local level. There was no conceptual distinction between local, territorial and central government, the local and territorial governing bodies forming an integrated part of the state apparatus.

Overall, therefore, Ukraine's indigenous, pre-Soviet tradition conflicted with the Soviet territorial model. The former included federalism and decentralization, while the Soviet Union bequeathed Ukraine a highly centralized system. The key question was how useful these models were for the project of state-building after 1991.

Failed Reforms, 1990–94

After the demise of the Communist Party of Ukraine (CPU) in 1991, the system of soviets (*rady* and their executive committees, *vykonkomy*) became the institutional backbone of the state. Undoubtedly, the councils were barely able to assume self-governing responsibilities, having functioned in the shadow of the CPU all their life. The perceived crisis of governability and Kiev's lack of control over the local level fuelled demands to 'reinstate authority at the local level' and 'increase the role and responsibility of the state in overcoming the crisis' (*Biuletyn*, 1992: 16). This resulted in the re-creation of a vertical chain of command from the centre to the local level modelled on the French system of prefects.

In March 1992 President Kravchuk established presidential representatives (*predstavnyky*) to act as a transmission belt for reforms from the centre to the local level and to prompt local soviets to 'stand up to the conditions of independence' (*Biuletyn*, 1992: 80). The 'Law on the President's Representatives' granted the president the right to appoint his representatives as heads of the *oblast'* and local state administration in *oblast'* and districts, and in Kiev and Sevastopol (Art.1). The representatives were to act both as the executive arm of local councils and as the agent of the centre in *oblasti* and regions. They were accountable upwards to the higher-level representatives and the president in a unitary vertical executive structure that co-existed with the regional and local *rady*. The unclear division of powers fuelled conflicts between the heads of *rady* who waged a struggle against curtailment of their powers by the representatives. By 1994, a coalition formed in parliament to press for restoring the executive authority of the *rady* in order to weaken President Kravchuk's control over the regions. As a result, presidential representatives were not re-appointed after the 1994 local elections, and were subsequently abolished.[3]

The ad hoc institutional changes led to confusion and uncertainty. In

June 1994, the 24 newly elected heads of *oblast*-level *rady* acquired extensive powers over their mandated territories, as, following the Soviet principle, a higher level council could decide on any issue of the lower level council. At the same time, it was unclear to whom the heads themselves were accountable. The juxtaposition of the elements of the system of soviets with presidentialism meant that regional leaders could decide on their own allegiance: either to the president, the prime minister or the chairman of the Supreme Council.

However, in a decree of August 1994, the newly elected president, Leonid Kuchma, eliminated this ambiguity. He restored the executive chain of command by subordinating popularly elected heads of *rady* at *oblast'* and *raion* levels (who were simultaneously the heads of executive committees, *vykonkomy*) directly to himself, and made them personally responsible for the execution of state powers. Symptomatically, this breached Kuchma's electoral slogan of decentralization of power to the regions (see below), as it limited democratically elected local authorities, but it evoked hardly any opposition because of fear of the centrifugal tendencies that had manifested themselves over the period 1991–94. The centralizing drive was also to be reflected in the provisions of the new constitution, despite the fact that none of the main political forces openly championed the centralized model of statehood.

Spectre of Centrifugal Tendencies

The regional elites' hopes that independence would bring not only economic prosperity but also greater autonomy from the centre were dashed by the first years of independence, which saw standards of living devastated by hyperinflation in 1992–93, and, instead of ending the *diktat* of an incompetent, all-powerful 'centre', merely shifted it from Moscow to Kiev. These disappointments galvanized concerted opposition to Kiev from Eastern and Southern Ukraine, which intensified in the run-up to the elections. Deprived of the support of these regional leaders, Kravchuk lost the 1994 presidential elections. At that time, fear of the disintegration of the state under the strain of centrifugal forces reached its peak. Even if discontent was widespread amongst Ukraine's regional elites, some were more determined than others to secure greater autonomy. The most adamant were regions such as Crimea, Donbas and Transcarpathia, each of which had close historical ties with other states.

Crimea stood out as a special case in Ukraine as it was the only region with an ethnic Russian majority, and had the strongest historical links with Russia. Crimea was incorporated into Ukraine in 1954 as an administrative-territorial unit (*oblast'*) after the Crimean Autonomous

Soviet Republic was abolished in 1945 (following the deportation of the Crimean Tatars in 1944). On the eve of Ukrainian independence in spring 1991, the status of the Crimean Autonomous Republic was renewed by the Supreme Council of Ukraine. However, after the 1991 Ukrainian referendum on independence, Crimean separatist tendencies intensified, with the encouragement of Russia's political elites, who viewed Crimea as a historical part of Russia. In May 1992 the Crimean leaders passed the Constitution of the Republic of Crimea, which proclaimed the peninsula a sovereign state that 'enters into the state of Ukraine and defines its relations with Ukraine on the basis of contract and agreements' (*Vedomosti Verkhovnovo Sovieta Kryma*, 1991–92). In 1994 separatism peaked with the election of a pro-Russian Crimean president, Yurii Meshkov. This resulted in a clampdown by Kiev. The first step was the 'Law on the Autonomous Republic of Crimea' of 17 March 1995, which reduced the autonomy of Crimea, abolished the Crimean presidency and cancelled the 1992 constitution. Then Kuchma issued a decree placing the executive institutions of Crimea directly under 'executive authority of Ukraine'. In November 1995 the Supreme Council of ARC adopted a new constitution, a number of articles of which were rejected by the Ukrainian parliament on the grounds that they contradicted the laws of Ukraine in such spheres as Crimean citizenship, state symbols, control over key ministries, property rights, and state language.

Donbas, in turn, is a region consisting of two *oblasti*, Donetsk and Luhansk in the Donbas basin (15 per cent of which is within the Russian Federation), with the highest proportion of ethnic Russians outside Crimea: 45 per cent in Luhansk and 44 per cent in Donetsk, according to the 1989 census. Moreover the majority of ethnic Ukrainians are Russian-speakers. In 1990–91 some attempts were made here to establish an inter-front organization, modelled on the separatist Russian-speakers' movements in the Baltic republics, as well as to form a union of 12 eastern and southern Ukrainian *oblasti*. In March 1994, a local referendum in Donbas, held simultaneously with the parliamentary elections, tested public support on four proposals: 1) full membership of Ukraine in CIS; 2) a federal structure for Ukraine; 3) the introduction of Russian as a second language; 4) the immediate introduction of Russian in Donbas as an official language alongside Ukrainian. Each of those questions obtained over 50 per cent of votes. Nevertheless, Donbas, in contrast to Crimea, has not pushed for secession from Ukraine.

Another region that raised demands for political autonomy was Transcarpathia, dealt with by Judy Batt in this volume. These centrifugal tendencies added urgency to the issue of resolving the question of the territorial distribution of power, but precisely because of the challenge they seemed to pose to the territorial integrity of the state, far-reaching decentralization was unlikely to be implemented by the constitutional reformers. At best, an ambivalent compromise between centralization and decentralization would be achieved.

THE CONSTITUTIONAL DEBATE ON THE TERRITORIAL-ADMINISTRATIVE FRAMEWORK

The vexed question of the territorial division of power had thus reached the top of the agenda in the aftermath of the parliamentary and presidential elections of June 1994, but these did not deliver a configuration of political forces conducive to rapid constitutional reform.[4] Apart from a large contingent of deputies with nebulous ideological convictions, two hostile ideological blocs emerged in parliament – the right and the left – both of which were, moreover, at odds with the newly elected President Kuchma, who thus lacked a stable parliamentary power base. Three tasks confronted these forces: choosing a unitary or federal model of the state; defining the position of Crimea; and (once the unitary model was chosen) working out the form and competences of local and regional self-governing bodies.

Federalism

Between 1989 and 1994, the idea of federalism had surfaced in different regions and among certain ethnic minorities. However, these failed to unite in a coherent pro-federal alliance. The March 1990 local elections brought to power non-communist elites in three Galician *oblasti*, who began to advocate federalism as a way of decentralizing the Soviet empire, at a time when Ukraine's independence appeared only a dim and distant prospect. Viacheslav Chornovil, then chairman of Lviv *oblast'* council, and subsequently a leader of the national-democratic movement *Rukh*, advocated Galician autonomy in order to protect the region from the pro-communist forces which still controlled Kiev in 1990–91. But once Ukrainian independence became a reality in 1991, the national democrats (whose ranks were largely made up of Galicians) not only swiftly discarded the idea of federalism, but – as will be argued below – vehemently opposed it as an 'anti-state' ploy devised by Southern and Eastern Ukrainian elites.

In 1990–91 the notion of a federal Ukraine also appeared in the programmes of several smaller parties, which, however, failed to get elected to the parliament (see Zolotariov, 1994). Prior to the 1994 elections, the pro-federal 'camp' was reinforced by liberal parties and leaders from Eastern Ukraine, such as Donbas politicians Zviagilskyi (the deputy prime minister) and Valentyn Landyk, both close to the Labour Party, which represented the 'red directors' and leaders of the local state structures. These regional parties failed, however, to win more than a few seats in the new 1994 parliament. Therefore the hopes of the federalists were pinned on Volodymyr Hryniov, a close political ally of President Kuchma from the Interregional Bloc for Reform (IRBR). Hryniov propounded the economic benefits of federalism, and argued against the tendency to view unitarism as a recipe for state strength and the federal state as 'weak, tending towards disintegration' (Hryniov, 1995: 27). Regional economic autonomy would provide incentives for a more efficient use of Ukraine's potential, and would stimulate bottom-up economic reforms, especially by fostering 'organic' privatization and entrepreneurship. Federalism would counteract Ukraine's regional disparities and overcome grievances occasioned by Kiev's arbitrary redistribution of resources. According to Hryniov, 'the very idea of unitarism carries a threat to the statehood of Ukraine' as the centre's drive to control declining resources in the midst of economic crisis would only intensify centrifugal, separatist forces. He also argued that federalism would enhance the democratic credentials of the new state, and that the ultimate cause of separatism lay in the 'centralising tendencies of apparatchiks' in Kiev, whose policies forced regional elites to resort to 'federalism' to defend themselves against the centre (Hryniov, 1995: 36).

While economic motives prevailed amongst the Eastern Ukrainian elites, representatives of national minorities, such as the Romanian deputy from the Chernivtsti *oblast'*, Ivan Popesku, suggested that a federal structure should be a long-term goal for Ukraine in light of its multi-ethnic composition. As a stepping stone towards federalism, Popesku advocated territorial autonomy (*natsionalno-terytorialni utvorenia*) for those national minorities living in compact settlement (Popesku, 1996: 7). Similar views were espoused by the Hungarians in Transcarpathia, as Batt shows. However, the proponents of federalism were very weakly represented in parliament, and, moreover, focused on their narrow regional or ethnic perspectives at the expense of forming a supra-regional alliance to promote federalism. The Eastern Ukrainian elites were internally divided between the pragmatic regional leaders, who favoured economic liberalism, on the one hand, and the left-wing parties, which represented these regions in parliament but rejected federalism. On the other hand, President Kuchma's support for federalism, if it ever existed, proved short-lived. His links (via IRBR) with Hryniov and his, albeit vague, calls for decentralization, had seemed to put him in the camp of federalists during the election (Tomenko, 1995: 54), but once elected he not only failed to support federalism openly, but actually advocated the centralized model of the state.

Unitarism

Federalist ideas met with a rebuff from the president and major parliamentary forces, including the national democrats and the left, albeit for very different reasons. As we shall see, the rejection of federalism did not entail a consensus on other issues pertinent to the territorial-administrative model. The left (the communist, socialist and the peasant factions) opposed on principle even the use of the terms 'unitarism' and 'federalism' (see Politburo UkrSSR, 1991: 10), intent instead on safeguarding 'socialist achievements', including the hierarchical soviet system inherited from the USSR. Federalism, however, was also discarded by those who wanted reform of Soviet-era institutions, above all the national democrats, who were assisted in their task by prominent constitutional lawyers. The president opposed federalization as it would be contrary to his overarching agenda of building a vertical executive chain of command. The centrist factions in parliament, in turn, remained divided on the issue.

The national democrats rejected federalization on the grounds that Ukraine needed to become a unified, integrated political entity. Allocating the Russified regions substantive political, economic and cultural autonomy would deepen the already pronounced historical, cultural and linguistic cleavages (Baltarovych, 1994: 3) by encouraging the differentiation of territorial identities (through educational systems and the use of iconographic symbols such as a flag and emblem), in competition with central government's efforts to foster national allegiance. Institutionalizing regional differences would provide centrifugal forces with symbolic legitimacy and material resources. In other words, regional interests would prevail at the cost of the consolidation of the new state. The national democrats insisted that a strong national identity had first to be built capable of withstanding regional interests that would jeopardize the nation-building process and endanger Ukrainian independence. These arguments revealed the national democrats' lack of trust in the allegiance to the new state of the East and South Ukrainian elites, whom they believed prioritized regional over national interests, and favoured re-integration with Russia. The connection seemed clear: calls for territorial autonomy originated from regions that had historically been part of other states, some of which – namely, Russia and Romania – did not recognize Ukraine's borders until 1997 (on Romania, see Wolczuk, 1997). In particular, there were fears of Russia's imperial ambitions and its readiness to support separatist movements in Ukraine (as it had in Moldova). The way the formally federal USSR had broken up, and subsequent separatist movements in the Russian Federation (including the war with Chechnya) were cited as further proof of the disintegrative potential of federalism (Kornienko, 1996: 141).

The national democrats' position was backed by constitutional lawyers, who presented arguments to the effect that 'federalism is a means of unifying separated regions, not decentralising their integrity'. It was argued that in the case of the USA, federalism was synonymous with centralization. Ukraine had no need of federal arrangements, because it already existed as a legally bounded territory; in post-Soviet Ukraine, federalism would amount to disintegration rather than integration (Kornienko, 1996: 141; see also Shapoval, 1996: 135). Curiously, examples of other federations, such as Germany and Austria, were dismissed as 'of a more or less artificial character', because these states were 'artificially' federalized (although the historical roots of those federations in the nineteenth-century German principalities and Austro-Hungarian provinces were acknowledged). In line with Soviet theory, only federations built on ethnic principles were regarded as genuine.

Ukraine's regional differences should be overcome through a uniform system of local self-government. Only after a period of centralization could the gradual devolution of power to popularly elected regional assemblies be contemplated. Amongst the European states, France was viewed as the template for Ukraine;[5] and 'European' traditions of state building were frequently invoked, for example:

> The establishment of a modern nation-state requires a unitary political system that would allow for the implementation of a general methodology of state building and for the functional co-ordination of central and regional governmental mechanism. European constitutionalism dictates that a nation-state is built as a single, unitary organism (Baltarovych, 1994: 3).

However, enthusiasm for unitarism required the national democrats to distance themselves from the tradition of federalist political thought set by the intellectual fathers of modern Ukrainian statehood, such as Mykhailo Drahomanov and Mykhailo Hrushevskyi. According to Professor Volodymyr Shapoval, one of the leading constitutional lawyers involved in constitution-drafting, the federalist ideas of Drahomanov and Hrushevskyi originated in the specific circumstances of Ukraine at the time:

> In the second half of the nineteenth century, the idea of federalism was fairly popular among the progressively thinking Ukrainian intelligentsia. However, those who upheld the idea of federalism

were attracted only by its external aspect, therefore the role and place of the Ukrainian nation and its land was stressed in the context of a so-called federation of Slavic republics, rather than the territorial division of the authority of state bodies. (Shapoval, 1996: 130).

In other words, federalism then was conceived as a means of carving out Ukrainian autonomy within the Russian empire; it was not to be regarded as a model for the internal organization of the Ukrainian state. Moreover, federalist thinkers had encountered the problem that:

> There were no clear-cut principles to delineate the historical boundaries of the regions between the subjects of the federation and neither their number nor competencies were specified. This justifies the cautious approach to the tendency to 'absolutize' the federal conception of statehood in Ukrainian political thought (Shapoval, 1996: 135).

Instead, the national democrats evoked the tradition of the Ukrainian People's Republic (UNR) of 1917–20, which was defined as a decentralized unitary state, as more appropriate for post-Soviet Ukraine. The unitary model was viewed as sufficiently flexible to integrate Ukrainian 'ethnographic lands' with their various political traditions. While it was acknowledged that the 1918 draft constitution had envisaged 'national personal autonomy' for ethnic minorities (that is the right to form non-territorial, national unions with self-governing competence in issues affecting the 'national way of life'), this was not to be confused with territorial autonomy.

Confining federalist ideas to the dustbin of history was a significant break with the indigenous intellectual heritage. As Rudnytsky pointed out:

> The strength of the old federalist concept was its breadth of vision. It placed the Ukrainian problem within a wide international context, organically connecting the goal of national liberation with the cause of political liberty and social progress of Eastern Europe as a whole (Rudnytsky, 1977: 218).

While by the end of the twentieth century, new forms of cooperation and integration within the 'Europe' of the EU were confirming the complementarities of federal and national modes of governance adumbrated by earlier Ukrainian political thinkers, circumstances in Ukraine led the national democrats to give primacy to *samostiinist* (independence) over their intellectual forebears' more open, pluralistic ideals of statehood.

However, the elaboration of the unitary model was no straightforward matter either. First of all, the case of Crimea had to be dealt with separately; and second, the institutional framework for the regional and local levels still had to be defined.

Crimea

The question of Crimea divided the 'unitarists': while all of them conceded Crimea's special condition as the only region of Ukraine with an ethnic Russian majority and strong historical links with Russia, they differed on the institutional means by which to manage its specificities. The new constitution had to define the peninsula's name, its official language and property regime, as well as whether it would have rights to its own constitution, budget and tax-raising powers, special citizenship, separate security forces, and diplomatic relations with other states.

President Kuchma, the leftist and centrist factions conceded that extensive autonomy was indispensable to placate Crimea's centrifugal forces and avert separatism. The left and the Interregional Group of Deputies (MDG) supported the Crimean elites on issues such as the name 'Autonomous Republic', the constitution, the law-making prerogative of the Supreme Council of Crimea, citizenship and language. They also supported the creation of a permanent representative of the CAR in Kiev as an attribute of its 'sovereignty'. In contrast, the national democrats vehemently opposed any such concessions on the grounds that they would reinforce separatism in the peninsula. Recognition of the sovereignty of Crimean institutions over the territory of the peninsula would usurp the sovereignty of the Ukrainian state. While radical right-wing parties called for Crimea to be reduced to the status of an *oblast'*, the two national democratic factions, *Rukh* and *Derzhavnist'*, conceded that Crimea required tailor-made arrangements, but stressed that integrating Crimea into Ukraine required Kiev to have the upper hand in the division of power. They envisaged only 'autonomy' (*avtonomia*) instead of the status of a 'republic' on the grounds that the latter was incompatible with the unitary state. 'Autonomy' would not entail attributes of statehood such as a presidency and constitution (although it might have a special *Statut*). Rather than a fully fledged parliament with law-making and tax-raising powers, the Supreme Council of Crimea was to be a regional representative organ issuing 'decisions and resolutions'.[6]

However, apart from the pro-federal MDG, the differences between the president and centre-right factions in parliament were not irreconcilable. There was broad agreement that Crimea required political autonomy but would not be allowed to have its own (or dual) citizenship, security forces, or to foster diplomatic links bypassing Kiev. It was firmly held that Crimea's situation was exceptional and no similar provisions were to be made for other regions of Ukraine, such as Donbas, Transcarpathia or Bukovina. Even if the details remained under dispute until the last day of constitution-making, the broad agreement paved the way for a hybrid territorial-administrative system – a unitary state with a federal component, Crimea.

The Unitary Model: 'Reformers', 'Restorationists' and Decentralization

While 'unitarists' rejected federalism, they did not discard the idea of decentralization, as long as this did not undermine the sovereignty and territorial integrity of Ukraine:

> In a decentralized form of autonomy, there exists at first an independent, already existing sovereign power, which gives up a part of its rights and attributes to certain territories. Autonomy is the next developmental stage following the establishment of the central power system, and does not contradict the unitary form of government (Kornienko, 1996: 139–45).

However, the scope of decentralization was neither agreed nor fully spelled out in the constitution, and in practice turned out to be limited to the lowest, local level of self-government in Ukraine.

All apart from the leftist factions agreed on the abolition of the system of soviets, seen as incapable of providing genuine self-government because its hierarchical form defeated the principle of autonomy. In practice, after the demise of the Communist Party, the councils (*radas*) were not politically accountable at the local level, and obstructed economic reforms. The 'reformers', that is the centre-right factions and the president, shared the conviction that new life had to be breathed into local self-government in villages and cities. In that respect, they took on board the obligations stemming from Ukraine's admission to the Council of Europe in November 1995, which, among other things, required implementation of the European Charter on Local Self-Government. The Charter stipulated the independence of local community self-government as the basis of the state.

Despite the broad support for this at the level of local communities, the intermediate, regional layer proved more difficult to agree upon. The concept of decentralization does not imply any particular scope for devolved power at the regional level. In Ukraine, local self-government (*mistseve samovriaduvania*) denotes both regional and local self-government and many proponents of decentralization championed self-governing powers for basic, municipal units rather than intermediate, regional units. The European Charter of Local Government did not provide clear cut-guidance, being much less specific about regional autonomy than about local self-government. Overall, the debate on decentralization centred on three interrelated issues: 1) the type of regional units; 2) the powers of regional self-governing bodies *vis-à-vis* the centre and the regional bodies of state administration; 3) the representation of regional self-governing bodies at the centre.

Regional Units

The fundamental issue was the type and size of units to be granted territorial self-government. The reformist constitution-drafters faced a conundrum. On the one hand, the Soviet-era *oblasti* were unsatisfactory as they lacked legitimacy and cut across historical regions; on the other hand, the historical regions proved not only difficult to define but their institutional delineation would highlight the weak territorial cohesion of independent Ukraine. The fact that concerted calls for territorial autonomy originated in historical regions with the strongest regional identities and long ties to other states (Crimea, Donbas and Transcarpathia) exacerbated the sense of threat to territorial sovereignty.

In the end, under the strain of the sheer number of issues to be dealt with, and the pressure of time to finalize the constitution, the task of elaborating new territorial units proved intractable. For lack of an agreed, viable alternative, the Soviet-era *oblasti* were retained in the new constitution; but, because of their weak historical legitimacy, they were only accorded the most limited powers.

The Role and Powers of the Regional Self-Governing Bodies

Once the 'path of least resistance' had been chosen, the key questions were how much autonomy, and what kind of representative institutions the *oblasti* should have. The problem boiled down to the balance of power between the agencies of the centre (state administration) and representative institutions at the *oblast'* level.

The right was prepared to devolve power only as long as the territorial integrity of Ukraine was not threatened. The national democrats opted for the preservation of *oblasti* (despite their Soviet pedigree) as a lesser evil, provided they were not granted extensive powers. They opposed the creation of directly elected regional assemblies, and preferred indirectly elected *rady* with weaker legitimacy *vis-à-vis* the centre – thus side-stepping their professed commitments in principle not only to decentralization (except at the lowest level), but also to 'Europeanization' in as much as directly elected regional self-government had, by the mid-1990s, become a clear trend in many European states. For the national democrats, state-building necessitated the circumscription of regional autonomy. In particular, they feared regional challenges to the centre's policies in language, education and culture, such as the Donbas local plebiscite in 1994 (see above). They also argued that indirect election would recruit new people from below, in place of the *nomenklatura* (Bezsmertnyi, 1996: 25–8).

In this respect, the right found a powerful ally in President Kuchma, who stressed the imperatives of control and efficiency:

> Practically, [today] nobody rules Ukraine. [At the regional level] everybody is interested in his own welfare. The interests of the people and the practical issues of running the state are pushed to the side. There are the first signs of the disintegration of the state. Some *oblasti* and even districts (*raiony*) have taken decisions on the level of their contributions to the state budget. This means that one of the most important laws of Ukraine is not being implemented...

> The fully-fledged executive vertical structure is needed to end 'anything goes' (*vsedozvolennist'*), and cronyism practised by a number of *raion* and city heads. At this level mismanagement prevails, and an ordinary person is left without any protection, support, or justice. We have to eliminate such manifestations of contemporary local feudalism, take radical measures to restore order, [and] protect our citizens (Kuchma, 1994: 3).

In the president's view, only the creation of a rigid vertical executive structure could alleviate the problem, simultaneously weakening the *oblast'* and *raion* councils. He therefore also favoured indirect elections to weaken the councils' popular legitimacy; and revived the presidential representatives (*predstavnyky prezydenta*) at *oblast'* and *raion* level, who would simultaneously head the executive – the regional state administration – and chair the councils. Strict control of the *predstavnyky* from above would allow delegation of 'important decision-making, such as the management of state property, to the regional level' (Kuchma, 1994: 3). In other words, decision-making power could only be devolved to regions if they were under the control of state officials subordinated to the president. Essentially the president advocated a highly centralized model of state, even though (like the national democrats) he professedly favoured 'de-statization' (*vidderzhavlenia*) of the self-governing bodies in place of the unified Soviet-style system. In the event, v*idderzhavlenia* meant replacing the latter with a consolidated network of French-style prefects to oversee regional self-government.

As pointed out above, the left's aim was to restore the system of soviets, with the *radas* (soviets) continuing to be subordinated to the central state authorities:

> We support the preservation of the system of councils of the working
> masses with a clear division of functions between the various levels
> … and the vertical subordination of the executive organs of councils
> to the higher level up to the Council of Ministers in matters of
> national importance (Symonenko, 1996: 3).

At the same time, the Left cited the European Charter on Local Self-
Government in order to maintain that 'the Councils of People's Deputies
(*rady*) are one of the most powerful and effective forms of self-
government' (Kriuchkov, 1995: 5). However, the left wing passed over the
incompatibility of local and regional self-government autonomy with the
principle of 'democratic centralism', which they continued to espouse;
and glossed over the problem that traditional soviets could not be
autonomous from the state, as they *constituted* the state. In particular,
strict financial subordination had meant that councils had no independent
resources to perform their functions and the resources were instead
allocated by the centre to the *oblast'*, and thence to the lower level. The
councils had no independent revenue-producing sources, such as taxes or
municipal property.

The left opposed the institutional 'duality of power' at the regional
level, that is the co-existence of popularly elected councils with local state
administrations headed by the presidential representative. In particular,
the latter contradicted their understanding of *narodovladia* ('people's
power'). Furthermore, the left consistently argued in favour of direct
election to all levels of councils, a move that the national democrats and
the president opposed. The left even invoked the World Declaration of
Local Self-Government, which made explicit references to self-
government of larger territorial units, while the national democrats
preferred the European Charter's vagueness on the question of regional
autonomy. Paradoxically, insofar as it supported directly elected *oblast'*
councils, the left turned into a champion of decentralization:

> [R]ejecting demagogy and politicking, and striving for democratic
> principles, there is no need to abolish Councils, but to divide clearly
> – most of all in the Constitution – the spheres of competence of the
> centre, regions and the local level, of the representative and
> executive bodies; to transfer the right to decide local matters to the
> local level; and to give regions and localities maximum autonomy
> (*samostiinist*) (Kriuchkov, 1995: 5).

Representation of Regions at the Centre

The final questions were how regions were to be represented at the centre,
and whether the upper chamber of the legislature would be designed for

this purpose. The idea that pronounced regional differences made a strong case for bi-cameralism in Ukraine reappeared sporadically during the constitutional process over the period 1990–96, but did not command the favour of the parliamentarians for the same reasons that federalism and regional autonomy had been rejected. Some national democrats feared the Senate would become a first step towards the federalization of Ukraine 'through the back door'. It was commonly asserted that upper houses were only needed in federations, whereas Ukraine was a unitary state. *Oblasti* were purely administrative units and as such they did not need to be represented at the centre. As Serhiy Holovatyi, a national democrat deputy, argued 'we have *oblasti* and not regions. Let's create regions and only then represent them' (The Materials of the Constitutional Commission, 1991: 8). To the argument that even some unitary states, such as Poland, had an upper chamber, opponents responded that bi-cameralism in Poland was sanctioned by traditions that did not exist in Ukraine.

The left rejected bi-cameralism as incompatible with its model soviet system, and also used the argument that 'the creation of a Senate would stimulate separatist and centrifugal forces' (Kriuchkov, 1995: 4). Even the centrist Interregional Group of Deputies (MDG), otherwise favouring far-reaching devolution of power to regions, rejected bi-cameralism on the grounds that it would 'split Ukraine' and 'because of the threat of instability, exacerbate regional differences and complicate the legislative process'.[7] However, the MDG's scepticism stemmed from its objection to the president's formula for the upper chamber in the constitutional drafts of 1995–96, giving each *oblast'* three senators. This would not reflect the weight of the densely populated East and South, and would give undue prominence to the West and Central Ukrainian *oblasti*. For example, in Donetsk *oblast'* one senator would represent 1,300,000 voters, as opposed to 226,000 voters in Chernivtsi. In face of this centrist and leftist opposition, the supporters of bi-cameralism, including the president, found themselves in a minority, and an upper chamber was not created.

Overall, the constitutional debates on the territorial model revealed a high degree of agreement between the national democrats and the president to ensure the prevalence of the centre over the periphery. Doggedly adhering to the system of soviets, the left was hardly a constructive opposition, while the centrist forces were too weak and divided to promote devolution of power to the regions. The single most important factor that determined the outcome of the constitutional debates was the fear of separatism amongst the national democrats and trust in a strong centre (under the tutelage of the presidency) as an engine of the state-building project. The example of Crimea, where demands for territorial autonomy in 1991 escalated to full-blown separatism by 1994, fuelled fears that devolution of power to other regions would not serve to accommodate differences but would foster separatism, and thereby threaten Ukraine's territorial integrity. Even if Crimea was granted political autonomy, this was not to apply to the rest of Ukraine. Hence, unitarism carried the day. Although decentralization was also advocated by the majority of forces, there was no agreement on what this meant and no essential principles or mechanisms in place to put a brake on strong tendencies in practice to centralize power.

THE CONSTITUTIONAL OUTCOME: THE TERRITORIAL-ADMINISTRATIVE MODEL OF THE STATE

The chapter on the territorial-administrative system in the 1996 constitution is strikingly succinct. In general, constitutions in unitary states either regulate local self-government in detail or outline only the basic framework. In the case of Ukraine, the latter path was chosen primarily because of the lack of a coherent conception of an appropriate territorial distribution of power. The Soviet-era administrative division was upheld in the constitution and the country's four-tier grid of *oblasti*, districts *(raiony)*, cities and villages was retained (Art.133), as shown below.

Decentralized local self-government was explicitly guaranteed for villages and cities (Arts.7 and 140). In particular, article 140 replaced the system of soviets by 'de-statizing' their councils *(radas)*, defining local government as 'the right of a territorial community ... to resolve independently issues of local character within the limits of the Constitutions and the laws of Ukraine'.

Constitutional debates, however, did not finally clarify the regional tier of government *(oblast'* and district). Federalism had been discarded as too

TABLE 2

Tier	Territorial Units
1st	Central government: legislature and executive
2nd	*Oblasts* (24); and The Autonomous Republic of Crimea; and Cities of Kiev and Sevastopol (directly subordinated to central government)
3rd	*Raiony* (mainly rural districts); and bigger cities (subordinated to *oblasts*)
4th	Villages and smaller cities (subordinated to districts)

dangerous to the new Ukrainian state, yet at the same time, some degree of devolution of power to the regions remained on the agenda insofar as none of the key actors openly advocated a centralized state model. The result was an ambiguous declaration:

> The territorial structure of Ukraine is based upon the principles of unity (*yednist'*) and cohesion (*tsilisnist'*) of state territory and the combination of *centralisation and decentralisation* in the exercise of state power [emphasis added] (Art.132).

This allowed for the continuation of a centralized system. According to article 140, the councils of *oblasti* and *raiony* 'represent the common interests of territorial communities of villages and cities', indicating that the mandate of regional representative bodies is limited to advancing the common interests of the basic units of local self-government. Symptomatically, the concept of regional self-government is absent from the constitution and other legislative acts. The constitution did not grant democratic legitimacy to regional institutions, as it did not stipulate whether either *oblast'* or *raion* councils were to have popularly elected representative bodies (Art.141).[8] This was finally resolved in the 1997 'Law on Local Self-Government in Ukraine', according to which *oblast'* and *raion* councils were to be directly elected. The law was drafted by the parliamentary Commission on State-building, Councils and Self-government, which was dominated by the communists, who took the initiative to assert the powers of the intermediary layer of self-government. They did so, however, without securing a sufficient financial basis for real autonomy from the centre (Sayenko *et al.*, 1997). After the parliament adopted it, the president vetoed the 'Law on Local Self-government' three times but finally capitulated and signed it in 1997.

The only region of Ukraine which was explicitly granted territorial autonomy, was the Autonomous Republic of Crimea (ARC), an anomaly in an otherwise unitary state. The ARC was granted the right to its own constitution, a parliament with the right to issue 'normative acts', and a Council of Ministers. Nevertheless, Kiev's authority on the peninsula was asserted and Crimean autonomy circumscribed in a number of ways.[9] The chapter on the ARC served as a basis for the drafting of the Crimean Constitution, which was approved by the Supreme Council of Ukraine in December 1998. Despite granting political and economic autonomy to the peninsula, Kiev retains control over the Republic by resorting to applying financial pressure – Crimea, like the rest of Ukraine, relies on Kiev for financial resources. Even if in reality Crimean autonomy is a far cry from what was demanded in the early 1990s, Crimea was in practice recognized as a federal component in the otherwise unitary state, and thus serves as a powerful symbol of an alternative model of organizing centre–periphery relations in Ukraine.

Centralization has been achieved through administrative subordination and financial instruments realized through the vertical executive pyramid of 'regional state administration' envisaged by the constitution and the 1999 'Law on Local State Administration'. According to the constitution, the heads of the local state administration at *oblast'* and *raion* level are appointed by the president and are subordinated to heads of administration at higher levels (Art.118). Local state administrations were vested with wide-ranging powers (listed in Art.119 in the constitution), including the drafting and implementation of *oblast'* and *raion* budgets,[10] and serve as executive bodies of *oblast'* and *raion* councils. In six *oblasti* heads of councils double as heads of state administrations, and as such are directly subordinated to the president, despite being popularly elected (see *Ukrainskyi Regionalnyi Visnyk*, 2000: 8). Even if the practice of combining two posts existed between 1994 and 1996 (in the first two years of Kuchma's presidency), it violates the 1996 constitution, which envisaged the separation of the posts.

Budgetary processes are used as a powerful and highly effective instrument of control by the centre over the regions. Regional and local self-government does not have sufficient autonomous revenue sources, and remains highly dependent on the centre for financial handouts (Parkhomenko, 1999). The budgetary system is not only centralized, as the centre jealously guards tax-raising powers, but also arbitrary and changeable. The centre ensured its prevalence over the *oblasti* and *raiony* to the extent that regional decentralization has become a mere constitutional figure of speech.

CONCLUSION

By dismantling the remnants of the system of soviets, the new constitution brought Ukraine into the domain of Western models of statehood in terms of the form of government and the territorial-administrative model. The constitution amounted to a landmark for the 'European option' in Ukrainian politics. Yet Ukraine's claim to the status of a 'normal' European nation-state does not mean that its peculiarities as a new state, coping with the legacies of its past – including profound regional differences – have been left behind. The upsurge of centrifugal forces following independence in 1991 convinced the elites of the need to adopt a unitary model of state (with special status for Crimea) to ensure national consolidation.

'Catching up with Europe' did not entail skipping any stages in the process of state-building. Even if most Western European states moved from centralized to more decentralized models by the 1990s, the Ukrainian elites were convinced Ukraine had to replicate the Western Europe trajectory of state-building, which meant that regionalization would only be contemplated once the national territory was fully integrated under a unified 'sovereign'. The imperative of unity took priority over the assertion of Ukrainian indigenous political tradition, which favoured federalism and decentralization over the centralized, unitary state model. Most tellingly, the national democrats' search for continuity with the pre-Soviet statehood tradition ultimately gave way to the overriding political objective of territorial integrity and unification. This was only too welcome to the president, who sought control over the periphery as a pivotal element in his carefully constructed edifice of executive powers.

As a result, the constitution is heavily skewed in favour of centralization, which in practice, especially on the part of the executive branch, means arbitrary intervention in the affairs of the regional level. So greater political and economic independence from the centre remains on the agenda of regional elites. Even if in 1990–96 the Ukrainian national elites saw 'Europe' as a grid of nation-states, it is only a matter of time before the regional elites begin to look to a 'Europe of the Regions' as a rich reservoir of models for regionalization in Ukraine. These models advance on Ukraine as neighbouring countries, such as Poland (Ukraine's 'strategic partner' and an importance source of advice on 'Europeanization'), carry out a territorial-administrative reform in preparation for EU membership. However, in contrast to its western neighbours, EU membership is not on the cards for Ukraine for the foreseeable future, so Kiev does not have the same incentive to accelerate the process of 'catching up with Europe' in territorial-administrative reform or in other fields.

NOTES

1. The nine gubernias included: Kiev, Podila, Volynia, Chernihiv, Poltava, Kharkiv, Katerynoslav, Kherson, Taurida, but without Crimea; it also included some western districts of the Don Army province. In 1924 within Soviet Ukraine, the Autonomous Socialist Republic of Moldova was created of several *raions* adjacent to the border with Romania, and territorial adjustments in favour of the Russian SFSR were made in 1925, when Southern Kursk and Voronezh, as well as Taganrog and Shaklty regions were transferred to Russia (See Laba, 1995).
2. Before its annexation in 1939 Western Galicia's territorial division was inherited from the Habsburg empire. In Volynia the territorial units originated in the 1864 territorial reform in tsarist Russia, while Bukovina formed part of the Romanian territorial system. As result of the 1939–45 border changes the following *oblasti* were created: L'vivska, Volynska, Rivenska, Ivano-Frankivska, Chernivetska, Ternopilska, Akermanska (Izmail), and Zakarpatska.
3. See *Holos Ukrainy*, 16 February 1994.
4. In principle, the parliament comprised three political blocs: left, right and centre. Yet only the factions on the left and the right, which were created on the basis of political parties, had a more or less clearly identifiable ideological orientation. On the right, the national-democrats

accounted for 27.2 per cent of deputies, and were grouped mainly in two factions, Rukh and Statehood (*Derzhavnist*), which formed on the basis of the People's Movement of Ukraine (Rukh) and the Ukrainian Republican Party respectively. They were assisted by '*Reformy*' (Reforms), the faction which was joined by (mainly Ukrainophone) liberals from other regions of Ukraine and thus became the only faction in the new Supreme Council that drew its members from the majority of *oblasti* (the rest of the factions had a pronounced regional bias). The Left comprised three factions – the communists, Socialists and SelPU – which together controlled 147 seats (43 per cent). The independent deputies united in parliamentary groups such as '*Yednist*' (Unity), which represented the Dnipropetrovs'k *oblast*', '*Tsentr*' (Centre), which consisted of apparatchiks from central state structures, or '*Nezalezhni*' (Independents), which attracted a heterogenous mass of deputies. The Interregional Group of Deputies (MDG) emerged from the defeated centrist-liberal, Russophone Interregional Block for Reforms (IRBR) and contained the large contingent of Crimean deputies.

5. Author's interview with Roman Bezsmertnyi, member of parliament, April 1996.
6. Moreover, Rukh advocated the recognition of the Crimean Tatars as the 'indigenous people'. The Tatars, who were returning from Central Asia to Crimea after the deportation by Stalin in 1944, were viewed as the rightful, 'indigenous' people of the peninsula, in contrast to the recent migrants – ethnic Russians. However, in contrast to its initial stance in 1992, Rukh stopped advocating the Crimean Tatars' right to self-determination through the creation of territorial autonomy in Crimea.
7. Author's interview with Galina Starovoitova, the member of parliament, July 1997.
8. The norm on the indirect mode of elections, as favoured by the Right and the president, was excluded during the final stages in order to appease the left wing and some centrist parliamentarians. Yet, this concession did not go so far as to include a provision on direct elections. Article 141 only states that the chairpersons of district and *oblast*' councils are elected by the respective councils and lead the executive staff of the council.
9. First of all, the ARC was declared 'an inseparable constituent part of Ukraine [which] decides on the issues ascribed to its competence within the limits of authority determined by the Constitution of Ukraine' (Art.134). Secondly, the Constitution of the ARC has to be approved by the Ukrainian parliament in Kiev (Art.135). Thirdly, the Prime Minister of the ARC can be appointed and dismissed by the Supreme Council of ARC only with the consent of the president of Ukraine (Art.136). The Supreme Council of ARC can issue 'normative' or 'legal' (as opposed to legislative) acts only in specified areas, and even then they have to comply not only with the Constitution of Ukraine but also with laws passed by the Supreme Council of Ukraine. In case of their 'nonconformity' the president has the right to suspend and file a case to the Constitutional Court to determine their constitutionality (Art.137). Thirdly, the decisions of the Council of Minister of the ARC have to comply with the acts of the president and the Cabinet of Ministers of Ukraine (Art.135). Fourthly, the court system of Crimea belongs to a unified system of courts of Ukraine (Art.136). And finally, the ARC was refused the right to raise taxes and to have separate (or dual with Russia) citizenship.
10. However, the *oblast*' or district councils obtained a degree of leverage against the centre as under certain circumstances they can force the president to recall the head of the respective state administration (Art.118).

REFERENCES

Arel, D. and A. Wilson (1994), 'The Ukrainian Parliamentary Elections', *RFE/RL Research Report*, Vol.3, No.26.

Baltarovych, Y. (1994), 'Ukraine: A Federal or Unitary State', *Demos*, Vol.1, No.7 (28 Nov).

Bezsmertnyi, R. (1995), 'Konstytutsiya Garantuie Samovriaduvania', *Nova Polityka*, No.5, pp.25–8.

Birch, S. and I. Zinko (1996), 'The Dilemma of Regionalism', *Transition* (1 November), pp.22–5.

Birch, S. (2000), 'Interpreting the Regional Effect in Ukrainian Politics', *Europe-Asia Studies*, Vol.52, No.6 (September), pp.1017–41.

Biuletyn Verkhovnoi Rady Ukrainy (1992), Fifth Session, No.23.

Bruski, J.J. (1997), 'Miedzy Sobornoscia a Separatyzmem. Funkcjonowanie I Rozpad Ukrainiskiej Federacji Galicyjsko-Naddnieprzanskiej, 1918–1919 (Between Sobornist' and

Separatism: the Functioning and Fall of the Galician-Dnieper Federation, 1918–1919)', in Stawowy-Kawka I. and W. Rajka (eds), *Ku Zjednoczonej Europie*. Krakow (Cracow): Wydawnictwo Uniwersytetu Jagiellonskiego, pp.37–52.

Hesli, V.H. (1995), 'Public Support for the Devolution of Power in Ukraine: Regional Patterns', *Europe-Asia Studies*, Vol.47, No.1.

Hryniov, V. (1995), *Nova Ukraina: Yakoiu Ya Yiyi Bachu*. Kiev.

Kopylenko, O. (1996), 'De Shukaty Koreni?', *Uriadovyi Kurier*, 30 April.

Kornienko, M. (1996), 'Regional Autonomy: Federation or Decentralization', *Ukrainian Law*, No.3, pp.139–45.

Kriuchkov, H. (1995), 'Shche Odyn Krok to Dyktatury', *Kommunist*, No.49 (December), pp.4–5.

Kubicek, P. (2000), 'Regional Polarisation in Ukraine: Public Opinion, Voting and Legislative Behaviour', *Europe-Asia Studies*, Vol.52, No.2 (March), pp.273–94.

Kuchma, L. (1994), 'Address of the President of Ukraine Leonid Kuchma to the Supreme Council', *Holos Ukrainy*, 24 December, pp.3–4.

Laba, R. (1995), 'The Russian–Ukrainian Conflict: State, Nation and Identity', *European Security*, Vol.4, No.3 (Autumn), pp.457–87.

'Law on the Formation of Local Power and Self-Governing Organs', *Holos Ukrainy*, 16 February 1994.

'Law on Local Self-Government in Ukraine', *Uriadovyi Kurier*, 14 June 1997.

Liber, G. (1998), 'Imagining Ukraine: Regional Differences and the Emergence of an Integrated State Identity, 1926–1994', *Nations and Nationalism*, Vol.4, No.2 (April), pp.187–206.

Lindheim, R. and G. Luckyi (eds) (1996), *Towards an Intellectual History of Ukraine: An Anthology of Ukrainian Thought From 1710 to 1995*. Toronto, Buffalo, London: University of Toronto Press, pp.171–83.

Materials of the Constitutional Commission (1991), Fourth Meeting, Archives of the Constitutional Commission, (March).

Nemiria, G. (1996), 'Regionalism and Ukrainian Nation-state Building', Unpublished Conference Paper, CREES, (Birmingham, June).

Parkhomenko, V. (1999), *Problemy Mistsevoho Samovriaduvania v Ukraini 1990-kh Rokiv*. Kiev, pp.162–206.

(Politburo UkrSSR) Meeting of Politburo on 2 July 1991, the Central State Archive of Civic Associations of Ukraine, FOND 1, OPYS 11, Delo.2278.

Popesku, I. (1996), 'Ludyna v Derzhavi: Harmonia Prava', *Holos Ukrainy*, 3 December, p.7.

Rudnytsky, I.L., (ed.) (1952), *Mykhaylo Drahomanov. A Symposium and Selected Writings*. The Annals of the Ukrainian Academy, New York, pp.193–205.

Rudnytsky, I.L. (1977), 'The Fourth Universal and Its Ideological Antecedents', in Taras Hunchak (ed.), *The Ukraine, 1917–1921: A Study in Revolution*. Cambridge, MA: Harvard University Press, pp.186–219.

Rudnytsky, I.L. (1987), *Essays in Modern Ukrainian History*. Alberta: Canadian Institute of Ukrainian Studies.

Sayenko, Y., A. Tkachuk and Y. Pryvalov (1997), *Mistseve Somovraduvanya v Ukrainii: Problemy i Prohnozy*. Kiev.

Shapoval, V. (1996), 'The State System of Ukraine: Political and Legal Aspects', *Ukrainian Law*, No.3, pp.130–38.

Sliusarenko, A. and M. Tomenko (eds) (1997), *Istoria Ukrains'koi Konstytustyi*. Kiev.

Solchanyk, R. (1994), 'The Politics of State-Building: Centre–Periphery Relations in Post-Soviet Ukraine', *Europe–Asia Studies*, Vol.46, No.1, pp.47–68.

Symonenko, P. (1996), 'Komunisty za Taku Konstytutskyi Yaku Vidpovidatyme Voli Bilshosti Narodu', *Kommunist*, No.17 (April), p.3.

Tomenko, M. (1995), *Ukrainska Perspektyva: Istoryko-Politolohichni Pidstavy Suchasnoi Derzhavnoi Stratehii*. Kiev.

Ukrainskyi Regionalyi Visnyk (2000), East–West Institute, 15 November.

Vedomosti Verkhovoho Sovieta Kryma (1991–1992), No.7.

Wolczuk, R. (1997), 'Relations Between Ukraine and Romania in the Context of NATO Enlargement', *The Ukrainian Review*, Vol.44, No.4 (Winter), pp.34–41.

Zolotariov, V. (1994), 'A Federative System of Government as a Means of Resolving the Present Crisis in Ukraine', *Demos*, Vol.1, No.7 (28 November).

Narva Region within the Estonian Republic: From Autonomism to Accommodation?

DAVID J. SMITH

In the period since 1991, Estonia's north-east border city of Narva and its surrounding county of Ida-Virumaa has been most notable for its large concentration of 'non-titular' national groups. Today, only 18 per cent of the region's inhabitants are Estonian by ethnic nationality. The remainder of the (predominantly urban) population consists of Russians and a variety of other ethno-national groups, although a majority speaks Russian as a first language (Ida-Virumaa County, 1997). The Russian-speaking concentration is especially marked in the city of Narva, where Estonians number only four per cent. As in the other towns of the region, Narva's population consists mainly of Soviet-era settlers and their descendants. For this reason, a majority of inhabitants did not obtain automatic rights to Estonian citizenship following the restoration of independence.[1]

Narva shares its name with the river that separates the city from its neighbouring town of Ivangorod. Today, this narrow watercourse marks the *de facto* state border between Estonia and Russia, a line that corresponds to the Soviet-era boundary dividing the ESSR from the RSFSR. For 300 years prior to 1945, however, Narva and Ivangorod constituted a single administrative unit. *De jure*, the current frontier still has no official status: an Estonian–Russian border treaty has been awaiting full ratification by the two parties since 1996, but continues to form the subject of an inter-state dispute. The original essence of this disagreement lies in Russia's refusal to admit to the illegal annexation of Estonia by the USSR in 1940 and, by extension, to recognize the borders of the inter-war Estonian Republic fixed under the 1920 Tartu peace treaty with Soviet Russia. These inter-war borders encompassed Ivangorod and a strip of territory to the east of the Narva river, as well as the south-eastern region of Pechora which had historically formed part of Russia proper. Following the Soviet reoccupation of 1944, these latter territories were detached from Estonia and incorporated into the neighbouring RSFSR. However, insofar as the restored Estonian state of today considers the Tartu treaty to be the sole legitimate document governing relations with Russia, its borders are deemed to correspond to those established in 1920. In practice, Estonia dropped its symbolic claim to the 'lost territories' back in 1996. Russia, however, still refuses to ratify the agreement, citing alleged infringement of the rights of 'Russian-speakers' living in Estonia.

Historically, it has been Narva's misfortune to be located at a point where the interests of many states collide (Weiss-Wendt, 1997: 22). Founded by the Danes during the thirteenth century, the city came under the control of the Livonian Order in 1346. In the course of the Livonian Wars, it passed into the hands first of Russia (1558), then of Sweden (1581), which finally relinquished the Livonian provinces to the tsarist empire following the Great Northern War of 1700–21. Swedish and Russian overlords both confirmed the rights and privileges of the Baltic German nobility, which continued to exercise political hegemony until the Russian Revolution paved the way for the emergence of an independent Estonian Republic. In administrative terms, Narva was transferred to the neighbouring Russian *Guberniia* of Saint Petersburg during 1802. Its status was finally resolved through a referendum held in July 1917, when the population of the Narva district – by this time roughly divided between ethnic Estonians and Russians – voted to attach the town to the newly autonomous province (later independent republic) of Estonia (Weiss-Wendt, 1997: 36–40).

Local government in the new republic was constructed on the basis of the administrative divisions inherited from the Tsarist period. Narva and Ivangorod were therefore incorporated into the expanded eastern county of Virumaa. Unitary in character, the inter-war republic initially provided for local self-government at both county and district (parish, borough, town) level (Reino, 1998; Elango *et al.*, 1998: 208–9; Raun, 1991: 112). Alongside generous territorially based provisions for its national minorities (12 per cent of the population during 1918–40), Estonia also introduced a system of non-territorial cultural autonomy. Unique in inter-war Europe, this legislation was restored to being in 1993 and forms the centrepiece of minority rights provision in present-day Estonia (Von Rauch, 1995: 135–45; Smith, 1999: 455–74; Smith, 2001: 9–36). Growing political instability in the wake of the Great Depression, however, strengthened the already widely held contention that the state order was 'too democratic for its own good' (Lieven, 1993: 62). In March 1934 the acting president Konstantin Päts suspended parliamentary rule before going on to consolidate his own personal dictatorship during the second half of the decade. Although not completely abolished, local self-government and minority rights were severely curtailed at this time (Elango *et al.*, 1998: 208, 280–82; Ruutsoo, 1993). Whatever semblance of local democracy remained was swept away entirely following the Soviet annexation. In terms of administrative structure, the 11 former counties were replaced by 15 *raiony*, whilst primary level units consisted of 193 village Soviets, 27 boroughs and 35 towns by the end of the Soviet period (Kaldmäe *et al.*, 1999: 4). As towns of 'republican significance', Narva and Sillamäe were placed under the direct supervision of the ESSR Council of Ministers (Raun, 1991: 169–70).

The face of the region was utterly transformed after 1944, when Narva was reduced to rubble during fierce fighting between occupying German forces and the advancing Red Army. The city's inhabitants, previously evacuated by the Germans, were for the most part not permitted to return to their homes, and were replaced by refugees and workers administratively mobilized from western Russia, Belarus and Ukraine. Post-war industrialization exploited the region's extensive reserves of oil-shale, with mines in nearby Kohtla-Järve providing fuel for two new power stations in the environs of Narva. Narva's Kreenholm mill and a range of new enterprises drew further migrants attracted by the relatively high living standards obtainable in the ESSR. Whilst much emphasis has been given to the transient nature of post-war immigration, 69 per cent of Narva's population during the early 1990s had either been born in Estonia or had lived there for over 30 years (Kirch *et al.*, 1993: 177). Despite the lack of any obvious affinity with 'titular' culture, these more established residents were widely identified as 'Baltic Russians' distinct from their ethno-national kin in the neighbouring RSFSR. According to some local commentators, Narva developed a particular 'niche' identity within the Soviet state.[2] At the same time, the city's industrial base was also deeply dependent upon the highly centralized all-union economy for its markets and supply of essential raw materials.

POST-SOVIET ESTONIA: A 'NATIONALIZING' STATE ON THE ROAD TO EUROPE

The identity and affiliation of Narvitians only really became an issue during 1988–89, when the Estonian Supreme Soviet took a number of steps affirming the republic's sovereignty within the USSR. These measures were adopted under growing pressure from the Estonian Popular Front (which captured power in the March 1990 republican elections) and other more radical nationalist groups whose demands quickly shifted to outright independence. Post-Soviet state-building in Estonia reflected the growing prevalence of 'nation-state' (*rahvusriik*) ideology in the run-up to independence (Smith, 2000: 68–74). If the Law on Citizenship appeared firmly at odds with the multi-ethnic character of the population, the same might be said of the 1992 constitution, which provides for a unitary model of statehood and establishes Estonian as the sole official language of state and local government.

In all but exceptional cases, offices in state agencies and local governments are to be filled by Estonian citizens. Hopes that cities such as Narva might be deemed exceptional in this regard were dispelled by the May 1993 Law on Local Elections, which stipulated that only citizens would be allowed to stand for office (all permanent residents are allowed to vote in local elections, regardless of citizenship status). This decision by the Estonian parliament ran counter to recommendations by the Council of Europe, and contradicted assurances given by the government prior to Estonia's accession to that organization in May 1993 (Pettai, 1993: 30). By the same token, the 1996 Law on Public Service enforced the citizenship requirement with regard to other state agencies. Knowledge of the Estonian language had been made a requirement for public sector employment as early as 1989. Once again, the state generally adopted a pragmatic line towards this issue prior to 1996. Subsequently, however, a series of legislative amendments have sought to reinforce the position of the state language, most notably through a stipulation that candidates standing in local and national elections must possess a working knowledge of Estonian. This move elicited considerable opposition from the small group of Russian-speaking MPs, who argued that the proposed measures contravened the European Charter on Local Self-government and the European Framework Convention for the Protection of National Minorities. However, whilst EU pressure has led to the deletion of certain language requirements for private sector employees, those pertaining to local government office became law in 1999 (Smith, 2001: 22–5; EU Commission, 2000: 20).

Provision for national minorities under the 1992 constitution centres on the cultural autonomy paradigm. In territorial terms, inhabitants of localities where 'at least half of the permanent residents belong to a national minority' have the right to receive responses from state agencies, local governments and their officials in the relevant minority language. Legally speaking, the term 'national minority' applies only to citizens of Estonia. However, the constitution also states that in localities where the language of the majority of permanent *residents* is not Estonian, local governments may use the majority language as an internal working language (Constitution of the Republic of Estonia, 1996). Since local authorities also have the right to determine the language of instruction in municipal primary and lower secondary schools, basic education in Russian looks set to continue in cities such as Narva. Under recent amendments to the 1993 law on education, 60 per cent of upper secondary state schools (for pupils aged 16–19) must teach entirely in Estonian by the year 2007 (EU Commission, 2000: 19). The original law had provided for a complete transition to Estonian-language instruction in these schools by 2000 (subsequently extended to 2007). This goal, however, proved wholly unrealistic given the continued shortage of personnel qualified to teach in the state language.

Attempts to resurrect democratic local self-government were an integral part of the campaign for Estonian independence during 1988–91. A November 1989 law created a framework for the post-independence era, instituting a two-tier system of administration similar to the one that existed in 1920s Estonia. At the secondary level were 15 self-governing counties (formed on the basis of the pre-existing Soviet *raions* in 1990) whilst the primary level consisted of smaller towns, boroughs and rural municipalities. Initially, at least, the six 'republican cities' (Tallinn, Tartu, Narva, Kohtla-Järve, Pärnu and Sillamäe) were also given second-tier status (Gorokhov 2000: 10–11; Estonian Institute, 1995: 1–2). However, little genuine progress towards the restoration of local self-government was made before 1993, when the right-of-centre nationalist coalition headed by Mart Laar introduced further legislation covering the conduct of local elections, the functions, responsibility and organization of municipalities and the preparation, adoption and implementation of local budgets (Kaldmäe *et al.*, 1999: 9). Despite this consolidation of the legal base, municipalities have found it hard to achieve financial autonomy (Estonian Institute, 1995: 2; Gunter, 2000). In the initial period of post-communist reform, the premium was placed firmly upon the restoration of local democracy. Subsequent experience, however, suggested that far-reaching decentralization was at odds with considerations of both administrative efficiency and unitary state-building. Such concerns informed the June 1993 Act on Local Government Organization, which transformed the counties into a branch of national government charged with ensuring cohesion and administrative efficiency. Under the same law, the six republican cities lost their special status and became ordinary first-tier municipalities. At the time of writing, the question of local government has again come to the fore, with plans afoot to reduce the number of local governments from 247 to 85 in order to save on administrative costs (Sindrich, 2000b; Gunter, 2000).

The 1993 rationalization was consistent with the Thatcherite principles of the Laar government, whose opponents complained of an undue centralization of state power. At the same time, the nature of local government reform clearly reflected the apparent threat to state integrity posed by Russian-speaking former communist elites in Narva and Sillamäe (Marran and Vungo, 1999: 100). For the most part, the leadership of these towns still did not possess Estonian citizenship. By ensuring that they would now not be eligible to stand for re-election, the 1993 Law on Local Elections triggered the open confrontation between Tallinn and Narva that had been brewing for the previous five years.

'AVOIDING TRANSDNIESTR NORTH': NARVA AND IDA-VIRUMAA 1988–93

The Narva executive – headed by Vladimir Chuikin from December 1989 – had been resolute in its opposition to Estonian independence during the late Soviet era. Key actors from the city assumed a prominent role in a range of organizations (e.g. the Interregional Committee of the ESSR) dedicated to the defence of Soviet power. At the heart of their campaign against the Estonian government were proposals for a wholesale redrawing of administrative boundaries. A request for autonomous self-financing status, presented by the Narva city soviet to the ESSR government in April 1989, was merely the first of a number of similar projects unveiled during the next two and a half years (Gorokhov, 2000: 15–16). The boundaries of the proposed autonomous area showed considerable variation over time. The notion of a Narva Special Economic Zone, unveiled in April 1990, was quickly widened to include all the local governments of north-eastern Estonia. At its most ambitious, the Interregional Committee sought to create a 'new state-territorial formation' embracing Narva, Sillamäe and Kohtla-Järve from the ESSR and Ivangorod, Kingisepp and Slantsy from the RSFSR. For the most part, the various autonomy proposals were based upon the network principle, whereby participation was deemed open to self-governing units at varying levels and even to individual enterprises. In all cases, however, Narva, and its adjoining territories containing the two power stations, was to form the centre of the region (Gorokhov, 2000: 18; Kionka, 1990: 20–21). Common to all proposals were demands for: full autonomy in the spheres of taxation, culture, education, healthcare, social provision and electoral law; local authority ownership of social and productive infrastructure; a visa and tariff-free regime at the state border; special consultative voting rights in the Estonian parliament (Gorokhov, 2000: 15–20).

As a basis for their demands, local leaders frequently invoked the spectre of possible inter-ethnic violence. In July 1991, for instance, Tallinn was warned that the option of forming a breakaway 'Transnarovan SSR' was becoming increasingly popular amongst the inhabitants of north-eastern Estonia. This contention, however, was not borne out by surveys conducted around this time, which found that 87 per cent of the region's inhabitants were in fact opposed to the idea of secession from Estonia (Gorokhov, 2000: 11–12). The pragmatic stance adopted by Edgar Savisaar's Popular Front-led government (April 1990–January 1992) must be cited as a major factor behind the maintenance of ethnic peace during this crucial period. In power (and subsequently in opposition during 1992) Savisaar argued for the creation of a new post-Soviet 'Third

Estonian Republic' in which citizenship would be made available to all residents of the former ESSR (Smith, 2000: 54). Whilst rejecting the federal model advanced by leaders in the north-east, the Savisaar government did recognize the expediency of creating a Narva Special Economic Zone with a favourable tariff regime (Gorokhov, 2000: 18, 22). However, when legislation was put before parliament in June 1991, the rising influence of the Estonian 'national radicals' ensured that it was not adopted. Following Russia's recognition of Estonian independence on 24 August, the city councils of Narva and Sillamäe pledged to recognize the laws of the Estonian Republic, but were nevertheless dismissed on the basis of their previous refusal to do so during the period after March 1990. This exclusion from power, however, proved only temporary, since extraordinary local elections held in October 1991 returned most of the former deputies to the council. In Narva, the old executive committee, headed by Chuikin, was subsequently re-elected.

That the central government made no attempt to challenge the outcome of the elections – indeed, the fact that the old council was allowed to stand for re-election at all – is symptomatic of the Savisaar government's continued efforts to build bridges with the Russian-speaking population after independence. The state's actions in this regard were also significant in providing non-titular actors with perhaps the sole effective 'opportunity structure' permitting them to attempt political mobilization and challenge the centre after 1992 (Smith and Wilson, 1997: 851). Pointing to an upsurge in support for Estonian independence amongst non-Estonians during 1989–91, Savisaar continued to advocate an inclusive citizenship policy as the best guarantee of a stable state order (Savisaar, 1999: 69; Smith, 2000: 72–3).

The failure of this vision was exemplified by Savisaar's fall from power in January 1992 and the nature of the citizenship law adopted the following month. In Narva, widespread popular opposition to the law prompted the local Trade Union Centre to organize a one-day 'political strike' at the two local power stations. Whilst both Chuikin and the leaders of the strike committee alluded to the risk of a 'Transdniestr North', these thinly veiled threats had no discernible impact upon the course of state building. Nevertheless, it is notable that, despite calls to take up arms from some quarters, the city leadership and the TUC made no incitement to violent action (Gorokhov, 2000: 34–6).[3] That this was the case says much about political culture in Narva, where, 'for all their headline-grabbing intransigence officials [took] seriously their ability to keep the city under control' (CSCE, 1992: 61). Talk of an impending eruption of violent conflict in any case appeared exaggerated during 1991–92: surveys from this period suggested that levels of social tension were higher in the capital Tallinn, which is far more ethnically diverse and home to a larger concentration of recent settlers (Kirch *et al.*, 1993: 177). Also, uncertainties arising from the Law on Citizenship were mitigated at least partly by the new constitution, which stipulated that all permanent residents would continue to enjoy social and economic rights. For the time being, non-citizens could continue to live and work in Estonia on the basis of the old Soviet *propiska*.

In the case of the north-east, Raivo Vetik claims that the new constitutional arrangements provided for a degree of decentralization appropriate to a territorially concentrated ethnic group (Vetik, 1993: 276). This belief was, however, clearly not shared by local elites in Narva. The summer of 1992 thus witnessed the first calls for a referendum on achieving the kind of 'special status' which Narva had enjoyed during earlier periods of its history (Marran and Vungo, 1999: 100–103; Gorokhov, 2000: 37–41). The subsequent formation of a 'North-East Estonia Autonomy Committee' clearly enjoyed the tacit approval of council leaders, who sought to capitalize on discontent engendered by the citizenship law and the worsening economic situation. The collapse of the Soviet economy and the instigation of 'shock therapy' had disastrous consequences for employment, prompting the council to call for greater support for local enterprises and closer links with the CIS. If the state refused to deviate from its strict monetarist policies, the temporary government under Tiit Vähi (February–October 1992) did establish a special commission on Ida-Virumaa in an attempt to impose the new constitutional order and stabilize the economic and social situation. To this end, Vähi also granted 'citizenship for special services' to key members of the Russian-speaking elite, including Narva mayor Vladimir Mizui. It was a policy which his radical nationalist opponents characterized as 'bribery' (Marran and Vungo, 1999: 98).

From October 1992, Mart Laar's centre-right 'Fatherland' coalition adopted an altogether different approach towards the north-east and the 'Russian question' more generally. In the words of one commentator, it was decided that the 'shock therapy' approach should now be extended to Estonia's non-citizens in order to force this group to decide its citizenship status and national affiliation (Marran and Vungo, 1999: 103). By the summer of 1993, with the hurdle of Council of Europe membership now safely negotiated, the Laar government felt freer to pursue its own domestic nationalist agenda. In June, it introduced new legislation stipulating that holders of Soviet passports must apply for new residence and work permits within a year or else face the status of illegal immigrant and the possibility of deportation from the country. In its initial form, this 'Law on Aliens' seemed calculated to heighten insecurity amongst the non-citizens who were to be issued with temporary five-year residence permits in the first instance. Applicants were also required to possess a 'legal source of income', yet it was unclear whether, say, unemployment benefit would fall into this category. As such, the law caused particular anxiety in Narva, where the true rate of unemployment was estimated at 30–35 per cent in mid-1993 (Hanson, 1993: 21). By this time, Narva had replaced the capital, Tallinn, as the area of greatest social tension within Estonia. The fervent opposition expressed by local residents only served to increase the concerns of international observers, who also voiced deep concern over many provisions of the new law. In the light of this criticism, Estonian President Lennart Meri refused to promulgate the law, referring it instead for consideration by legal experts at the CSCE and the Council of Europe.

The Narva and Sillamäe Referenda

For the Narva executive, this so-called 'aliens crisis' provided the ideal pretext for advancing the cause of local autonomy. On 28 June, the city council agreed to put the question 'do you want Narva to have the status of national-territorial autonomy within the Republic of Estonia?' in a referendum to be held on 17 July. The essence of the autonomy proposal was that state legislation should only come into force in Narva after confirmation by the city council. Although the council cited the aliens law by way of formal justification for this step, its declaration also made reference to several other pieces of legislation. Especially notable in this regard was the May 1993 Law on Local Elections, which had formed the object of an earlier appeal to Western governments (Gorokhov, 2000: 42–4). The referendum gambit is therefore best regarded as a last, desperate attempt by the city leadership to hang on to power after it had been ruled ineligible for the October 1993 local elections. Although the referendum has been widely portrayed as a secessionist move, available evidence suggests that this was not in fact the case. Rather, it seems, Chuikin *et al.* were seeking to bring additional pressure to bear upon the Estonian government to amend its nationalities legislation and redraw the existing state order. The evidence also suggests that these aims were to be achieved by peaceful means (Sootla, 1993a).[4]

Above all, the initiators of the referendum were looking to capitalize on the wave of Western criticism that had followed the adoption of the Law on Aliens. The announcement of the poll was timed to produce the greatest possible effect internationally, coming shortly after President Meri had decided to refer the Law on Aliens to international scrutiny, and coinciding with a visit to Germany by Prime Minister Mart Laar. Laar for his part characterized Narva's leaders as agents of Moscow, calling developments in the region 'a reflection of the Karaganov doctrine' (Sootla, 1993a: 15).[5] Estonia's reorientation towards the East would not have been an unwelcome development as far as the leadership of the Russian Federation was concerned.[6] However, active support for the Narva referendum, possibly sparking secessionist demands, would also have been a gift to Yeltsin's domestic nationalist opponents at a time of growing political tension within Russia itself. In this regard, Moscow was careful to portray the referendum as strictly an internal affair of the Estonian state, declaring that should the population of Narva and Sillamäe vote in favour of territorial autonomy, the possibility of union with Russia was excluded. Like their 'compatriots' in north-eastern Estonia, then, Russia's leaders relied mainly on indirect pressure via the intermediary of the CSCE and individual Western governments. Laar's point regarding the 'Karaganov doctrine' thus seems a valid one (Sootla, 1993c: 53).

On 5 July, Narva council expressed its 'satisfaction' with the response of international organizations to the north-east crisis, and declared its support for a series of proposed amendments to the Law on Aliens tabled by the CSCE High Commissioner on National Minorities, Max Van der Stoël. When the law went back before parliament the following day, Sillamäe town council upped the ante by announcing that it too was to hold a referendum on autonomous status for the town. The Estonian government, however, showed itself unwilling to make any further concessions. From the point of view of the centre, there could be no question of compromising the unitary model of statehood established under the 1992 constitution (see also Gorokhov, 2000: 49).[7] Already on 29 June, the government decreed that the Narva referendum was contrary to the constitution, and stated that it did not exclude the possible forcible dissolution of Narva council. The latter option enjoyed the backing of more radical nationalist factions within parliament, and was clearly considered. Ultimately, however, the government decided to follow the advice of the chancellor of law, who ruled that although the result of the referendum could have no legal force, there was no impediment to its actually being held.

The question now was whether the council leaders would obtain a majority vote in favour of autonomy; and, if so, whether they would abide by the legal chancellor's ruling. In the event, the referendum of 17 July failed to provide a clear popular mandate. Firstly, the impact of the polls was lessened by the fact that the council of neighbouring Kohtla-Järve – a town far more multi-ethnic in complexion – declined to hold its own referendum. Secondly, although 97 per cent of participating voters in Narva and Sillamäe endorsed the autonomy proposal, this must be set against officially recorded turnouts of only 54.8 per cent and 61.4 per cent, as well as evidence of ballot rigging. This outcome confirms earlier suggestions that, although the local population had preferred 'the devil they know' in October 1991, the city governments did not in fact enjoy the wholehearted backing of local residents (Hanson, 1993: 17–23; Hanson, 1994: 10). That there was – and still is – significant support for territorial autonomy is undeniable. However, research conducted in 1993 found that a majority of those in favour believed that such status should be realized through acts and decisions of the bodies of state power rather than on the initiative of the local authorities (Gorokhov, 1994: 13–14; see also Smith and Wilson, 1997: 857).

As the October local elections approached, Chuikin and his allies were fast becoming marginalized within the town councils as well as the influential Trade Union Centre. In the eyes of many prominent members of the local elite, the picture of political instability that Narva presented to the outside world was clearly deterring outside investment and hindering the economic development of the region (CSCE Mission, 1993c). In the midst of the 'aliens crisis', the Laar government had agreed to examine the possibility of 'accelerated naturalization' for non-citizens wishing to present themselves as candidates in the local elections. Although this option was never likely to be extended to the likes of Chuikin, Tallinn ultimately found a sufficient number of 'loyal' representatives, prepared to stand for election in the north-east (CSCE Mission, 1993d).

CSCE Mission representatives in Narva did 'not preclude strong reactionary activities during the [electoral] campaign should Chuikin and his associates get support from across the bridge' (CSCE Mission, 1993e). However, the possibility of aid from the 'external national homeland' diminished following the (albeit temporary) resolution of the Russian power struggle in Yeltsin's favour at the start of October. The events in Moscow apparently soothed the political situation in Narva, and the local elections went ahead unhindered, with a strong turnout by voters (CSCE Mission, 1993f). In Sillamäe, a list of eligible candidates prepared with the backing of Vähi's Coalition Party (at that time the leading national party of opposition) won 13 out of 21 seats. In Narva, on the other hand, the most successful electoral lists were generally formed on the basis of local interest groups rather than national parties. These were the Trade Union Centre, the Democratic Party of Labour (DPL) – successor to the Communist Party of Estonia) and the Narva Estonian Society (NES).

1993–2000: TOWARDS ACCOMMODATION?

In the light of these results, Philip Hanson claimed 'it would be absurd to say that the Estonian government's difficulties in Narva have been resolved by the new local elections: 'The success of the TUC and the DPT suggest that the old discontents and allegiances of the population still matter' (Hanson, 1994: 13). If opposition forces have maintained their high profile, the most recent local elections of October 1999 at least dispelled the impression of local particularity. On this occasion, almost half the seats in the council (14 out of 31) went to the principal national opposition party (Edgar Savisaar's Centre Party) a further seven to an alliance of the two main Russian-speaking parties in Estonia, and only three to the DPL. More significant is the fact that, notwithstanding their political complexion, successive city councils since 1993 have eschewed confrontation and focused squarely upon promoting political stability and economic development. These were certainly the principal goals during 1993–96, when two local Estonians from the NES list (Raivo Murd and Anatoli Paal) were appointed to the posts of executive mayor and city council chairman respectively (CSCE Mission, 1993e). Neither men were prone to question the existing state order.[8] Paal's 'Narva' list later went on to win 12 seats in the October 1996 local elections, compared to eight for the DPL and six for the Russian-speaking United People's Party. Developments since 1993 thus seem to bear out the contention that the town's citizen elites have acted as '"gatekeepers", moderating and redefining what appears on the local political agenda' (Smith *et al.*, 1998: 114). Local elites have engaged in 'rights-based politics' during this period – in 1996, for instance, they appealed to the president to veto initial attempts to impose Estonian language requirements for candidates to municipal office. For the most part, however, this politics has been more concerned with gaining greater resources to ease the plight of non-citizens and facilitate their integration into the polity (Smith and Wilson, 1997: 852; Smith *et al.*, 1998: 114). In this regard, it appears typical of the stance taken by Estonia's Russian-speaking elite as a whole (Smith, 2001: 23–4).

This 'depoliticization' of Narva and Sillamäe was aided by the fact that Chuikin and other hardliners departed to pursue careers in business after October 1993. Since this time, the principal torchbearer for the politics of the old guard has been the Union of Russian Citizens of Narva (URCN) headed by Iurii Mishin, former ideology secretary of the city's Communist Party committee and a continued staunch advocate of regional autonomy. URCN was established in 1992 to defend the rights of local residents who opt to take Russian citizenship.[9] Its potential constituency expanded greatly during 1994–96, when as many as 100,000 non-citizens applied for Russian passports – the majority of applications coming from north-eastern Estonia (Smith and Wilson, 1997: 859). However, all the evidence suggests that most of those who applied did so for purely instrumental reasons – i.e. this was the quickest means of obtaining a valid travel and identity document. For this reason, the number of applications decreased dramatically once the Estonian state began to issue 'alien's passports' in 1996. Talk of URCN as a major and potentially destabilizing political force appears greatly exaggerated (Smith, 1997: 266–72). Similarly, reports of significant support for LDPR and Communist candidates in Russian parliamentary and presidential elections (Smith and Wilson, 1997: 860) should be seen in the context of a negligible turnout by Russian citizens living in Estonia.

Proof that Narva had shed its image as a confrontational 'red' city came in January 1995, when Swedish textile firm Boras Wäfveri acquired a 75 per cent stake in the city's Kreenholm mill. After long and tortuous negotiations, the American company NRG Energy is currently poised to take over the two local power stations. Whilst privatization should help to secure the long-term future of these enterprises, the rationalization of local industry – especially the highly polluting energy and mining sectors – looks set to increase unemployment (estimated to be running at close to 20 per cent in 2000) even further. In the course of 1999/2000, plans for further job cuts in the power sector provoked a series of demonstrations by local workers (Sindrich, 2000a; Smith, 2000).

As well as highlighting the critical situation with regard to employment, the unrest of June 2000 focused upon what is perceived as undue centralization of power and indifference on the part of national government. The Estonian government's long-term vision for the region hinges upon the promotion of small business and tourism. In this regard, Ida-Virumaa is at the centre of a pilot project under the EU PHARE 2000 scheme (Sindrich, 2000a: 7). In the eyes of many local leaders, however, the attempts to bring about economic regeneration have been further complicated by the 'nationalizing' policies of the Estonian state. The extent to which the language law is observed in practice is open to question. However, local commentators in Narva complain that many experienced and potentially effective candidates are currently excluded from office on the grounds that they lack Estonian citizenship and/or knowledge of the state language.[10] At a time when many Russian-language schools are still ill equipped to integrate their students adequately into an Estonian-speaking milieu, language legislation has also become a source of social closure for Russian graduates of Russian-language basic and upper secondary schools. 'Exit' rather than 'voice' seems to be the prevailing strategy on the part of Narva's young people, who are seeking to move to the West in increasing numbers.

This 'brain-drain' is understandably a source of great concern within the city. Whilst virtually all local actors agree that integration is necessary, most question the current law on education and feel that existing provisions for territorial autonomy should be greatly expanded.[11] This view is representative of Estonia's Russian-speaking politicians as a whole (Smith, 2001: 20–21). What is certain is that cultural autonomy is not regarded as a workable paradigm for the defence of minority rights. Firstly, the relevance of this model is necessarily limited at a time when the majority of the non-titular population does not possess Estonian citizenship and the Russian community lacks the necessary resources to implement the scheme (Smith, 2001: 25–6).[12] Of the several minority groups eligible to establish cultural autonomy, none had done so by the end of 2000.[13] At the same time, state and local government has extended fairly extensive support to minority groups outside the framework of this law, and a thriving network of cultural societies now exists in Narva and the surrounding region. This suggests that the state strategy of breaking down an amorphous 'Russian-speaking' population into smaller and more manageable ethno-cultural groups has met with a fair amount of success (Smith, 2001: 26).

FUTURE PERSPECTIVES: IDA-VIRUMAA WITHIN A 'EUROPE OF THE REGIONS'?

Could Estonian EU membership actually be conducive to the attainment of greater national-territorial autonomy for the region? This at least was the conclusion drawn from an international seminar on 'interethnic dialogue in a regional perspective', which took place in Narva during November 2000. Addressing the gathering, a representative of the Institute of Ethnic Groups of Süd-Tyrol declared that 'from a European point of view, it is normal that a national minority becomes a majority in its own region'. In future, he added, each inhabitant of Europe will need to speak three languages – their mother tongue and neighbour's language as well as a 'language of international communication' such as English, Russian or Spanish. Delegates from the Ida-Virumaa county government, present at the meeting, welcomed the fact that processes of integration in Estonia are occurring within a European context. However, an advisor to the Estonian Ministry of Education insisted that Russian is very quickly losing its status as a language of international communication, and that the Estonian national integration strategy is designed to facilitate this (Totskaia, 2000).

In a report on the seminar, a local journalist noted the contrast between putative 'European' regionalism and the existing Estonian model of local administration, adding that 'here, I recalled the year 1993, when we held a referendum on Narva's independence (*samostoiatel'nost'*). The question did not receive a positive response (from the central government), but now

Europe is offering us almost the same thing' (Totskaia, 2000). Demands for legislative modifications in the sphere of local government have indeed been advanced by some representatives of European international organizations. Former Council of Baltic Sea States Commissioner on Human Rights Ole Espersen, for instance, has suggested that Estonia should amend its legislation on state service and political parties in order to allow non-citizens greater participation in the political life of the country. In Espersen's view, such a move would conform to the corresponding convention of the Council of Europe (*Narvskaia Gazeta*, 10 November 2000). However, despite the periodic frictions over citizenship and language legislation, the twin goals of 're-nationalizing' the state and 'returning to Europe' have appeared far from mutually incompatible. The EU and other European organizations clearly view the current integrationist paradigm as the best guarantee of stability, and have not questioned the fundamental bases of Estonian state- and nation-building. Estonian governments foi their part have had few problems in fulfilling the necessarily vague EU provisions governing 'respect for and protection of minorities'.

Cross-Border Cooperation

The future of Narva and Ida-Virumaa is of course inexorably linked to the wider question of Estonian–Russian relations. It is the perceived threat to Estonia from the 'eastern neighbour' that does much to explain the current preoccupation with unitary nation-statehood and the attempts to secure EU and NATO membership. Ida-Virumaa currently derives significant benefit from East–West transit trade passing through the Estonian ports, and its enterprises would obviously profit from an increase in exports to Russia. Unfortunately, the longstanding state of virtual 'cold war' between the two countries has prompted Russia to levy double tariffs on imports from Estonia.

EU-sponsored moves to promote stability and 'region-building' in the Baltic sea area have attached considerable importance to cross-border cooperation between sub-state actors as a means of fostering greater engagement with Russia. The desire for such links has been readily apparent on both sides of the Estonian-Russian frontier; according to some accounts, it was an important factor behind the advance of inter-state negotiations on the border during 1996 (Alekseev and Vagin, 1999: 43–64). For Narva, cooperation with the neighbouring towns and *raions* of the Russian Federation is a question of day-to-day necessity in view of the curious situation occasioned by the collapse of the USSR. In practical terms, Narva and Ivangorod formed part of a single agglomeration prior to 1991. Numerous residents from the Russian side worked in Narva and vice versa. The total number of people needing to cross the border on a regular basis is estimated at around 7,000 (Belov, 2000). Following the start of a functioning border regime in 1992, the municipalities of Narva and Ivangorod were able to gain approval for a simplified procedure allowing local residents to cross the river visa-free on the basis of a special permit.

Representatives of the Narva town government pointed to the development of constructive links with Ivangorod and other neighbouring Russian municipalities during 1999/2000.[14] This activity has been developed within the framework of wider Baltic sea regional initiatives such as ESTRUFIN and the 'Community Development and Cross-Border Cooperation in the Estonian/Russian Border Area' (Centre for Transboundary Cooperation, 2000: 2).[15] The latter project was established by the Narva Centre for Transboundary Cooperation (financed by the Swedish government) and the Danish Institute for Border Region Studies using money from the Danish government and the European Union. A 'Peipsi Forum' conference held in November 1999 united actors from all of Estonia's eastern border regions (including representatives of the second city, Tartu) with their counterparts from the Leningrad and Pskov oblasts of Russia. The aim was to facilitate cross-border initiatives between these border areas and to impart experiences of cooperation in the Danish-German border region during the past half century (Centre for Transboundary Cooperation, 2000: 1–3).[16]

In the light of these activities, it is intriguing to speculate whether the 1990 proposal for a 'network region' linking north-eastern Estonia and Russia could be revived within the wholly different context of EU–Russian cross-border cooperation. At the time of writing, however, this still appears a distant prospect. In November 2000, local actors in Narva responded positively to the idea of creating an Estonian-Russian Euroregion, yet noted that closer cooperation would be difficult in the continued absence of a formal inter-state border treaty.[17] Such comments merely confirm that the scope of problems in the border area go far beyond the competence of the local authorities directly concerned (Centre for Transboundary Cooperation, 2000: 2). In this regard, Narvitian actors pointed to a need either for greater autonomy to resolve local questions or for more support for cross-border initiatives from the state centre. One member of the city government noted that of the 12 funding applications submitted by Ida-Virumaa to PHARE via Tallinn, only one had been supported, as against three out of five successful applications by the western city of Pärnu. Whether this was due to political factors or merely a case of inadequate preparation on the part of local actors could not be ascertained.[18] The Deputy Chair of the city council, for his part, stated that although the centre understands the need to develop the region, 'negative stereotypes' still persist. In this regard, he added, the simplified border regime between Narva and Ivangorod had undoubtedly contributed to a growth in drugs trafficking and organized crime in the region.[19]

In Kulikov's view, the most positive aspect of Estonia's prospective EU membership – aside from an expected increase in inward investment – derived from the 'normal and positive' state of Russian–EU relations. This, he said, could not fail to have a positive effect on Russian policy towards Estonia.[20] As he himself admitted, however, EU membership will most likely entail a significant hardening of the current border regime once EU membership is attained. Such hardening has indeed already been apparent within the context of the accession process. In September 2000, the Estonian side moved to abolish the simplified border regime between Narva and Ivangorod, citing preparations for EU entry by way of justification. Residents of both towns who need to cross the border on a regular basis are now obliged to obtain a new, multi-entry visa that allows the bearer to spend up to 90 days in the neighbouring state during any one year (Belov, 2000). Around the same time, Russia announced plans to end its policy of granting free visas to holders of 'aliens passports' residing in Estonia (Panfilenok, 2000).[21]

CONCLUSIONS

Claims of significant popular support for secessionism in Narva and Ida-Virumaa between 1988 and 1993 appear to have been greatly exaggerated. The experience of these years suggests that under Soviet rule, local residents acquired a sense of territorial identification with the ESSR that sharply differentiated them from their neighbours in Russia. What a majority could not subscribe to, however, was the 'restorationist' philosophy of state-building adopted after independence. From the standpoint of late 2000, the prospect of major ethno-political instability appeared to have receded significantly, yet Narva and its surrounding region continued to face considerable socio-economic problems. If the current regional development plan for Ida-Virumaa has been accorded particular significance within the accession process, the implications of EU membership for the region remain unclear. For the time being, the accent remains firmly upon the 'integration' of the non-citizen population. Whilst few Russian-speaking actors would question the desirability of this goal, full integration into a monolingual nation-state framework remains a problematic concept in areas where little or no Estonian is spoken. As the number of naturalized Soviet-era settlers grows progressively, the current 'minority rights' paradigm based on cultural autonomy is clearly not regarded as sufficient. For the time being, the titular ruling elite remains committed to a unitary model of statehood. The most notable change in attitudes during the EU accession process has been a growing acceptance that integration of non-citizens is a necessary course of action. In the early 1990s, legislation on citizenship and aliens' status seemed explicitly designed to exclude Soviet-era settlers from influence over the state-building process and to pressure them into leaving Estonia. In this regard, the term 'integration' denoted a one-way process whereby non-citizens were expected to assimilate themselves into Estonian culture. The state integration strategy published in March 2000 makes it clear that this understanding has changed, and that the scope of the term has been widened to denote the integration of society as a whole.[22]

In recent times, the opposition (still principally Estonian) Centre Party has again begun to challenge the prevailing *rahvusriik* orthodoxy.[23] According to Elsa Suikanen, Centre Party member and Chair of Narva City Council, the current problems in the north-east would not have arisen had citizenship been given to all residents at the start of the 1990s. In this regard, she expressed a hope that EU entry might lead to a further softening of citizenship policy towards Soviet-era settlers. In particular, Suikanen was concerned that EU membership might open the door to an influx of new, possibly non-European migrants, something which 'would not be good' for the city.[24] Such views have previously been expressed by other members of the Eurosceptic Centre Party (Smith, 2001: 31–2). Anecdotal evidence suggests that they are also increasingly common across society as a whole: in the light of the country's declining demographic profile and the need to find skilled labour from somewhere, it appears that many titular actors are slowly beginning to reappraise their attitudes towards the Russian-speaking population. The pace of future accommodation will of course depend to a large extent upon the future course of international relations between Estonia and the Russian Federation. In the most optimistic scenario, Ida-Virumaa could profit enormously from a growth in trade between Russia and the EU, especially within the context of a trans-national Baltic sea region. However, other local actors point to the EU policy on external borders – not to mention the prospect of Estonian entry to NATO – and fear a 'new iron curtain' running along the line of the Narva river.

NOTES

1. Estonia's current statehood rests on the principle of legal continuity, which holds that the inter-war Estonian Republic (founded in 1918) was illegally occupied and annexed by the USSR in 1940. By this reading, Estonia remained a *de jure* independent state under foreign occupation throughout 1940–1991. The mass immigration which occurred under Soviet rule meant that the proportion of non-titular (mainly Russian or Russian-speaking) national groups in the total population rose from 12% to 39% during 1940–1989. On 20 August 1991 the Estonian Supreme Council (parliament) declared the legal restoration of the inter-war republic rather than the creation of a new, post-Soviet state. Under the citizenship law of February 1992, automatic citizenship was granted only to citizens of the inter-war republic and their descendants. Soviet-era settlers and their descendants who wish to obtain Estonian citizenship must undergo a process of naturalisation that requires them to demonstrate a working knowledge of the Estonian language. The nature of Soviet nationalities policy, however, meant that in 1989, only 12% of non-titular residents were conversant in Estonian. For a full discussion of citizenship and nationalities policy see: Smith, Aasland and Mole (1994); G. Smith (1996); D. Smith (2000: 65–112). By late 2000, almost 113,000 of the 500,000-strong non-Estonian population possessed Estonian citizenship (EU Commission, 2000: 17). At least 100,000 have taken Russian citizenship; the remainder have yet to define their status, and reside in the country on the basis of Alien's passports.
2. Interview with Iurii Maltsev, Chair of the Russian Cultural Society in Estonia, Tallinn, 3 June 1994. As Collias (1990, 72–90) reminds us, Soviet 'nation-building' emphasised the importance of local and regional identities as well as loyalty to the USSR. Rose and Maley (1993: 51) found that for 52% of Russian-speakers living in Estonia in 1993, town or locality constituted the primary basis for self-identification.
3. Interview with Vladimir Alekseev, Chair of the Narva Trade Union Centre, Narva: 24 February 1995.
4. Interview with Vladimir Chuikin, Chairman of Narva City Council, December 1989–October 1993, Narva, 26 April 1996; interview with Aleksandr Maksimenko, Chairman of Sillamäe City Council, October 1991–October 1993, Narva, 26 April 1996.
5. In an article published in autumn 1992, Sergei Karaganov, the Deputy Director of the European Institute in Moscow, stated that Russia could usefully further its geo-strategic aims within the FSU by purporting to defend the human rights of Russian-speakers living in Russia's 'near abroad' (See Smith, 1997:149–150). Laar's remarks came amidst fresh allegations of 'ethnic cleansing' and threats of economic sanctions by Russian Foreign Minister Andrei Kozyrev following the announcement of the referendum.
6. Interview with Vassilii Svirin, head of the Russian delegation to inter-state negotiations with Estonia, Moscow, 21 May 1995.
7. Interview with Peeter Olesk, Estonian Minister for Citizenship and Migration October 1993–June 1994, Tallinn, 17 June 1994.
8. Interview with Raivo Murd, Mayor of Narva 1993–96, Narva, 12 October 1994; interview with Anatoli Paal, Chair of Narva City Council 1993–96, Narva, 12 October 1994.
9. Interview with Iurii Mishin, Narva, 14 October 1994.
10. Interview with Olga Ivanova, editor of *Narvskaia Gazeta*, Narva, 19 November 2000.
11. Interview with Nikolai Kulikov, deputy chair of Narva City Council 1993–, Narva, 22 November 2000; also interview with Ivanova.
12. Interview with Alla Matvejeva, member of Narva City Council and representative of the Russian cultural society *Svetogor*, Narva, 22 November 2000.
13. Cultural autonomy is available to Russians, Germans, Swedes, Jews and other minority groups numbering more the 3,000. Under the system, the relevant group sets up an elected cultural council with full administrative and supervisory powers over minority schools and other activities. The council has the power to levy taxes on registered members of the minority group. This income supplements funding received from central and local government.
14. Interview with Kukilov.
15. Interview with Svetlana Legkodym, Counsellor to the Mayor of Narva, Narva, 23 November

2000. ESTRUFIN is a joint PHARE and TACIS-funded project set up in 1999 to promote closer cooperation between the towns of Narva, Lappeenranta (Finland), Vyborg and Ivangorod (Russia).
16. Interview with Andrei Pershin, representative of the Centre for Transboundary Cooperation, Narva: 21 November 2000.
17. Interview with Kulikov.
18. Interview with Legkodym
19. Interview with Kukilov
20. Ibid.
21. Interview with Matvejeva.
22. Interview with Stephan Heidenhain, First Secretary of the OSCE Mission to Estonia, Narva, 22 November 2000.
23. *RFE/RL Research Report*, 14 March 2001.
24. Interview with Elsa Suikanen, Chair of Narva City Council October 1999–, Narva, 21 November 2000.

REFERENCES

Alekseev, Mikhail and Vladimir Vagin (1999), 'Russian Regions in Expanding Europe: the Pskov Connection', *Europe–Asia Studies*, Vol.51, No.1, pp.43–64.
Belov, Leonid (2000), 'Granitsa vse sil'nee rezhet po zhivomu', *Narvskaia Gazeta*, 14 September.
Centre for Transboundary Cooperation (2000), 'Community Development and Cross-Border Cooperation in the Estonian/Russian Border Area', *Lake Peipsi Quarterly*, Winter, pp.1–3.
Collias, Karen (1990), 'Making Soviet Citizens: Patriotic and Internationalist Education in the Formations of a Soviet State Identity', in Henry Huttenbach (ed.), *Soviet Nationality Policies: Ruling Ethnic Groups in the USSR*. London: Mansell, pp.72–90.
'The Constitution of the Republic of Estonia', Estonian Translation and Legislative Support Centre (1996), translation into English, www.rk.ee/rkogu/eng/epseng.html#1p
CSCE (1992), 'Russians in Estonia: Problems and Prospects'. Washington: CSCE.
CSCE Mission to Estonia (1993a) Internal Memo from Narva Office, 20 July.
CSCE Mission to Estonia (1993b), Internal Memo from Narva Office, 17 August.
CSCE Mission to Estonia (1993c), Internal Memo from Narva Office, 22 September.
CSCE Mission to Estonia (1993d), Internal Memo from Narva Office, 28 September.
CSCE Mission to Estonia (1993e), Internal Memo from Narva Office, 6 October.
CSCE Mission to Estonia (1993f), Internal Memo from Narva Office, 25 October.
Elango, Õie, Ants Ruusmann and Karl Siilivask (1998), *Eesti maast ja rahvast. Maailmasõjast maailmasõjani*. Tallinn: Olion.
Estonian Institute (1995), *Estonia in Facts: Local Government Reform*. Tallinn: Estonian Institute.
European Union Commission (2000), 'Regular Report from the Commission on Estonia's Progress towards Accession', www.europa.eu.int/comm/enlargement/dwn/report_11_00/pdf/en/es_en.pdf
Gorokhov, Sergei (1994), 'Analysis of Changing Social Statement and Socio-Political Activity in Narva', *The Monthly Survey of Baltic and Post-Soviet Politics*, June, pp.3–14.
Gorokhov, Sergei (2000), *Gorodskoe Samoupravlenie Narvy: za Deciat' Let Peremen 1989–1999*. Narva: Narva City Council.
Gunter, Aleksei (2000), 'Less Local Government Needed', *The Baltic Times*, 7–13 December.
Hanson, Philip (1993), 'Estonia's Narva Problem, Narva's Estonia Problem', *RFE/RL Research Report*, Vol.2, No.18, pp.17–23.
Hanson, Philip (1994), 'Estonia: Radical Economic Reform and the Russian Enclaves', unpublished draft document.
Ida-Virumaa County Government (1997), 'Developmental Plan of Ida-Viru County 1998–2003', www.ida-virumaa.ee/kava/basis-of.htm

Kaldmäe, Madis, Ave Poom, Ülari Alamets, Krista Kampus, Priidu Ristkok, Kaidi Roots, Jaanus Tärnov (1999), 'Local Government in Estonia', draft document prepared for Estonian Ministry of Internal Affairs, www.juhan.ell.ee/english/materials/ELLkogumik_MK.doc

Kionka, Riina (1990), 'Integral and Estonian Independence', *Radio Free Europe Report on the USSR*, Vol.2, No.30, pp.20–21.

Kirch, Aksel, Marika Kirch and Tarmo Tuisk (1993), 'Russians in the Baltic States: To Be Or Not To Be?', *Journal of Baltic Studies*, Vol.24, No.2, pp.173–88.

Kochenovskii, Oleg (1991), *Narva. Gradostroitel'noe razvitie I arkhitektura.* Tallinn: Valgus.

Lieven, Anatol (1993), *The Baltic Revolution.* New Haven, CT and London: Yale University Press.

Marran, Mikk and Eve Vungo (1999), *Eesti Pöördub Läände.* Tallinn: Avita.

Panfilenok, Mikhail (2000), 'Vozmozhny izmeneniia v zakone ob inostrantsakh', *Narvskaia Gazeta*, 28 September.

Pettai, Vello (1993), 'Contemporary International Influences on Post-Soviet Nationalism: the Cases of Estonia and Latvia', paper presented at the American Association for the Advancement of Slavic Studies, 25th National Convention, Hawaii, 19–21 November.

Raun, Toivo (1991), *Estonia and the Estonians.* Boulder, CO: Westview Press.

Reino, Üllar (1998), '*Eesti omavalitsusüksustest 1920. Aastate esimisel poolel*', in Jüri Ant (ed.), *Kaks algust. Eesti Vabariik – 1920. Ja 1990. Aastad.* Tallinn: Eesti Riigiahiiv.

Rose, Richard and William Maley (1994), *Nationalities in the Baltic: a Survey Study.* University of Strathclyde: Centre for the Study of Public Policy.

Ruutsoo, Rein (1993), 'Rahvusvähemused Eesti Vabariigis', in *Vähemusrahvuste Kultuurielu Eesti Vabariigis.* Tallinn: Olion.

Savisaar, Edgar (1999), *Usun Eestisse.* Tallinn: TEA.

Sindrich, Jaclyn M. (2000a), 'Light at the End of Ida-Virumaa's Tunnel', *Baltic Business District*, June 2000, p.7.

Sindrich, Jaclyn M. (2000b), 'Radical Administrative Reform for Estonia?', *The Baltic Times*, 5–11 October.

Smith, David J. (1997), 'Legal Continuity and Post-Soviet Reality: Ethnic Relations in Estonia 1991–95', unpublished Ph.D. dissertation, University of Bradford, 1997.

Smith, David J. (1999), 'Retracing Estonia's Russians: Mikhail Kurchinskii and Interwar Cultural Autonomy', *Nationalities Papers*, Vol.27, No.3, pp.455–74.

Smith, David J. (2000), *Estonia: Independence and European Integration.* Amsterdam: Harwood Academic Publishers.

Smith, David J. (2001), 'Cultural Autonomy in Estonia: a Relevant Paradigm for the Post-Soviet Era?', *One Europe or Several?* Working Paper 1901. Brighton: Economic and Social Research Council.

Smith, Graham (1996), 'When Nations Challenge and Nations Rule: Estonia and Latvia as Ethnic Democracies', *Coexistence*, No.33, pp.25–41.

Smith, Graham, Aadne Aasland and Richard Mole (1994), 'Statehood, Ethnic Relations and Citizenship', in Graham Smith (ed.), *The Baltic States: the Self-Determination of Estonia, Latvia and Lithuania.* London: Macmillan, pp.181–205.

Smith, Graham and Andrew Wilson (1997), 'Rethinking Russia's Post-Soviet Diaspora: the Potential for Political Mobilisation in Eastern Ukraine and North-East Estonia', *Europe–Asia Studies*, Vol.49, No.5, pp.845–64.

Smith, Graham, Vivien Law, Andrew Wilson, Annette Bohr, Edward Allworth (1998), *Nation-building in the Post-Soviet Borderlands. The Politics of National Identities* Cambridge: Cambridge University Press.

Sootla, Georg (1993a), 'Estonian Chronology', the monthly survey of Baltic and Post-Soviet Politics, July, pp.3–32.

Sootla, Georg (1993b), 'Estonian Chronology', *The Monthly Survey of Baltic and Post-Soviet Politics*, August, pp.34–44.

Sootla, Georg (1993c), 'Political Background and Possible Consequences of the Summer Crises in Estonia', *The Monthly Survey of Baltic and Post-Soviet Politics*, August, pp.49–57.

Totskaia, Yulia (2000), 'Mezhnatsional'nye Otnosheniia u nas I v Evrosoyuze', *Narvskaia Gazeta*, 14 November.

Vetik, Raivo (1993), 'Ethnic Conflict and Accommodation in Post-Communist Estonia', *Journal of Peace Research*, Vol.30, No.3, pp.271–80.
Von Rauch, Georg (1995), *The Baltic States. The Years of Independence*. London: Hurst.
Weiss-Wendt, Anton (1997), 'Komu prinadlezhit Narva? K voprosu o territoriaľno-administrativnoi prinadlezhnosti goroda 1858–1917 gg.', in I. Belobrovtseva (ed.), *Baltiiskii Arkhiv* (Tallinn, Avenarius, 1997), pp.22–46.

Upper Silesia:
Rebirth of a Regional Identity in Poland

LUIZA BIALASIEWICZ

Despite a decade of fundamental constitutional reforms, the question of the restructuring of the institutions of local governance continues to dominate the political scene in post-communist Poland. A far-reaching administrative reform of the Polish state was, at long last, implemented on 1 January 1999. The reform created 16 new regions (*województwa*), completing the process of administrative decentralization begun in 1990, and granting a whole series of capabilities to the new regional councils including, for the first time, responsibility for developing and implementing regional economic policies (see Kisielowska-Lipman's contribution). The enactment of the new institutional architecture, however, has only further ignited the debate over the proper division of competences between the various levels of territorial governance and their relation to the national state. Decentralization holds high symbolic value in the post-communist political imagination and, since 1989, has been touted both by representatives of the Polish state and by citizen groups as a key indicator of the transition to participatory democracy. This phenomenon is not unique to Poland (see for example, Fowler's discussion of the Hungarian case in this volume) and, just as in other post-communist contexts, in Poland too there exists broad consensus across party and ideological divides on the need for decentralization, a principle also enshrined by the new Polish constitution that 'guarantees the decentralization of public authorities' and recognizes the municipalities (*gminy*) as the basic units of territorial self-rule.

Calls for territorial-administrative reform also reflect the rediscovery of historical-cultural regional and local specificities within a national space declared homogeneous during the 45 years of communist rule. Such a rediscovery is emotionally charged, and opens up new opportunities for collective self-definition, with the articulation of local and regional difference becoming a key locus of cultural politics as people reclaim their past and declare their belonging. It should also be noted, however, that internal reforms in the post-communist states do not proceed in a geopolitical vacuum, and much has been written about the weight of 'Western' models in shaping domestic political and economic choices in

Central and Eastern Europe (see Pickles and Smith, 1997). The symbolic weight granted by post-communist elites to administrative decentralization and regionalization and the 'natural' association of these processes with democratization draws, in fact, upon received wisdom in Western 'transitology' (Burawoy, 1992) which identifies the devolution of state powers as 'a natural progression in the evolution of representative democracy' (Sharpe, 1993: 8). External actors, both states and transnational organizations, influence the processes of institutional reform not only by setting the conditions for accession to membership or allocation of funds, but also by functioning as the 'legitimate repositories of knowledge about the democratic state' (and thus its proper political, economic and cultural organization). The dominant model guiding the association of regions with 'democratic progress' remains that furnished by the European Union, which has done much to encourage the development of regional governance. At the level of the national state, administrative regionalization has come to be represented as a 'European' practice; within the new territorial units, the practice of regional governance has come to mark its practitioners as 'Europeans'. It is a symbolic as well as a practical association: a variety of Union financial transfers and agreements are administered at the regional level, as local leaders are well aware. In Poland, as elsewhere, regions are overwhelmingly seen as a 'European thing' and I shall devote considerable attention to the long shadow of Europe – both as a conceptual and an institutional entity – in my examination of Polish regionalism.

My focus lies with the articulation of regional difference as a key locus of identity politics in one portion of Polish state territory – Upper Silesia – that has been progressively 'regionalized' in the post-1989 era: that is, legitimated as a distinct 'historical-cultural region'. My approach is informed by recent theorizations in political geography that understand regionalization not simply as the administrative apportionment of segments of space but, rather, as the dynamic *process* of constituting regions as particular 'imagined communities' in space, legitimating distinct territorial divides and allocating governance (for an overview, see Paasi, 1986, 1991, 1996; Thrift, 1990).

The Plebiscite and the Inter-War Years: The National Question in Silesia

The territories of today's Upper Silesia have always been a contested border area. From Polish and Bohemian rule in the 900s and 1100s, to later Prussian and Austrian domination (from the 1500s on), imperial ambitions have often clashed at this Central European crossroads. The struggles over Silesia's 'ownership' by the Czechoslovah, Polish and

German states at the beginning of this century form only the most recent chapter in a long history of contested belonging. The end of the First World War, however, forms a useful starting point for a discussion of the region's distinct past.

BECOMING UPPER SILESIA I

With the re-establishment of the Polish state in 1918, the question of Upper Silesia's proper place in the international state system became a crucial political issue. Appealing to the principles of national self-determination consecrated at Versailles, Poland argued that the significant Polish-speaking population of the region should be regarded as 'nationally Polish' and thus annexed to the new Polish state. The German authorities rejected this, arguing that in a border region long characterized by multiple national belongings, the language criterion was an unreliable marker of national status. The task of allocating the territories of Upper Silesia lasted nearly three years (1918–21), one of the most contentious episodes of boundary settlement in recent European history. After a highly controversial plebiscite carried out in March 1921 (in which almost 60 per cent of the regional population voted for annexation to Germany and 40 per cent for inclusion within the new Polish state), and two Polish uprisings that were violently repressed, 30 per cent of the Silesian territories (along with 46 per cent of the regional population) were assigned to Poland. The borderline left over 530,000 Poles and the cities of Bytom, Gliwice and Zabrze on the 'German' side and a significant German population in Poland. In the ten years following 1918, over half (following Brubaker's (1996) figures, approximately 600,000) would eventually emigrate. Upper Silesia's national mosaic and its special legal status in the inter-war period merit further discussion, however, for it is during these years that the various visions of the region that inspire present-day Silesian regionalists were first formulated and became the object of intense struggles.

In July 1920, a special act of the newly reborn Polish state (the *Ustawa Konstytucyjna*) assigned the Polish portion of Upper Silesia a distinctive 'organic status', with wide-ranging powers and competencies (the only such autonomous region in inter-war Poland). Upper Silesia was given its own parliament (*Sejm*) with devolved regulatory and administrative powers both at the level of the region (*województwo*), and its counties (*powiaty*) and municipalities (*gminy*). Local authorities were able to regulate the public use of the Polish or German language and had control over police, schooling, and all public services within the region. The Silesian *Sejm* also won authority over the collection of taxes and public fees, with a special formula to calculate the percentage of monies to be returned to the Polish state for 'national purposes' and the amount that was to remain in the regional treasury, the *Skarb Ślaski* (see Ciągwa, 1979, 1988). Decision-making autonomy was further enhanced by the wide-ranging powers of the Silesian regional governor (*wojewoda*), who was free to exercise complete control over regional administration and schooling.

Besides its legal specification in the Polish constitution, the region's status was also formally regulated by the Geneva Convention, ratified by Poland and Germany in May 1922. The Convention enumerated a set of measures to assure the continuity of economic and cultural life in the region and the protection of minority rights within both the Polish and German territories, guaranteeing a 'soft' division of the region between the two national states. Germany was obliged, for example, to purchase one million tons of Polish coal per annum, while in Polish Silesia legal constraints were placed upon the expropriation of German-owned industries. The Convention also assured bilingual schooling, and freedoms for minority political and cultural organizations. These guarantees, however, prevented the full legal and political integration of Upper Silesia into the Polish state. Until 1937 (when the terms of the Convention expired), Silesia was governed by an entirely different set of laws regulating mining, labour relations and even land ownership, and subsequent attempts by the Polish state at legal unification were strongly resisted (see Ciągwa, 1988; Nawrocki, 1993). Indeed, some historians have described the reunification of Upper Silesia with Poland as a 'de facto union of two nations' (*unia realna dwóch państw*) (see Leszczyńska, 1990), noting the almost 'civilizational' divides that lay between the region and the rest of the new Poland. As Nawrocki (1993) suggests, Upper Silesia's unique status after 1922 granted it opportunities for economic and cultural development that only augmented its distance from the rest of the Polish state and prevented its full incorporation into the Polish economic, political and national-cultural spheres.

The place of Silesia *vis-à-vis* the inter-war Polish state was expressed within two broadly contrasting visions: that of the Silesian *chadecja*, a distinct brand of Catholic conservatism that argued for Silesia's special nature and, in particular, its role as a 'proper' model of development for the rest of the newly born Polish state; and that of the *sanacja*, insisting on the absolute necessity of integrating the region into the national whole (see Kopec, 1986). For the *chadecja* (the term comes from the Christian Democratic tradition), the rest of the new Polish state had to 'catch up' with Silesia, the most developed region of the country with a large, highly educated and organized elite that, according to the *chadecja*, could lead the *whole* of the new Poland. Silesian society was portrayed as a highly egalitarian one, where the rule of law was part of everyday life and universally accepted, unlike the other partition areas where legal norms and institutional arrangements were 'foreign' and had been imposed from above. Finally, the Silesian *chadecja* placed great emphasis on the work ethic as a distinguishing characteristic of local society that contributed to its economic success and its egalitarian nature. In Silesia, they argued, one's status was determined by one's achievements, not national or class attributes. The *chadecja*'s bourgeois conservatism was also closely tied to Catholic values, seen by its ideologues as the bulwark against social disaggregation, and with its leading figures coming from the circles of the local Catholic intelligentsia.

The *chadecja* enjoyed relative superiority in the Silesian Sejm until 1926, when, following the May coup, the forces of the *sanacja* came to power. Passing to the opposition, the *chadecja* opted for a defensive strategy: Silesia had to preserve its identity from the encroachments of the Polish state, and its distinctive values from utter Polonization. This platform found broad support among the regional population, largely dissatisfied with Polish rule after 1922 (Długajczyk, 1983; Kopeć, 1986). It is interesting to note that many elements of the *chadecja*'s vision and, in particular, their inscription of the regional identity would resurface in the voices of latter-day Silesian regionalists. Alongside evocations of Silesians' distinct social values and work ethic, perhaps the most evident echo of this vision is the emphasis on Silesia's distinct 'border culture', which had 'produced individuals who are not only bi-lingual but also bi-national – just like the pear trees that line the frontier and bear fruit on both sides' (Fr. Emil Szramek, cited in Nawrocki, 1993).

The *chadecja*'s relations with the German minority were ill defined, fluctuating according to political needs and the prevailing social climate. Although the German community was often enlisted in their struggle against the forces of the *sanacja*, regional leaders were well aware of the 'German threat' to Silesian autonomy, and most alliances with minority leaders were based on pragmatic considerations. As will be seen below, this sort of ambivalent attitude towards the Silesian Germans has, indeed, resurfaced in the narratives of present-day regionalists.

The proponents of the *sanacja* – of the full integration of Silesia into national structures – were considerably more diverse in their approaches. Overall, however, this political/ideological bloc was driven by the conviction that the region's 'organic' status was a serious barrier to its full incorporation into the Polish state. *Sanacja* leaders did not reject Silesian distinctiveness entirely, however, but saw it as an integral part of the cultural mosaic that made up the new Polish state. They argued that

Silesians should abandon the temptations of separatism for a 'modern cultural regionalism' (see Nawrocki, 1993) that would allow them to reconcile their otherness with the framework of the national state.

Sanacja proponents concentrated on several key issues. The first was the need to integrate the region's legal system with the national one (Długajczyk, 1983). A second was to enforce Polonization of the regional economy and administration and, above all, of the industrial elite: a necessary 'nationalization of Silesian capital' (*unarodowienie śląskiego kapitału*). Such visions were very often explicitly anti-German: unlike the *chadecja*, *sanacja* proponents rejected the multi-national and multi-cultural nature of the region and conducted a concerted campaign against purported German dominance in both the economic and cultural realms, drawing criticism from the League of Nations and German leaders upon more than one occasion (Rechowicz, 1971).

Another key locus of struggle was the question of regional boundaries. After 1926, numerous proposals were advanced for enlarging the Silesian *województwo*, adding to its territories several other neighbouring *powiaty*. Although the proposals were presented with the rationale of unifying the various industrial infrastructures of Poland's south-western territories under one administration and creating more compact transport and communication linkages, the thinly veiled aim was, in fact, the 'dilution' of Silesia's particularisms by increasing the number of Poles and thus consolidating its 'Polishness' (Rechowicz, 1971). Such proposals were vociferously opposed by Silesian regional leaders (both the *chadecja* and more radical separatist groups such as the *Związek Obrony Górnoślązaków*), who rightly feared the likely dilution of the region's culture and autonomous status, and the weakening of their own political support with an inflow of non-autochthonous Poles. The boundary question would again resurface in the 1990s with regionalists' proposals for the creation of a new Silesian region.

The heated regional political debates of the inter-war years contributed to a gradual 'dilution of the common feeling of a distinct regional belonging that had previously united most Silesians, regardless of national identification' (Błaszczak-Wacławik, 1990: 29). The Polish state's attempts at Polonization, coupled with the German minority's increasingly reactive stance, led to a progressive 'nationalization' of the regional population (Błaszczak-Wacławik, 1990: 27), and when Silesia was incorporated into the Third Reich in 1939, the question of national identification had already become paramount. The census of the Silesian population by the occupying forces in 1941 placed further emphasis on national belonging. The *Deutsche Volksliste* identified those individuals who could be formally conscripted for military service as 'national

Germans', while also marking out those whose national identification was considered 'labile' (estimated at over 60 per cent of the population in the 'Polish' Silesian provinces – see Błaszczak-Wacławik, 1990: 48). Although often discounted in post-war histories as facile opportunism, the extent of Silesians' collusion with German authorities remains a complex question, for the choices forced upon the local population by the occupying forces were often tragic.

The 'Workers' Eldorado'

> When my father went into the army during the war, the Germans asked him who he was. He said he was a German. So they told him that he could not speak German properly, that he was just a stupid Ślązok. When the Poles came after the war, you know, people from outside [the region], they considered us half-Poles or simply Germans ... They would glare at me at work if by mistake I let a word in dialect slip out. They would say: 'Listen to how these Germans ruin the Polish language ... They would call us 'Hitler's sons', 'the Wermacht', '*Szwaby*' ... (cited in Szczepański, 1997: 11).

The events of the Second World War gave the post-war Polish authorities ample room to argue for the need to ensure the region's 'full loyalty to the Polish state' (see Błasiak, 1990; K. Wódz, 1995). This was to be achieved through mass population transfers and a number of legal measures designed to erase all traces of the German past and assure Polish national homogeneity. In the immediate post-war years, over 3.5 million Germans were expatriated from Silesia as well as the territories of what was once East Prussia. Their place was taken by 1.5 million Poles 'repatriated' from lands in the east (Magocsi, 1993; Bialasiewicz and O'Loughlin, 2002; Kordan, 1997). A subsequent series of inter-governmental agreements for 'family reunification' allowed the remainder of those choosing to declare German nationality to emigrate in large numbers: between 1955 and 1989, it is estimated that over 1,198,000 people left for the Federal Republic of Germany under a system of 'exchanges' that provided substantial economic compensation to the Polish state for each re-patriant.

Between 1945 and 1946, thousands of Silesians accused of ties with Germany were arrested and deported to forced-labour camps in the Soviet Union (including many former 'Polish patriots' who had been imprisoned during the war years for anti-German activities – see Błasiak, 1990). In the years following the war, a set of laws designed to excise all memory of the region's German population stipulated ten-year jail sentences for any *'odstępstwo od narodowości'* – any 'treason' against Polish nationality. Such 'treason' was broadly construed by the special 'Commissions for the

Fight against Manifestations of Germanness' (*Komisje do Zwalczania Przejawów Niemczyzny*) called up to enforce the new laws. 'Police patrols would go through our houses and look for anything with German script on it – books, of course, but also porcelain, medicine bottles, anything', recalls Dietmar Brehmer, founder of the German minority organization *Pojednanie i Przyszłość* in Katowice.[1]

In communist Poland, the memory of Silesia's special character as a multi-national borderland where several cultural and political worlds came together was erased, and 'the region became simply a framework for economic planning. It was a space for the production of certain goods, a space within which a certain set of exchanges took place, a space containing a certain workforce' (Pulinowa, 1998: 10). It became the *Górno-Śląski Okręg Przemysłowy* (or GOP – the Upper Silesian Industrial District), an industrial agglomeration that at the end of the 1980s housed over four million people. It was a place whose 'identity' was marked exclusively by its economic role: the Polish Eldorado where in the 1970s and 1980s over one-quarter of the entire Polish GNP was generated. Its symbols were the *Huta Katowice* steel-mill, where workers from all around the country would build the socialist dream; and the expanses of new housing projects that irreversibly transformed the turn-of-the-century urban landscapes of Katowice and other towns. 'The hard physical labour of coalminers and steelworkers placed them in the vanguard of the civilizational mission of real socialism. With their toils, they were to embody the new Poland' (Szczepański, 1999b: 7). Upper Silesia was to be 'the model region of "socialism with a human face"'; it was to provide 'a living proof that we could easily reach – and overtake – the industrial successes of the corrupt West' (Karwat, 1999: 29).

The thousands of workers who arrived in the GOP from all around Poland did, indeed, enjoy a number of privileges – better housing, vacation homes, even access to scarce goods through a network of special shops for miners (the famous *gewexy*). 'The image of the region in the rest of the country was that of servile conformists, opportunists, "the guiding force of the nation"', notes Katowice journalist Krzysztof Karwat (1999: 29) – 'we were nothing but workers – *Ślązoki-robole* – loyal to the authorities and just thinking of filling our always empty stomachs'. 1980 brought an end to such myths. The symbols of the workers' paradise fast became symbols of workers' revolt, with *Huta Katowice* becoming one of the most active centres of *Solidarność* in the early 1980s. It was also in Silesia, at the *Wujek* mine, that the brutality of the regime showed its face after martial law was declared.

For post-communist Poland, Upper Silesia became an economic nightmare. The GOP's industrial complexes became the target of endless restructuring proposals and the symbol of the economic disasters wrought by central planning. But it was also here, where only 30 per cent of the 'local' pre-war population had remained, that the most vehement regional identity claims in post-1989 Poland began to be articulated. In the past decade, Silesians have rediscovered themselves and their region. 'We have spent the past ten years looking for Silesia', Wojciech Sarnowicz, documentary film-maker and the director of TV Katowice, has stressed in numerous public appearances: 'the Ślązak [the Silesian] did not exist in the party propaganda. We were all workers – working side by side for the good of the nation. We had to dig our past, our culture out of this web of lies.'[2] In the pages to follow, I will trace some of the processes that have accompanied this 'excavation' of the regional identity. My focus will not lie, however, with the overt autonomist proclamations that captured Polish media attention in the early 1990s as these proved only a marginal and transient phenomenon (see Błasiak, 1993; Nawrocki, 1993; and Szczepański, 1993a, 1993b). I will highlight, rather, the more diffuse practices of 'banal' regionalism (to twist Michael Billig's (1995) term) that, since the 1990s, have sought to present and represent the region in the everyday lives of its inhabitants, 'institutionalizing' the regional representation and consolidating it as a locus of identity.

BECOMING UPPER SILESIA II: 'I LOVE ŚLĄSK'

It is the most banal, everyday acts of 'naming' that constitute the first step in regional 'becoming'. As Paasi (1996: 35) reminds us, the act of naming the region 'brings together its historical development, its important events, episodes and memories and [joins] the personal histories of its inhabitants to this collective heritage'. Naming both expresses the 'character' of the region and also serves to reproduce it. It evokes powerful feelings of identification with the newly constituted territorial grouping and is thus capable of generating agency.

The repeated 'naming' of Upper Silesia in the past decade has certainly constituted a fundamental step towards the region's institutionalization. The variety of political movements which arose in the early 1990s such as the *Ruch Autonomii Śląska* (Movement for Silesian Autonomy) and the *Związek Górnośląski* (Upper Silesian Association) defined themselves by evoking Upper Silesia as a distinct territorial ideal. Such overt acts of regionalization have been accompanied, however, by a series of more 'banal', everyday practices of representation that, over the years, have naturalized the idea of Upper Silesia in popular perception. An active protagonist in this naturalization has been the Katowice bureau of the *Gazeta Wyborcza*, Poland's largest newspaper. In summer 2000, the

Gazeta began giving out a bumper sticker to its readers sporting the region's new coat of arms emblazoned with the words 'I love *Slask*'. The sticker, as the newspaper announced, was intended 'for all those who care about this region and want to show it'. Although the emblem provoked a whole series of polemics, the initiative was 'on the whole very successful', according to editor-in-chief Andrzej Stefański, 'it made people happy to be able to say "I care about this place"'.[3] The Katowice *Gazeta* has also held annual competitions among local schoolchildren on the themes of 'Why I love Silesia' and 'What it means to be Silesian', and has co-sponsored and heavily publicized other initiatives such as the 'Festival of Local Homelands' (*Festiwal Ojczyzn Lokalnych*) that brought together over 2,000 local schoolchildren and featured theatre and music performances in Silesian dialect as well as 'regional' food and music (*Finał 2000*, 2000).

The regional dialect or *gwara* is enjoying a vivid revival, in fact. Apart from a variety of folkloric events and *gwara*-speaking contests sponsored by Radio Katowice and countless other cultural organizations (*Godka, choby w doma*, 1999), the years since 1990 have also witnessed the appearance of numerous scholarly works and dictionaries (most importantly, the work edited by Cząstka-Szymon *et al.*, 1999). The *gwara*, actively repressed during communist times as an 'aberration of the Polish tongue'[4] and relegated to the private sphere of family conversations, is now, according to regional activists, a matter of local pride, a way of 'being finally ourselves'.[5] Efforts to codify the dialect in printed form – be it in the form of children's books, dictionaries or academic treatises – have become an important focus of local authors and publishers.[6] Best known is certainly the 'trilogy' tracing the 'cultural history of the region' published by Rybnik lyceum history teacher, editor of the *Gazeta Rybnicka* and self-styled Silesian scribe Marek Szołtysek (1998, 1999, 2000). Szołtysek's books, which mix local dialect and 'standard' Polish and contain numerous photographs and cartoons illustrating the 'Silesian world', to use the author's own words, 'were written to finally tell us who we – *Ślązacy* – are'. As Anderson (1983) has noted, it was the advent of print capitalism that contributed to the establishment of the 'imagined communities' of nationhood through the creation of a common and permanent national language. The written codification of the Upper Silesian *gwara* (however partial, as it is a 'living' and territorially variegated dialect as its scholars note – see Synowiec, 2000a, 2000b) thus not only serves to confirm the dialect's existence but, indeed, also that of a distinct (regional) community associated with it.

The wide success of such popular initiatives suggests that the set of regional representations and symbols upon which they draw is, to some extent, 'recognizable and recognized', to paraphrase Paasi (1996). Certainly, it is just such representational practices that act to *construct* Upper Silesia as a region, as a distinct community of belonging. Yet any such identity-constituting practices can only be successful if they are recognized and legitimated by at least a portion of the population – and thus if they draw upon pre-existing iconographies, pre-existing regional 'collective memories'. The re-assertion of a regional collective memory that counters communist historiography has been fundamental in Upper Silesian regionalism over the past decade. It is by making recourse to the past that Upper Silesia's distinct identity has been asserted, delimited through an articulation of *difference* from the rest of the Polish state and *affinity* with the broader European whole.

INVENTING REGIONAL TRADITION: THE SILESIAN PAST

The processes of constructing a regional community can be likened in many respects to those of nation-building. Just as modern nationalism is, above all, 'a discourse about space and time', a 'mode of constructing and interpreting a determinate social space – and its historical past' (Williams and Smith, 1983: 502), so too is the constitution of regional 'imagined communities' (Anderson, 1983). In constructivist understandings, modern nationalism has been inescapably tied to what Hobsbawm and Ranger (1983) have termed 'the invention of tradition': a declaration of the national community's emergence from a set of (usually glorious) origins; origins which are located within the national territory and discursively bound to particular geographical locations. It is such a framing of a national past that helps to represent the national unit as a taken-for-granted, 'natural' continuity in time and space; as the only possible form of social organization to 'evolve' within that territory.

As Paasi (1986, 1996) notes in his theorization of regional institutionalization, narratives of the past form a vital facet of the regional story as well. In Upper Silesia, the past is everywhere: as Katowice mayor Piotr Uszok insists, 'one cannot understand our region without understanding its history'.[7] In the discourse of political leaders, cultural figures and other active 'regionalists', present-day Silesia is represented as but a 'fragment of its true self',[8] if not 'a historical mistake'.[9] To understand the 'true region' one must thus look to the past. The past, in fact, is much more orderly than the present, and fits better with the idealized picture of the region that its proponents paint. Historical narrative is used to specify the distinctive traits that make the region 'what it is', while also marking its difference from the remainder of the Polish state. The key trope in the regional story is certainly Silesia's place within a broader European heritage – or, perhaps more accurately, the indivisibility of Silesian and European histories, whether conceived as distinct trajectories of economic development or political and social 'progress'.

Scholars of nationalism have long stressed the social role of historians and other 'writers' of the historical imagination of the nation (see Anderson, 1983; Hobsbawm, 1990). Upper Silesia has its own scribes, both popular (such as Szołtysek, cited above) and academic. Sociologist Marek Szczepański, one of the most prolific academic commentators of Silesian regionalism, has repeatedly stressed in his work the place of Silesia in European history, and the distinctiveness of its 'developmental path' as compared to that of the rest of Poland. 'It is well known', he wrote in a recent issue of popular regional monthly Śląsk (Szczepański, 1999b: 6; see also Szczepański, 1997, 1998), 'that Silesia, since time immemorial, formed an integral part of the Old Continent, not only in geographical but also in cultural and civilizational terms ... Its path to Europe has always been different from that of the remainder of the current Polish state.' In his recent articles, Szczepański (1997, 1998, 1999a, 1999b) has inscribed the region's history and its 'civilizational path' within a series of 'developmental phases', a narrative of Rostowian progress which not only serves to explain Silesia's current condition but that also, he notes, can tell us much about the region's 'possible' future.

Szczepański is a figure of some import on the regional cultural and academic scene and, I would argue, his work provides an important theorization (and thus legitimation) of popular 'collective memories', of popular 'ways of knowing' the region, its past and, therefore, its identity. For the sociologist, the fundamental shift that would forever mark the fortunes of the region occurred two and a half centuries ago, when Upper Silesia abandoned its plebeian roots and started on the road to rapid industrialization. 'It was already in the mid-1700s that the current shape of the Upper Silesian landscape began to take form. Factories and mines replaced stalls; peasants became miners and steelworkers' (Szczepański, 1999a: 6). This shift not only transformed the regional economic landscape, but also firmly placed Upper Silesia 'within the progress of European civilization' (Szczepański, 1999a: 7).

Silesia's place within the flow of European history and, in particular, within 'European progress', forms a recurrent theme in the narratives of regional political leaders as well as cultural figures. Kazimierz Kutz is perhaps the best known 'Ślązak', both within the region and in Poland as a whole, the man considered by many as the creator of the 'mit Śląskości' – the 'myth of Silesian-ness'; in the words of Katowice journalist Michał Smolorz,[10] someone who 'finally told Silesians who they were'. Award-winning film director, theatre producer, self-defined 'all-around hell-raiser', Kutz is now the region's Senator representing the *Unia Wolności* (Freedom Union):

> Silesia was an integral part of Europe when its most important transformations were taking place. It participated in the birth of the industrial revolution, of modern capitalism and of democracy with the rest of Europe – it was the Reich's second-largest industrial area when the remainder of partitioned Poland was still just fields ... And when the rest of Poland was just beginning its path to modernization, Silesia was already entering the second phase of capitalism – with the birth of trade unions, cooperatives, just as the rest of the West. Here, the proletariat was born just as it was being born in the rest of Europe – and with it, a new model of man, of society... A certain work ethic, but also a certain understanding of political culture, of social responsibility. Which still has not arrived in the remainder of the country.... But Silesia had already begun to move away from Poland in the Middle Ages; it left the Polish state as the Polish state was being born. So it has always been free of the absolutist traditions of the East.[11]

It would be foolish to deny the role of the industrial past (and present) in giving shape to the region, of course. At the turn of the twentieth century, Upper Silesia was the Reich's second most important industrial heartland (after the Ruhr), and it remains Poland's most heavily industrialized area, although hundreds of thousands of workers have been forced to leave the mines and steel mills during the past decade of restructuring. In communist times, it was the mythology of the heroic coal miners and steel workers that defined this region, while its industry exemplified communist progress (see Kubik, 1994). In the post-1989 processes of regional institutionalization, however, reference to the region's industrial past has become a means of differentiating Upper Silesia from the rest of Poland by stressing an identity indelibly bound to industrial progress, but having little to do with the glorification of the latter by the (national) communist state. In fact, the re-signification of Silesia's industrial past by today's regional actors serves to locate the region in Europe while marking its distinction from the remainder of the Polish state.

Silesia's 'European' industrial heritage is being celebrated in newly created museums and exhibitions (Jasnorzewski, 2000; Szczepańska, 1999) and forms a key part of regional education programmes in local schools (Pulinowa, in print; Nawrocki, 2000; Szczepański and Nawrocki, 1998). Moreover, in present-day narratives of the region, this heritage is rhetorically transposed into a series of attributes, loosely deriving from a certain *sort* of industrial development and endowing its participants (i.e. the inhabitants of the region) with a series of traits that, in turn, define their, and the region's, identity. Traits such as cleanliness, diligence, an 'iron-clad work ethic' that 'emerged from the Prussian factory ethos' (Szczepański, 1999a: 7) have, according to regional commentators, 'survived even 50 years of communism'.[12] *Ślązacy*, therefore, 'don't have to learn about Europe – they have always felt it in their toils, in their bones (*mają ją w gnatach*)' for they have always 'worked like Europeans – quite unlike the Asian work habits which seem to characterize other Poles'.[13] To cite Senator Kutz, it is such values that make of Upper Silesia a 'European Other within the Polish state' (*obcość Europejska w Polsce*).

THE USES OF EUROPE

The ideal of Europe is firmly woven into the regional story narrated by Silesian regionalists over the past decade, serving to distinguish Silesia from the remainder of the Polish state and to locate it within a broader community of belonging. Echoing Paasi (1996), regional narratives always serve both to 'express where the territorial unit has come from', but also 'where it is going' – and Silesia's future is quite clearly painted in European colours.

I noted how Silesia's industrial heritage is being reconstructed as part of a European 'civilizational trajectory'. The past is also being adopted by Silesian regionalists, however, to argue for Silesia's belonging to a 'European community of values' by stressing, in particular, the region's *multi-cultural and multi-national history*. As a border region that changed rulers and political alliances many times during the past centuries, Silesia was always inhabited by a population characterized by multiple national belongings. As a booming industrial centre, it always attracted men of fortune from all around Central Europe.

> At the turn of the century, 12 languages were spoken in the territories of today's Upper Silesia. Of course Polish, German, Czech, Hungarian and Russian. But also Hebrew and Yiddish, as well as the three Upper Silesian dialects. And the educated classes all knew ancient Greek and Latin that were taught at every state gymnasium... This sort of linguistic and identity mosaic was always considered a great value. Here, social divides were dictated by social roles – and not by national or ethnic belonging.[14]

Former regional governor Wojciech Czech and the *Związek Górnośląski*, the regionalist movement with which he was associated in the early 1990s, have repeatedly stressed Silesia's 'multi-cultural and multi-national nature' in arguing for the region's 'rightful place in Europe'. 'Europe is easily transposed onto Silesia – and Silesia onto the European project. We do not need to learn how to live together with other cultures, other nations – we have always done it', echoes Katowice mayor Piotr Uszok.[15]

Europe not only provides the conceptual clothes-horse upon which to hang the regional representation, it is also a very real arbiter of the authenticity of Upper Silesia's regional identity and difference. It is, in fact, to European institutions that those revindicating 'Silesian nationality' in recent years have turned: such as the group of historians from the Silesian University in Katowice, who recently deposited a petition to the European Court of Justice. It is to Union institutions and funds that local actors look in order to support their region-building initiatives and to provide frameworks for cross-border cooperation. 'We do what we can to strengthen contacts with Union institutions as well as with the member states at the local level', notes Chorzów's mayor, Marek Kopel.[16] Students from Silesian schools have been by far the most numerous of all Polish participants in EU youth programmes (*Euroscola po polsku*, 1999; *Polacy na Świecie Europy*, 1999), while regional government employees were the first from among their Polish colleagues to seize the opportunity to travel to Brussels for EU training courses on the formal and practical aspects of accession (*Gazeta Samorządowa*, 2000). Finally, despite the exceptionally high social costs of the economic transition, as hundreds of thousands of miners and industrial workers were progressively laid off since 1989, Upper Silesia continues to show some of the highest levels of support for European accession from among all of the Polish regions – surpassed only by the large and economically successful urban centres such as Warsaw and Kraków (on the attitudes of laid-off miners, see Szczepański, 1999c). Surveys carried out by the Committee for European Integration of the Republic of Poland in 1999 noted that over 69 per cent of Silesian respondents saw EU membership as 'positive for the country', while 58 per cent thought it 'above all positive for their region' (*Śląsk bardziej Europejski*, 1999; 4).

A PRIVATE HOMELAND

As successful as the regional representation may have become in the past decade, however, there exists a curious disjunction between the diffuse adoption of Upper Silesia as a locus of political, economic and cultural organizing and the continuing lack of regional institutions to reflect this. Even after the 1999 reform, for the most part, 'regionalizing' activities have proceeded *outside* of the formal structures of the new *województwo*, and the new region's functionaries are generally perceived as marginal actors in the processes of regionalization.

The Silesian regionalists give two reasons for this. First, the Upper Silesian identity is portrayed as broadly anti-political or, at least, apolitical, located within the realm of private practices – the family, the Church, personal habits. It is here, in the private sphere, that *Śląskość* (Silesianness) was able to survive both earlier German domination and the subsequent repression by the Polish communist state. Secondly, as regional actors repeatedly assert, 'Upper Silesia does not have – and never has had – a regional elite' (Sarnowicz, personal interview, 2000; Stefański, personal interview, 2000; see also Szczepański, 1999a and the debate in the magazine *Śląsk*, Kijonka and Karwat, 2000) and thus cannot create a strong regional politics. A number of historical reasons are commonly cited: its industrial development at the peripheries of first the Prussian and later the Polish state, both of which deliberately prevented the development of institutions of higher education within *Śląsk*'s territories in order to import 'colonial' elites to run the region's business. Many also extend the 'colonial domination' thesis to Silesia's most recent past, arguing that 'outsiders' faithful to the regime were always imported to fill key political, cultural and economic leadership posts – mostly, to add insult to injury, from the neighbouring areas of the *Zagłębie Dąbrowskie*, just east of the Brynica river. The *Zagłębie* has always been considered a fundamentally 'alien' territory, historically separate from Upper Silesia because never part of the Prussian territories. In the post-war years, it was an area of heavy in-migration from other parts of Poland, and was popularly seen by Silesians as a zone loyal to the communist state.

The arguments for 'internal colonialism' and, especially, for the absence of a regional elite point, however, to an important omission in the regional narrative of felicitous multi-national co-existence. 'Saying that Silesia had no elite is equivalent to saying that only Poles are to be considered Silesians – because historically, the elite was, for the large part, German. Just as saying that there is no high culture here, only folklore. What about the five Nobel prize winners [all German] who came from *Śląsk*?' argues German minority leader Dietmar Brehmer.[17] It is important to note that while the German heritage is heavily stressed in regional narratives (and used to argue for Upper Silesia's 'Europeanness'), '*living* Germans are quite absent – they are not part of the vision of Slask that [the regional actors] paint'.[18] The ambivalent nature of Upper Silesian regionalists' relationship with the region's German past reflects, in part, the equally ambivalent nature of Polish–German relations in the post-1989 era. While Germany is perceived by many Polish state actors as the conduit to Europe and EU membership, such pragmatic considerations are often coloured by fears of a 'renewed' economic and cultural domination (articulated mostly by the Polish right wing).

Studies carried out in the post-1989 period have indeed confirmed that formal politics in Upper Silesia continues to be overwhelmingly associated with the (party) state (see, among others, K. Wódz, 1994; J. Wódz, 1995). Recent years have witnessed repeated calls in the regional press for a 'Silesian lobby' in the national parliament (see, for example, Kijonka, 1999), noting that the region's interests cannot possibly be well served by 'national parties'. What 'works' in Silesia, or, even better, *who/what best represents Śląsk*, are actors and organizations untainted by national politics, outside the sphere of formal politics. Although distrust in formal politics is widespread in post-communist societies, the underlying causes of such feelings in Silesia are somewhat different. Here, the actors and institutions of formal politics lack legitimation not only because they are still associated with party-state structures or with their often corrupt successors (as in other countries) but also, above all, because they are perceived as an 'external' incursion into the local territory.

Katowice political scientist Jacek Wódz has stressed repeatedly the absence of national parties from local and regional politics in Upper Silesia (J. Wódz, 1998, 1999a, 1999b; see also Wódz and Wódz, 1999a, 1999b, 1999c). The post-1989 Silesian political scene has been dominated instead by what Wódz terms 'proto-parties': loose associations or coalitions of actors which come together around specific local problems and enter formal politics only at election time (the best example is that of the *Związek Górnośląski*). Jacek Wódz also notes the strong personalization of Silesian politics, and the 'collapse of the representativeness of existing political structures'.[19] In Upper Silesia, he argues, 'representation is claimed, rather, by single individuals'. The most evident case is that of Józef Małosz, Rybnik's mayor for two consecutive terms, the sole representative of the 'Movement for Rybnik' (*Ruch na Rzecz Rybnika*). Małosz (according to Petaux and Wódz, 1996) was successful due to his distancing himself from the structures and discourses of formal politics and constructing his support base upon a highly personalized network of local associations. Upper Silesia's regionalization thus appears to proceed despite (or at least alongside) the new administrative structures of the Polish state.

COMING 'HOME'?

All through the communist years we, *Ślązacy*, continued to live in our homeland – but we never felt at home. Now we *are* at home.[20]

The progressive institutionalization of Upper Silesia as a legitimate locus of political, economic and cultural action is indisputable. To echo Senator Kutz's statement cited above, Silesians are 'returning home'. To what extent is this return, however, related to the new opportunities provided by the administrative decentralization of the Polish state? The regional 'becoming' of Upper Silesia in the past decade appears to have proceeded *alongside* processes of state decentralization. While these latter have provided the openings necessary for the articulation of various regionalizing aspirations, they have not been the motivating factor for regional revival. In fact, despite the decentralization of powers to the regional level, regional authorities continue to be perceived by many as agents of the central government and thus not the legitimate representatives of the regional whole.

This is for two reasons. Firstly, the new *Województwo Śląskie* is perceived as only a *partial* representation of Upper Silesia, for the regional borders consecrated on 1 January 1999 'do not correspond to anyone's idea here of where the region should be'. For some, like the *Związek Górnośląski*, the new *województwo* is 'too small', as it does not include the 'historical territories of Śląsk';[21] that is, those of the pre-war period. For others, echoing the arguments of the inter-war Silesian regionalists, it is 'too large', for it 'mixes up outsiders with Silesians'[22] including, for example, the territories around Częstochowa 'which were never part of Silesia'.

Secondly, the new regional government and its functionaries continue to be perceived as 'outsiders' tied to national party politics. This popular perception is rooted in the region's and the regional governor's longstanding institutional roles, which underwent transformation only in 1999. Prior to this, the governors of the then 49 *województwa* acted essentially as the territorial delegates of the central government whose function was to 'coordinate the activities of state administration on the territory of the *województwo* in order to assure their conformity with government policy' (Wollmann, 1997: 469). The role of the regional governor reflected the 'dual model' of local governance that developed historically in Poland, entrusting local government functionaries with the tasks of both local self-rule and of executing delegated national state functions.

The 1999 reform has, for the first time, delegated a whole set of competences and resources to the regional administrations that previously lay solely in the hands of central government. These include the rights to stipulate 'regional statutes' or 'contracts', to create strategies of regional development and to generate regional income. The new regions now also have responsibility for administering primary, secondary and higher education; healthcare; social security/welfare provision; and broadly conceived 'spatial planning' (although decision-making in the above must still conform to national guidelines established by state bodies). Finally, the reform has also enshrined a loosely defined principle of 'subsidiarity': 'where appropriate', competences may be devolved by the regional administration to the *powiat* (county) or the *gmina* (municipality) (Government Plenipotentiary for the Systemic Reform of the State, 1998).

It is perhaps too early to discern the effects of this reform on popular perceptions of the regional governor's role; yet, two years after the reforms, the figure remains 'an outsider', only peripherally related to the everyday problems of the region. When governor Marek Kempski was forced to step down in December 2000 following a corruption scandal, popular commentaries noted cynically that 'Silesia goes on without him anyway'. For most of the regional actors I have interviewed, the reforms have simply provided additional 'tools' for *on-going* processes of regionalization, tools most fruitfully put into practice not by the administrative region but by local authorities in the *gminas* or municipalities. It is within the municipalities (in the large urban centres of the GOP but also in the small country towns) that the most ambitious 'regional initiatives' have taken hold. It is municipal leaders who have been the most active 'regionalists', both in promoting the idea of Upper Silesia (through various celebrations of regional heritage and culture) as well as in creating the highly personalized and place-bound networks of association that inscribe the region in practice.

CONCLUSION

The disjunction between the administrative Upper Silesia (*Województwo Śląskie*) and Upper Silesia as constituted in socio-spatial consciousness points to the importance of the regional narratives traced above. Such narratives are revealing for they point to the *practices* that create the region – and not merely the *boundaries* that delimit it. It is just such narratives, articulated by those whom Paasi (1996) terms the 'specialists' in the production and reproduction of spatial distinctions (politicians, journalists, cultural and business elites, all those with the power to craft representations of territorial identity due to their social rank) that act to institutionalize the region as a territorial ideal. A territorial ideal that, in the case of Upper Silesia, appears only partially to correspond to the formal regional institutions sanctioned by the nation-state.

ACKNOWLEDGEMENTS

Research for this contribution was carried as part of an ESRC-funded project on Regional Identity and European Citizenship (ref. no. L21325 2031), part of the *One Europe or Several?* programme.

NOTES

1. Interview with Dietmar Brehmer, 3 Jan. 2001.
2. Interview with Wojciech Sarnowicz, 23 Oct. 2000.
3. Interview with Andrzej Stefański, 23 Oct. 2000.
4. Interview with Sarnowicz.
5. Interview with Kazimierz Kutz, 25 Oct. 2000
6. Interview with Stefanski.
7. Interview with Piotr Uszok, 30 Nov. 2000.
8. Interview with Kutz.
9. Interview with Wojciech Czech, 2 Jan. 2001.
10. Interview with Michal Smolorz, 27 Oct. 2000.
11. Interview with Kutz.
12. Interview with Sarnowicz.
13. Interview with Kutz.
14. Interview with Czech.
15. Interview with Uszok.
16. Interview with Marek Kopel, 30 Nov. 2000.
17. Interview with Brehmer.
18. Interview with Brehmer.
19. Interview with Jacek Wódz, 24 Nov. 2000.
20. Interview with Kutz.
21. Interview with Czech.
22. Interview with Kutz.

REFERENCES

Anderson, B. (1983), *Imagined Communities*. London: Verso.
Bialasiewicz, L. and J. O'Loughlin (2002), 'Re-ordering Europe's Eastern Frontier: Galicjan Identities and Political Cartographies on the Polish-Ukrainian Border', in D. Kaplan and J. Hakli (eds), *Boundaries and Place: European Borderlands in Geographical Context*. London: Rowman & Littlefield.
Billig, M. (1995), *Banal Nationalism*. London: Sage.
Błasiak, W. (1990), 'Śląska zbiorowość regionalna i jej kultura w latach 1945–1956', in M. Błaszczak-Wacławik, W. Błasiak and T. Nawrocki, (eds), *Górny Śląsk: Szczególny przypadek kulturowy*. Warsaw.
Błasiak, W. (1993), 'Społeczne zródła mobilizacji oraz demobilizacji regionalnej i lokalnej zbiorowośći Górnego Śląska i Zagłębia Dąbrowskiego', in Gorzelak G. and B. Jalowiecki, (eds), *Czy Polska będzie państwem regionalnym?*. Warsaw: Europejski Instytut Rozwoju Regionalnego i Lokalnego.
Błaszczak-Wacławik, M. (1990), 'Miejsce i rola regionalnej kultury w procesach zycia społecznego zbiorowości Górnego Śląska do roku 1945', in M. Błaszczak-Wacławik, W. Błasiak and T. Nawrocki, (eds.), in *Górny Śląsk: Szczególny przypadek kulturowy*. Warsaw.
Brubaker, R. (1996), *Nationalism Reframed: Nationhood and the National Question in the New Europe*. Cambridge: Cambridge University Press.
Burowoy, M. (1992), 'The End of Sovietology and the Renaissance of Modernisation Theory', *Contemporary Sociology*, Vol.21, No.6, pp.774–85.
Ciągwa, J. (1979), *Wpłow centralnych organów Drugiej Rzeczypospolitej na ustawodawstwo Śląskie w latach 1922–1939*. Katowice: Śląsk.

Ciągwa, J. (1988), *Autonomia Ślaska (1922–1939)*. Katowice: Slask.
Czastka-Szymon, B., J. Ludwig and H. Synowiec (1999), *Mały Słownik Gwary Górnego Śląska*. Katowice: LEKSEM.
Długajczyk, E. (1983), *Sanacja Śląska 1926–1939. Zarys dziejów politycznych*. Katowice: Uniwersytet Śląski.
Euroscola po polsku (1999), *Gazeta Wyborcza Katowice*, 12 June, p.4.
Finał 2000 (2000), *Gazeta Wyborcza Katowice*, 12 June, pp.1–9.
Godka, choby w doma (1999), *Gazeta Wyborcza Katowice*, 13 December, p.8.
Government Plenipotentiary for the Systemic Reform of the State (1998), *Effectiveness, Openness, Subsidiarity: A New Poland for New Challenges*, Chancellery of the Prime Minister of the Republic of Poland.
Hobsbawm, E. (1990), *Nations and Nationalism since 1780*. Cambridge: Cambridge University Press.
Hobsbawm, E. and T. Ranger (eds), (1983), *The Invention of Tradition*. Cambridge: Cambridge University Press.
Jasnorzewski, R. (2000), 'Muzeum Narodowe Ziemi Śląskiej', *Śląsk*, Vol.9, No.59, pp.32–3.
Karwat, K. (1999), 'Fałszywy mit', *Śląsk*, Vol.9, No.47, p.29.
Kijonka, T. (1999), 'Powrot posłow', *Śląsk*, Vol.3, No.41, p.3.
Kijonka, T. and K. Karwat (2000), 'Co czeka Śląsk? (roundtable discussion with A. Klasik, T. Sławek, M. Szczepański and J. Wojtyla)', *Śląsk*, Vol.2, No.52, pp.8–13.
Kopeć, E. (1986), *'My i oni' na polskim Śląsku. (1918–1939)*. Katowice: Uniwersytet Śląski.
Kordan, B. (1997), 'Making Borders Stick: Population Transfer and Resettlement in the Trans-Curzon Territories, 1944–1949', *Intl. Migration Review*, Vol.31, No.3, pp.704–20.
Kubik, J. (1994), *The Power of Symbols Against the Symbols of Power*. University Park, PA: Penn State University Press.
Leszczyńska, C. (1990), 'Wojewodztwo w II Rzeczypospolitej' in A. Kuklinski and P. Swianiewicz (eds), *Polskie województwo: doświadczenia i perspektywy*. Warszawa.
Magocsi, P.R. (1993), *Historical Atlas of East Central Europe*. Seattle, WA: University of Washington Press.
Nawrocki, T. (1993), 'Spor o regionalizm na Górnym Śląsku' in G. Gorzelak and B. Jałowiecki, (eds), *Czy Polska będzie państwem regionalnym?*, Warsaw: Europejski Instytut Rozwoju Regionalnego i Lokalnego.
Nawrocki, T. (2000), *Pomiędzy rodziną, szkolą i uniwersytetem. Refleksje socjologa o barierach edukacyjnych na Górnym Śląsku*. Katowice: Uniwersytet Śląski.
Paasi, A. (1986), 'The Institutionalisation of Regions: A Theoretical Framework for Understanding the Emergence of Regions and the Constitution of Regional Identity', *Fennia*, Vol.164, No.1, pp.106–46.
Paasi, A. (1991), 'Deconstructing Regions: Notes on the Scales of Spatial Life', *Environment & Planning A*, No.2382, pp.239–56.
Paasi, A. (1996), *Territories, Boundaries and Consciousness: The Changing Geographies of the Finnish-Russian Border*. London: John Wiley.
Petaux, J. and J. Wódz (1996), *Les acteurs de la vie politique locale*. Katowice: US.
Pickles, J. and A. Smith (1998), *Theorizing Transition*. London: Routledge.
Polacy na Świecie Europy (1999), *Gazeta Wyborcza Katowice*, 13 May, p.7.
Pulinowa, M. (1998), 'Region – podstawowe pojecię przy pisywaniu zjawisk przestrzennych na ziemi', Seminar paper. Wydzial Nauk o Ziemi, Uniwersytet Śląski.
Pulinowa, M. (in print). Dni Ziemi w Sosnowcu – Praktyczne Wdrożenie Zasad Edukacji Regionalnej.
Rechowicz, H. (1971), *Sejm Śląski 1922–1939*. Katowice: Uniwersytet Śląski.
Sharpe, L. (1993), *The Rise of Meso Government in Europe*. London: Sage.
Śląsk bardziej Europejski (1999), *Gazeta Wyborcza Katowice*, 15 December, p.4.
Synowiec, H. (2000a), 'Gwara Śląska – jezyk żywy', (interview with S. Szymutko), *Śląsk*, Vol.4, No.54, pp.26–8.
Synowiec, H. (2000b), 'Gwara w szkole Śląskiej', *Śląsk*, Vol.5, No.55, p.67.
Szczepańska, J. (1999), 'Czas odklamac Śląsk', *Śląsk*, Vol.7, No.45, pp.12–15.
Szczepański, M. (ed.) (1993a), *Dilemmas of Regionalism and the Region of Dilemmas: The Case*

of Upper Silesia. Katowice: Uniwersytet Slaski.
Szczepański, M. (1993b), 'Regionalizm górnośłaski w spolecznej swiadomosci', in Gorzelak G. and B. Jalowiecki (eds), *Czy Polska będzie państwem regionalnym?*. Warsaw: Europejski Instytut Rozwoju Regionalnego i Lokalnego.
Szczepański, M. (1997), Regionalizm Górnośląski: Miedzy Plemiennością i Systemem Globalnym. Unpublished conference paper. Institute of Sociology. Uniwersytet Slaski.
Szczepański, M. (1998), 'Regionalizm Górnośląski: między autonomią i Separatyzmem', in *Europa Regionum*, Vol.3. Szczecin: Polsko Niemieckie Towarzystwo Badan Regionalnych, Uniwersytet Szczecinski.
Szczepański, M. (1999a), 'Cultural Borderland in Sociological and Political Perspective (The Case of Upper Silesia)', in *Local Power and Modern Community Political Life: Sociological Essays.* Katowice: Uniwersytet Slaski.
Szczepański, M. (1999b), 'Kmiecie, robotnicy i technolodzy intelektu', *Śląsk*, Vol.2, No.40, pp.6–8.
Szczepański, M. (1999c), 'Odprawy gornicze albo "Bierz i uciekaj"', *Śląsk*, Vol.11, No.49, pp.14–16.
Szczepański, M. and T. Nawrocki (1998), 'Ludzie bez "ojczyzny prywatnej" i edukacja regionalna', *Polonistyka*, Vol.5, pp.264–78.
Szoltysek, M. (1998), *Śląsk, takie miejsce na ziemi (opisanie Ojcowizny Górnoslązaków).* Rybnik: Slaskie ABC.
Szoltysek, M. (1999), *Zywot Ślązoka Poczciwego.* Rybnik: Slaskie ABC.
Szoltysek, M. (2000), *Biblia Ślązoka*, Rybnik: Slaskie ABC.
Thrift, N.J. (1990), 'For a New Regional Geography 1', *Progress in Human Geography*, Vol.14, pp.272–9.
Williams, C. and A. Smith (1988), 'The National Construction of Social Space', *Progress in Human Geography*, pp.503–18.
Wódz, J. (1995), 'Une reflexion sociologique sur la notion de "representation politique" en Pologne des annees 1990–1993', in A. Jamroz (ed.), *Democratie hier et aujourd'hui.* Bialystok.
Wódz, J. (1998), 'Tożsamosc Śląska jako zjawisko polityczne', in W. Swiatkiewicz (ed.), *Regiony i Regionalizmy w Polsce Wspólczesnej.* Katowice: Zaklad Socjologii Wiedzy, Uniwersytet Slaski.
Wódz, J. (1999a), 'The New Local Elite in Poland – The Dynamics of Change (Some Results of Empirical Research in Upper Silesia)', in *Local Power and Modern Community Political Life: Sociological Essays.* Katowice: Wyd. Uniwersytetu Slaskiego.
Wódz, J. (1999b), 'Napiecia, niepokoje, konflikty', *Śląsk*, Vol.8, No.46, pp.8–10.
Wódz, J. and K. Wodz (1999a), 'Cultural Identity of Upper Silesians: The Difficult Relationship Between National and Regional Culture', in J. Mucha (ed.), *Dominant Culture as a Foreign Culture: Dominant Groups in the Eyes of Minorities.* New York: Columbia University Press.
Wódz, J. and K. Wodz (1999b), 'Transborder Regions in Central Europe as a Political and Social Problem. The Example of Upper Silesia in Poland', in *Local Power and Modern Community Political Life: Sociological Essays.* Katowice: Wyd. Uniwersytetu Slaskiego.
Wódz, J. and K. Wodz (1999c), 'From Cultural Identity to Political Revindications – the Case of Upper Silesia', in *Local Power and Modern Community Political Life: Sociological Essays.* Katowice: Wyd. Uniwersytetu Slaskiego.
Wódz, K. (1994), 'Tożsamość etniczna, tolerancja, społeczeństwo obywatelskie. Opcje identifikacyjne współczesnych mieszkanców Górnego Śląska', in J.Wodz (ed.), *Vie politique locale – Polityczne zycie lokalne.* Katowice: Slask.
Wódz, K. (1995), 'Revitalisation of the Silesian Identity – Chances and Threats', in K. Wodz. (ed.), *Regional identity – regional consciousness. The Upper Silesian experience.* Katowice: Wyd. Uniwersytetu Slaskiego.
Wollmann, H. (1997), 'Institution Building and Decentralisation in Formerly Socialist Countries: The Cases of Poland, Hungary and East Germany', *Environment and Planning C: Government & Policy*, Vol.15, pp.463–80.

Poland's Eastern Borderlands: Political Transition and the 'Ethnic Question'

MARZENA KISIELOWSKA-LIPMAN

'Borderland' generally indicates a peripheral territory located on or near a boundary or frontier, which symbolically marks the limits of influence transmitted by a variety of political, economic and cultural centres. As Babiński points out, the existence of borderlands is proof of the artificiality and low effectiveness of borders (Babiński, 1998: 42); and indeed, the essence of a borderland region is a constant diffusion and interweaving of social groups and their cultures, defined here in a broad sense to include economic, political, linguistic and religious factors. This contribution examines the impact on Poland's multi-ethnic eastern borderlands of the political transition initiated from 'above' since the collapse of communism. My analysis revolves around two questions: firstly, how the major political changes such as democratization, decentralization and EU and NATO enlargement were accommodated 'below'; and secondly, how they have affected inter-ethnic relations.

The research concentrates on the Polish regions bordering Ukraine, Belarus and Lithuania, constituting a vast expanse of the 'eastern wall', remnants of Poland's former historic Eastern *Kresy*. The research took place in Podkarpackie region, which covers a large part of the Polish–Ukrainian borderland, and in Podlaskie region, bordering on both Belarus and Lithuania. Both regions share features characteristic of peripheral borderlands, such as a relatively low level of economic and social development, demonstrated by low levels of industrialization and urbanization, as well as poorly developed educational, social and technical infrastructure as compared with other parts of Poland (Sadowski, 1995). As a result, these regions are still highly rural: for example, in Podkarpackie the share of population in villages is substantially higher (59 per cent) than in cities (41 per cent), whereas overall in Poland, the reverse is the case, with 38 per cent in villages and 62 per cent in cities (GUS, 1998: Table 61). The low level of investment and technical underdevelopment of agricultural units is reflected in low income per capita compared with other regions and in high unemployment, which more often than in other regions has a structural character. The limited potential for upward social mobility stimulates migration abroad and to other parts of Poland, which has remained at a high level throughout the post-war period (Sadowski, 1995).

In the cultural dimension, these two provinces are ethnically among the most diverse regions, reflected in a high degree of religious and linguistic heterogeneity as compared with other more homogeneous parts of the country. According to the Parliamentary Commission for Ethnic and National Minorities, in Podkarpackie there are approximately 5,000–10,000 Ukrainians and in Podlaskie 250,000–300,000 Belarussians and 10,000 Lithuanians (*Mniejszości narodowe w Polsce*, 1995). For centuries the north-eastern territories, now Podlaskie region, were a place of rivalry between the Catholic, Orthodox and Greek Catholic religions, and the Polish, Belarussian, Lithuanian, Ukrainian, Russian, Jewish, Roma and Tatar languages and nationalities (Nikitorowicz, 1995: 52). Similarly, Podkarpackie region has traces of multi-cultural influence with the remnants of Polish-Ukrainian and Lemko mixture, but these have been much reduced due to shifting borders, forced resettlement and expulsion.

The long history of inter-ethnic coexistence between diverse religious and linguistic groups, which often led to cultural diffusion, gave birth to specific forms of social and political behaviour among the inhabitants of the borderlands, and determined the nature of inter-ethnic relations. On the eastern borderlands, one could find all the types of inter-ethnic contact proposed by Alvin Bertrand, namely cooperation; opposition; accommodation; assimilation; and confrontation (Bertrand, 1973). As Józef Chlebowczyk points out, a specific mixture of social behaviour, in his term 'borderland consciousness', is characteristic for such territories, and can be identified by:

> a range of social attitudes and behaviour rarely witnessed elsewhere, from unreflective, national indifference to programmed, conscious universalism on the one hand, and on the other, from declared patriotism to the most drastic symptoms of nationalistic doggedness, fanaticism and chauvinism (Chlebowczyk, 1975: 24).

Although ethnic conflict can be moderated by strong consciousness of regional unity, which acknowledges the necessity of day-to-day contact with one's neighbour, irrespective of his ethnic origin, this is vulnerable to conditions determined by social, economic and, especially, political systems. And indeed, politics plays a key role in activating various types of inter-ethnic contacts in borderlands. The prevailing ideology, propagated from above, can undermine the importance of regional belonging by emphasizing the superiority of national unity, which, in an ethnically diverse area, can provoke inter-ethnic competition, rivalry or opposition; or it may accommodate regional consciousness as one of its values, and, as a result, accelerate the development of inter-ethnic cooperation or accommodation, which can range from compromise and tolerance to domination and subordination.

ETHNIC DIVERSITY VERSUS CLASHING IDEOLOGIES

The eastern borderlands of Poland were the setting for battles between various antagonistic states and empires, including the Polish Republic of Nobles, Tsarist Russia, the Austro-Hungarian Empire, the inter-war Polish Republic, the Soviet Union, Lithuania and Ukraine, all of which struggled to impose on the conquered territories clashing ideologies that accentuated cultural differences and activated various types of inter-ethnic relations in the region.

Until the end of the eighteenth century, the eastern territories were incorporated within the borders of the multi-ethnic Polish-Lithuanian Commonwealth, a feudal state, based on political and civic rather than ethno-national unity, which allowed the inclusion of a vast number of ethnic groups. This resulted in the creation of a dual type of identity, both civic and national, for example, identification as *'Gens Ruthenus, Natione Polonus'* or *'Gens Lituanius, Natione Polonus'* (Filipowicz, 1992: 9; see also Kłoskowska, 1993: 102–3), but such identifications only applied to literate members of society, which included the small number of upper and incipient middle classes. The partitions of the Polish-Lithuanian Commonwealth between 1772 and 1795 split the territory of the eastern borderlands between the two competing empires of Tsarist Russia and the Habsburg monarchy. The part of the Polish-Ukrainian borderland that is the contemporary province of Podkarpackie was annexed by the Habsburg dynasty and formed an administrative unit called *Regnum Galiciae* (Galicia), whereas the north-eastern borderland territories, including the Polish-Lithuanian and Belarussian regions, were incorporated into Tsarist Russia.

The liberal-reformist trend of Habsburg politics, which came to the fore especially in the late nineteenth century, guaranteed a relatively wide political and cultural autonomy to Galicia, manifested in the granting of a constitution in 1867 and the establishment of a regional parliament. Liberal policies securing the right of individual ethnic and religious groups to preserve their cultural distinctiveness aimed to oppose and liquidate growing separatist and revisionist national movements within the Monarchy. As Józef Chlebowczyk points out:

The main feature of such a model was that, leaving aside Switzerland, it went the furthest in Europe in respecting individuality and the rights of separate ethno-linguistic and national groups, with regard to both legislative and political practice… Such liberalism in the national sphere resulted in the absence on a larger scale of the atmosphere of disagreement and conflict in relations between the state administration and national movements … and in this way consolidated and even deepened the effect of the process of state assimilation, the sense of belonging to the state known as 'Austrian patriotism', which in some social circles and regions preserved the consciousness of ties to the dynastic state, personified by the Emperor and King, who enjoyed great popularity especially in the village (Chlebowczyk, 1975: 250–71).

Although the liberal policies did not manage to prevent ethnic revival and, on the contrary, often stimulated national awakening (notably in the Ukrainian case), nonetheless Galician quasi-parliamentarism provided a useful forum for inter-ethnic interactions, in which conflicts were played out in parliamentary debates, unlike in the other partitions of Poland (under Russian and Prussian rule), where bloody uprisings and Jewish pogroms took place.

According to Mach, ethnic separatism is a key component of ethnic identity, which unifies an ethnic group in a fight for cultural, political and territorial autonomy (Mach, 1993: 217–18). The collapse of the empires triggered off hopes for independence in the borderland ethnic groups, particularly in Galicia, where both Ukrainian and Polish national movements benefited from the more liberal national policies of Austro-Hungary and hence were stronger politically and better organized. They laid claim to the same territories, and attempted to gain military control of them. The conflict unfolded into the Polish-Ukrainian war in 1919 from which the Poles emerged victorious and the Ukrainians found themselves a minority in reconstituted Poland.

The rebirth of an independent Polish Republic in the aftermath of the First World War led to the reunification of both the south and north-eastern *Kresy* after over a century of separation. The newly adopted state policies of a 'nationalizing regime', based on the claim that 'the core nation legitimately "owns" the polity' and 'the polity exists as the polity *of* and *for* the core nation' (Brubaker, 1996: 83), were rather problematic for the culturally heterogeneous *Kresy* with their blurred ethno-linguistic borders. The dilemma of how to accommodate the ethnically mixed *Kresy* into the Polish state was manifested in the opposing visions represented by the main national inter-war leaders – Jozef Piłsudski and

Roman Dmowski. The former, a denizen of Vilna (Vilnius, Wilno), wanted to accommodate *Kresy* within the state by means of a federal model built on civic rather than ethno-national unity, albeit with Poles as the dominant partner. In this respect, Piłsudski was either naive or ill-informed about the social reality of the region, inflamed as it was by the awaking nationalisms of the Lithuanians and Ukrainians, who did not wish to be incorporated into any Polish polity, whether civic or national, but aimed to build sovereign states of their own. Dmowski, on the other hand, was perhaps more pragmatic. Though advocating the unity and homogeneity of the Polish nation, he was prepared to annex only those parts of *Kresy* which were inhabited mainly by Poles. However, the remaining ethnic groups would have to be assimilated into Polish culture, or, in the case of ethnic groups resistant to the processes of Polonization, such as Jews and Germans, would have to accept the status of second-class citizens.

In the event, both approaches were combined, as Piłsudski managed to retain those parts of *Kresy* which extended well beyond Polish ethnographic territory, while Dmowski's programme of assimilation and repression was subsequently pursued. Accordingly, the *Kresy* were to act as a front for Polish expansion eastwards and this required the adoption of policies to promote Polish as the *lingua franca* and the primacy of the Catholic religion; the colonization by Poles of 'disputed' ethnically diverse areas; and the control of upward social mobility, permitted only to members of the 'core Polish nation'. These policies in the *Kresy* aggravated the non-Polish population and either awoke nationalism (in the case of Belarussians) or accelerated already existing nationalism (in the case of Lithuanians and Ukrainians) and often led to extremist actions, such as terrorist attacks targeting the Poles, to which the Polish state responded with more repressive measures (see Vakar, 1956; Motyl, 1980; Lossowski, 1966; Lukomski, 1995).

The outbreak of the Second World War generated inter-ethnic conflicts taking the form of open war among the diverse groups. Firstly, Soviet invasion in 1939 after the Ribbentrop-Molotov Pact led to repression of the Polish civilians of the borderlands. This took the forms of discrimination, restrictions, forced expulsion to Arctic Russia, Siberia and Kazakhstan of two million Poles, and extermination, for example the massacres of war prisoners at Katyn and Miednoje (see Davies, 1986: 67). Secondly, the war stimulated the state-building aspirations of Lithuanians and Ukrainians, who fought against the Poles and, in some cases, collaborated either with the Nazis, hoping in return to establish sovereign states in parts of the disputed borderland territories (Chałupczak, 1998: 217). The Polish resistance movement, the Home Army (*Armia Krajowa*,

AK), which operated in the occupied east, was also engaged in military actions against not only Soviet and Nazi forces, but also Lithuanian and Ukrainian national forces (UNO and UPA), as well as against innocent non-Polish civilians in what they called 'revenge actions'. The scale of atrocities committed in the eastern borderlands, especially in the Polish–Ukrainian conflict, cast a dark shadow over inter-ethnic relations in the post-war period.

The end of the war led to increased instability and insecurity in the region with the threat of Soviet domination, a prospect viewed with dismay by Polish inhabitants of the eastern borderlands because of their experiences under the 1939–41 occupation. Secondly, insecurity was increased by the redrawing of Poland's eastern border between 1947 and 1951 according to the Curzon line, signifying for the Polish state the loss of 30 per cent of its former territory, inhabited by five million Poles and large number of Ukrainians, Belarussians and Lithuanians (in total 12 million) before the war (Davies, 1981: 489; see also Stępień, 1998: 45). Drastic border changes entailed mass migration which, in fact, had been agreed back in 1944 between the pro-Soviet Committee of National Liberation (PKWN) and representatives of the Soviet Ukraine, Belarussia and Lithuania, with the aim of pacifying regional nationalisms through the resettlement of citizens (Chałupczak, 1998: 281). This meant the resettlement of millions of Poles and Jewish survivors, who could claim Polish citizenship granted before the war, and the forced migration of Ukrainians and Belarussians into the new Soviet territories (Chałupczak, 1998: 28).[1] Forced migrations raised tensions by reinforcing and legitimizing the inter-war stereotypes among the borderland neighbours, which have proved difficult to eradicate to this day.

Thirdly, the region remained unstable, threatened by military actions between the Ukrainian Insurgent Army (UPA) and the Polish and Soviet armies. These conflicts threatened the population and deepened animosities between the Poles and the Ukrainians. The fighting ended with the so-called Operation 'Wisła' (Vistula), the forced resettlement of 150,000 Ukrainians and Lemkos from the eastern borderlands on lands in the west and north taken over from Germany. The purpose of Wisła was to liquidate the UPA and its base in the compact Ukrainian population; to disperse the Ukrainian population in order to make it more susceptible to assimilation; and to homogenize the ethnically diverse borderlands (Chałupczak, 1998: 282). The borderlands were stabilized by strengthening the borders, which restricted the flow of migrants into and out of Poland and prevented the return to their homelands of those resettled on the so-called 'recovered' German lands. In fact, the border regime was so strict that the expelled people were not only forbidden to return permanently to their former homelands, but even their holiday visits were limited to certain territories and places. This was evident in the cases of both Poles resettled from Soviet Ukraine, Belarussia and Lithuania, and non-Poles forced to move from Poland into the newly established or expanded Soviet republics. Special rules applied to Ukrainians expelled from the eastern borderlands as a result of Operation 'Wisła'; they were restricted in their movement not only back to their historic settlements, but also into the cities, which inhibited their social mobility (see Misiło, 1997). Despite the official propaganda of 'fraternal' cooperation with neighbouring Soviet Republics, there was no free movement across the borders. Both sides of the eastern border implemented policies and bureaucratic procedures aimed to complicate and discourage individual visits, in parallel with a rise in collective travel, designed primarily as a reward for high-achieving Communist Party members (see Stępień, 1998: 45–6).

Contacts among the local people were also inhibited by nationalistic propaganda, emphasizing the historical anti-Polish feelings of the eastern neighbours and their hostility to Polish émigrés wishing to visit their former properties in the Soviet Republics. Furthermore, local communist authorities manipulated local fears that former Ukrainian, Lithuanian and Belarussian inhabitants might return and claim the properties they had left. This propaganda legitimized the border regime among the locals and made them even more hostile and suspicious of visits by former inhabitants. The nationalistic propaganda was especially intense in the case of Ukrainians, who were presented as natural enemies of the Poles, 'traitors' or 'fascists', recalling the crimes committed by UPA forces against the Poles of Podole and Wołyńę during the war. The main channel for transmitting the negative image of Ukrainians was school, where children learnt about supposed Ukrainian 'atrocities' (Bonusiak, 1999: 49).

As far as the Lithuanians and Belarussians were concerned, although there was little acknowledgement of their existence in communist propaganda, local people who encountered them on an everyday basis either mistrusted them (in the case of Lithuanians) or belittled them (in the case of Belarussians). Poles' suspicions of Lithuanians resulted not only from their experience of the inter-war conflicts, but also from the fresh memories of wartime Polish-Lithuanian fights in the Suwalszczyzna region, now a part of Podlaskie province, which discouraged travel to Lithuania (Chałupczak, 1998: 217). The level of hostility towards Belarussians was relatively low, though the local Poles despised their participation in Communist Party activities and treated them as Soviet and communist puppets.

The social and cultural activities of borderland minorities were controlled by the Ministry of Internal Affairs, and reduced to the role of promoting communist ideology and strengthening the Party's monopoly.[2] The Party leadership treated them either as a 'politically unsound element', to be kept under control (in the case of Ukrainians), or an easy target of assimilation by social promotion (in the case of Belarussians).

The ethnically heterogeneous communities lived side by side in an ominous silence enforced by censorship, which forbade open, objective discussion that would have allowed an explanation of complex past events often fragmentarily experienced, but deeply rooted in the memories of survivors and solicitously transmitted to the next generation. Barriers between ethnically diverse groups grew also due to the lack of mixed local activities and joint projects that might have promoted social integration but which were blocked by the communist administration, which, scared of losing its monopoly, resorted to a 'divide and rule' strategy. Central control not only blocked initiatives and implanted into the local community the germ of apathy, but also wrecked the chances of establishing dialogue. This incapacitated the borderland communities and deepened regional ethnic divisions, pushing ethnic minorities into cultural ghettos. This was fertile ground for an outburst of ethnic stereotypes and prejudices, which could not be confronted and therefore proved difficult to overcome. However, the social exclusion of ethnic minorities also had the effect of preserving their specific cultures, subverting the Party plan of cultural assimilation.

DEMOCRATIZATION AND ETHNIC REVIVAL

The collapse of communism and the progress of democratization, accelerated by the desire to 'return to Europe' (i.e. gain EU and NATO membership), entailed a widening of the scope of freedoms and rights for citizens, and for all socially important groups, whether religious, regional or ethnic. Democratization brought a new constitution and laws guaranteeing political, religious and linguistic rights. The new political path was a catalyst for ethnic revival, providing legal instruments for the exercise of rights, and furthermore encouraging greater social inclusion and participation of the ethnic groups. The ethnic revival was accommodated within the Solidarity movement and its ethos of freedom and equality, which attracted the ethnic minorities, and drew them into the development of Solidarity agendas at the central and local levels. Solidarity's structure designated special 'ethnic minority group' units to encourage ethnic participation.[3] During the 1989 parliamentary election, minority activists appeared on Solidarity lists and managed to secure ethnic representation in the parliament. However, the fragmentation of the Solidarity movement, evident already in the presidential campaigns in 1990 and 1991 (see Michta, 1997), which revealed a sharp split between the intelligentsia and the working base, resulted in a reduction in the ethnic minority intellectual contribution. Furthermore, the electorally driven desire to appeal to the masses and to expose 'clear blue water' between them and the ex-communists, led to the promotion of conservative values associated with 'Polishness', especially the Catholic religion and Polish historic myths, which could not be adopted by ethnic minorities.

Nonetheless, the ethnic awakening was developing rapidly, as demonstrated by the number of new non-governmental minority associations, established especially in borderlands, the traditional place of minority settlement. Ethnic minorities in the eastern borderlands tried to re-establish their presence by setting up numerous cultural and religious organizations, erecting monuments commemorating their heroes, and reclaiming nationalized properties (such as religious properties, former schools and association premises) as a result of the new property law.[4] Democratization thus opened a 'Pandora's box' amid the communities of the borderlands. The dominant, culturally privileged Poles underwent the 'shock therapy' of discovering the real level of ethnic and cultural diversity in the regions. Though they had encountered ethnic minority traces in everyday life during the communist era (for example, Orthodox churches and cemeteries), these had been regarded merely as remnants of a blurred past, investigation of which was made taboo by the regime. Local Poles felt their dominant position and interests, secure under communism, threatened.[5]

Inter-ethnic relations were also inflamed by the process of re-defining 'self' amidst the identity crises that occurred in the aftermath of communism. The bankruptcy of communist dogma brought about an ideological vacuum, which had to be filled with new values and symbols departing from the traditions of the Polish Socialist Republic. Both Poles and ethnic minorities drew from their experience of the inter-war Polish Republic. This was the nearest pre-communist period they could refer to, informally coded in social memory through the channel of the family. Having been a historic taboo during communism, interest in the period revived insofar as it demolished the myth of a Polish–Soviet brotherhood. Moreover, it was the time of crystallization, to a large extent, of the modern national identity of both Poles and the ethnic minorities. The process of redefining national identity by reference to inter-war tradition – a prime 'bone of contention' in Polish–minority relations – was not conducive to social reconciliation. Communist national engineering had transformed the eastern borderland to a battlefield in the 'invention' of new traditions: giving new names to streets, public institutions (schools and organizations); demolishing old monuments and erecting new ones that symbolized opposing values for different groups – one group's 'heroes' were another's 'oppressors'.[6] Thus the symbols used to construct the identity boundaries of various groups clashed, as did their respective ideologies, which is an important element of self-consciousness (Mach, 1993: 217–18). Furthermore, the presence of ethnically different 'others', a crucial component of identity, was used as a natural base for comparing, defining and modifying 'self' in opposition to them, along ethno-religious or linguistic lines (Mach, 1993: 213). The strongly rooted 'ethnic' modes of identity had no opportunity to be counterbalanced and moderated by 'civic' modes, which did not have a base in an apathetic and passive society, deprived of civic culture by the communist monopoly.

Inter-ethnic conflict can become increasingly embittered by the pre-election activities of local politicians, who use ethnic divisions in their campaigns. This symptom is especially evident in the case of the Białystok region, where post-Solidarity parties are regarded as allies of the Polish community, whereas Belarussians compose a left-wing electorate supporting the Democratic Left Alliance (SLD). Although, according to Jerzy Syczewski (SLD MP and head of the Belarussian Cultural Association), Belarussian support for the SLD is a result of their social stratification: '90 per cent of Belarussians are of peasant origin. What do they associate with social promotion and prosperity? Obviously not Piłsudski's Poland, but people's [i.e. communist – MKL] rule and Gierek' (quoted by Wilk, 1998: 31).

Nonetheless, Belarussian intellectual elites are convinced that this political divide also has a wider cultural dimension: the strong link between Solidarity and Catholicism is a factor alienating the majority of Orthodox Belarussians.[7] In Przemyśl region, where the percentage of Ukrainians is low, on the other hand, nationalistic antagonisms are exploited by all political actors, from the right to the left of the political scene.[8]

Dialogue among ethnic groups is further complicated by socio-economic disparities, compared to the comparatively prosperous western borderlands, where the rapprochement between Poles and Germans was more successful mainly due to numerous cross-border initiatives with Germany. Cross-border cooperation can play a crucial role in normalizing the situation in the borderlands. Minorities on both sides of Poland's eastern borders have often been used as political hostages, and events which take place on one side of a border are immediately mirrored on the other side, with broader linkage to inter-state relations. For example, reconciliation between Poles and Lithuanians was threatened by charges of discrimination against the Polish minority in Lithuania, on the one hand, while the Polish construction of a border security post in Puńsk – 80 per cent inhabited by Lithuanians – aggravated Vilnius.[9] Parallels can be drawn in the case of Polish–Ukrainian relations, which are focused on Przemyśl (Peremyshl) and Lwów (Lviv): the Łyczakowski cemetery in Lviv contains the graves of the so-called Eaglets, who died resisting the Ukrainian take over of Lviv in 1919. The Polish graves in Lviv have suffered years of neglect, as have UPA monuments around Przemyśl (see Wolczuk, 2001). Similar cases afflict Polish–Belarussian relations. So far political elites in the centre on both sides have tried to avoid direct confrontation on the borderland question, and have successfully communicated above the heads of the local and regional self-government bodies at the Warsaw–Vilnius or Warsaw–Kiev levels. However, at the same time they have tolerated nationalistic rhetoric on the part of their party colleagues, which is exploited in parliamentary games and electoral politics (particularly evident in the bloc of former Solidarity parties (AWS) and its local representatives in Białystok).

DECENTRALIZATION VIEWED FROM 'BELOW'

Decentralization began in 1990, and culminated in the Administration Act of 18 July 1998 which led to the creation of 16 new regions (*województwa*), replacing the previous 49. Several criteria were used in delimiting the new provinces including: (a) functional, (b) security, (c) social consent, (d) geographical, (e) adjustment to EU standards, (f) cultural and historic, (g) reasons of state.[10] The establishment of the new regions aimed to create robust, self-sufficient and more independent regions able to develop regional politics; to improve efficiency, which had been hindered by the previous fragmentation of administration in the financial and regional spheres; and to enforce efficiently the *acquis communautaire* in order to receive increasing transfers from EU structural funds.

The creation of the new regions raised several concerns at the local level. Firstly, a number of local elites complained that the new regions lacked economic resources, or that they had weak historical basis; in particular, they charged that the administrative division unduly reflected the distribution of political influence within the state.[11] Though such allegations were to some extent exaggerated, the AWS–UW coalition did devote much effort to securing their political position locally instead of concentrating on an information campaign about the reform, which would target a wide social spectrum. As a result of lobbying and, more often, highly publicized debates in which a number of proposals were aired, ranging from 7–8 regions, or 12–15, as well as the final 16, the reform did not win public credibility, but instead was perceived as a way of securing seats for party's colleagues from the centre.

The local communities worried that decentralization would mean the curtailment of subsidies, and would therefore further disadvantage the already economically and socially underdeveloped 'eastern wall'. The centre responded that, despite the fact that the eastern provinces are weaker for historic reasons, their economic position is satisfactory, and drew unconvincing comparisons with the position of their eastern neighbours.[12] There were also accusations that the new division meant centralization as opposed to decentralization, especially in the case of small regions that lost their previous *województwo* status by amalgamation into the new larger regions.[13]

Decentralization at the local level in the borderlands also raises questions about power sharing. The Ukrainian minority, whose members are now scattered throughout Poland, fear they will not be able to secure local representation to look after their interests in the more powerful regional administrative units.[14] The Ukrainians, therefore, call for the centralization of subsidies for ethnic minorities in order to guarantee continued financial support for their local activities. On the other hand, decentralization can work to the advantage of the more compactly settled Lithuanian and Belarussian minorities, who already have seats in local governments and therefore better access to local resources, which can be used for minority educational or cultural activities (Zaucha, 1999: 69–70). The Lithuanians especially are pleased with the new administrative divisions at the level of the commune council (*powiat*), which increased the number of their representatives in the local governments (*powiat* and *gmina*) in Sejny and Puńsk.[15]

The other problem of decentralization lies in the psychological sphere, in the local mentality which is hostile to new initiatives. Passivity and apathy are legacies of the communist period, which the Chairman of the Centre for Business Initiatives in Przemyśl referred to as the 'post-communist illness'.[16] In this respect Poles and ethnic minorities could be united: although they are generally appreciative of political and cultural freedoms, nonetheless they are affected socially (in unemployment and the lower standard of living) by economic transition and therefore look with nostalgia to the socialist welfare state. Jerzy Syczewski (head of the Belarussian Cultural Associations and SLD member of parliament) recalled that under the 'People's Republic', the Belarussian Cultural Associations used to employ 20 staff members, but now their budget can only afford two people (author's interview, Bialystok, November 1999). Local elites welcomed more autonomy at the regional level, but still wanted a centralized system of financing and subsidies, which they saw as essential for underdeveloped regions. In this sense, decentralization in the eastern borderlands is realized only partially 'on paper', and 'only if it takes place in the mentality of the local people can it be successful', a Przemyśl business representative told the author in November 1999.

Mentality is crucial not only to spark much-needed initiative, but also to overcome historical animosities, which jeopardize the regional cooperation and cross-border cooperation needed for economic revival. A positive attitude on the part of local government to 'others' is a precondition for establishing cross-border cooperation. This is firstly because a hostile atmosphere discourages potential businessmen from the east, who bypass borderland cities and do business elsewhere. Secondly, local government initiatives, especially linking city councils across the border, are helpful in securing small- and medium-sized Polish investment in the east, where the economic and security conditions are not stable. The accreditation and approval of the local *nomenklatura* of the eastern neighbour can encourage business and build more trust.[17]

Although local borderland communities play a key role, the potential success of decentralization and the resultant regional cooperation will ultimately depend to a large extent upon the approach of the political centre. This is especially the case with cross-border initiatives, which are the domain of foreign policy and national government, and therefore extend beyond the competence of local and regional government. The Polish government has to define clearly its policy towards the 'eastern wall', and how this fits with its foreign policy objectives towards the eastern neighbours. At the moment such policy is still indecisive and therefore raises confusion in local communities and among potential investors. If the government puts its bet on decentralization, the natural economic opportunity for the 'eastern wall' lies in forging closer links with the eastern neighbours, which already, at least in terms of exports, have proved beneficial: for example, Podlaskie and Podkarpackie regions achieve the best export results with eastern countries. Therefore, many in these regions argue that the government should create incentives and encourage even small-scale local initiatives. Some local initiatives come to nothing due to state intervention. For example, a proposal to establish a Polish-Ukrainian University in Przemyśl (based on the model of Viadrina University on the Polish-German border) was dropped because the government favoured setting up such an institution in Lublin.[18] Similarly, the centre did not follow up the concept of erecting a trans-cargo port in Przemyśl. Local business in the borderlands was also hindered by such state decisions as the limits set on the amount of hard currency that can be bought by foreigners, which was designed to target visitors from east; and the imposition of a visa regime on visitors from Russia and Belarus (Kurcz 1999, 13–15). Local elites are convinced that the 'centre' should endeavour to develop infrastructure (roads, motorways, telecommunication, modernized border crossings), which exceeds the capacity of regional governments, but which is necessary to attract potential investors.

Though the government initiated the establishment of three cross-border 'Euroregions' in the eastern borderlands (the 'Carpathian', 'Niemen' and 'Bug' Euroregions), and invested funds in the development of regional infrastructure to support them, these met with a mixed reception in the parliament in Warsaw. The creation of the Carpathian Euroregion in particular raised objections in the parliament, being identified by some MPs with the partition of Poland (Orlof, 1999: 69; and Słomkowski, 1993: 88–93). Moreover, the Euroregions do not have sufficient budgetary resources, considering the large territories and populations they embrace, which is the main obstacle in the generally impoverished regions in which they operate (Orlof, 1999: 75–6; and Helinski, 1997: 129–38). According to Alyson Bailes, there are a number of political, security, domestic, economic and financial factors which discourage states from potential sub-regional co-operation (Bailes, 1999: 154–5). All of these have been apparent, at one time or another, in the case of the eastern borderlands.

THE IMPLICATIONS OF EU AND NATO ENLARGEMENT

The processes of joining NATO and the EU reverberated in the borderlands in quite different ways. NATO membership was regarded locally more as a matter for the central elites, as it did not have a direct impact on day-to-day life in the borderlands. Only during the Kosovo crisis did the Belarussian minority adopt a hostile view of NATO and at the same time show increased sympathy for President Lukashenko. This is to be explained by the religious factor. The Belarussian minority associates itself with the Orthodox Church, and military actions targeting their fellow believers, the Serbs, were understood as an assault on the Orthodox religion. In this sense President Lukashenko was viewed by Poland's Belarussian minority not as a leftover from communism, but as a protector of the Orthodox religion, as Yeltsin had been also.[19] The pro-NATO attitude of the Polish media irritated the local Belarussians, who took it as NATO propaganda and switched to Belarussian TV, which is widely accessible in the borderlands and was regarded as more objective.

A similar polarization of opinion between Poles and the Lithuanian and Ukrainian minorities did not occur, because the latter perceive NATO from the perspective of their respective kin-states' own aspirations for NATO membership.

The enlargement of the European Union, however, caused much more reaction than anticipated among the borderland communities, and was perceived differently here than in other parts of Poland (especially central Poland and the western borderland). At first the local communities took a positive approach to the idea of EU membership for various reasons. For Poles, EU membership had ideological connotations and it was identified with the idea of 'returning to Europe', that is, a return to Western civilization, to which it is believed Poland had always belonged (Mach, 1997: 35–50). Minorities, on the other hand, were attracted by the idea insofar as it promised a broadening of the scope of cultural and political rights for ethnic groups and guaranteed their practical implementation.[20] There was also the economic factor, as the locals hoped that EU funds would even out the socio-economic position of the 'eastern wall' and lead to a rise in the standard of living. Parallels were drawn with the western borderlands, which are flourishing due to contacts with the EU member state, Germany.

The positive attitudes soon disappeared, however, as a result of the implementation of a more restrictive regime at the eastern border in 1998, designed by the Polish government to bring Poland closer to the Schengen *acquis*. The 1998 Act on Foreigners, Migrants and Border Traffic, which introduced visas and vouchers, applied to Russian and Belarussian visitors. According to a report of Border Guard Forces, in January 1998 the number of Russians crossing the border dropped by 48.5 per cent, and Belarussians by 35.8 per cent ('MSWiA…', 1998).

The most visible consequences of the new law were empty bazaars in Białystok and Warsaw's Stadium of the Decade, which had prospered and been filled by visiting traders from Poland's eastern neighbours before the restrictions were imposed. Another highly publicized event was the deportation of Romanian gypsies and illegal workers from Ukraine. The latter case resulted in a protest by the Ukrainian Council in Warsaw, as well as unfavourable coverage in the Ukrainian press in Lviv, which dubbed the deportation 'Operation Wisła – *encore*'. Criticism of the new law was sharpest in Białystok, where the local community organized a blockade of border crossing at Kuźnica Białostocka, demanded the scaling down of the visa procedure by, for example, issuing visas at the border and dropping their price from $60 to $20 – note that $30 is an average monthly salary in Belarus ('Policja…', 1998).

Thus the prospect of Polish EU membership, bringing with it

implementation of the Schengen *acquis*, raises several issues for the borderland communities. Firstly, the borderland economy is at stake. The visa restrictions limit to a large extent cross-border cooperation and initiatives, especially the bazaar trade, which is the lifeblood of the regional economy. Bazaar trade, according to Professor Marek Dąbrowski (a member of the Monetary Policy Council), 'should not be disparaged by hackneyed arguments that it is an old-fashioned form doomed to disappear, because in our economic situation this type of trade is a standard phenomenon, which should not be limited' (Dąbrowski, 1998). Indeed, cross-border bazaar trade is beneficial for the borderland regions as it activates local small- and medium-sized businesses, such as manufacturers, wholesalers, and the service industry (e.g. hotels, catering, transport and travel). Once it is lost, the people who are engaged in it will become frequent visitors to the local social security services (or may contemplate emigration).

Concern over the negative repercussions of the Schengen *acquis* for the 'eastern wall' was expressed by the vice-head of Podłaskie province, who emphasized the contribution of Belarussian migrants to the regional economy.[21] He anticipated problems in implementing the migration law (e.g. restrictions on work permits), as this would hit local business, which absorbs Belarussians either in the lowest paid sectors unattractive to Poles, or in the more specialized sectors, which require a high level of expertise and knowledge of the Belarussian market, rare amongst the local Poles. The Schengen *acquis* would also threaten cross-border cooperation in the Carpathian, Bug and Niemen Euroregions, which are based on the premise of open borders. It could entail bankruptcy and the waste of large investments in infrastructure designed to develop the cross-border economy. For example, one of the busiest border crossings in Europe, between Poland and the Ukraine at Korczów/Krakowiec, could become moribund, and plans for a privately sponsored motorway from Krakowiec to Kiev could be jeopardized as such a motorway would be unprofitable (Bachman, 1998).

Another problem raised by the visa regime centres on social issues. Local elites, both Poles and ethnic minorities, are concerned that a strict border regime will work against social integration amongst ethnically diverse people and will lead to retrogression in inter-ethnic and inter-state relations to the level of the pre-communist or communist period.[22] So far the process of border opening initiated by the collapse of communism has stimulated locally the growth of cultural, economic and family group contact, which has allowed stereotypes to be checked against real personal experience, and has reduced longstanding historic animosities. The Ukrainians from Przemyśl, who struggled in the communist period to establish a school with Ukrainian as the language of instruction, recalled that as a result of the open border between Poland and Ukraine, the Ukrainian language began to appear alongside Polish in business, in shops and advertisements, which was unheard of and unthinkable before.[23]

Borderland minorities also believe that the border regime will hinder contacts with their 'mother countries'. This issue can have wider international implications as it contradicts the Council of Europe 1995 Framework Convention on the Protection of National Minorities, which commits signatory states (including Poland) to guarantee the unimpeded contact of ethnic minorities with 'kin-states' (see Amato and Batt, 1998: 12). Local Poles also raised concern about Polish minorities on the other side of the eastern border, whose access to their homeland would be restricted. This issue was also debated in the Polish parliament, when it was proposed to introduce a so-called 'Polish Card' which would give Polish minorities a privileged treatment at the border (analogous to the cases of Slovaks and Hungarians, as described in Batt's contribution on Transcarpathiain). However, the 'Polish Card' proposal was rejected because of the problems it raised, firstly, in defining 'who is a Pole?' and what criteria should be adopted. Linguistic criteria would not work as many Poles in former Soviet republics are not speakers of Polish. Nor would religion, as Poles in across the eastern border are members not only of the Catholic, but also Orthodox and Greek Orthodox Churches, and many are atheists. Self-declaration, on the other hand, could lead to abuse. Secondly, it was felt that positive discrimination in favour of the Polish minorities at the border would likely entail negative repercussions in their host states, reawakening social prejudices and perhaps justifying cultural discrimination.

Above all, the local elites argue that the border regime will have serious political and security implications not only at the regional and domestic levels, but also for international relations. The idea of tightening the border regime, which is synonymous for them with another 'iron curtain', may solve some short-term problems which affect mainly the western EU members (e.g. illegal human traffic); but in the long term it will lead to the re-establishment of the 'Soviet cocoon – a danger sooner or later', as one interviewee told the author. Serious concerns are raised about the future of Ukraine and the lack of firm commitments to it from the EU, which some fear could lead to a tightening of its economic links with the Russian Federation and, in consequence, growing political and military dependence.[24] Therefore, local elites strongly support the priority accorded to Ukraine in Poland's foreign policy, but still see scope for a more proactive approach. In this sense, they are united with politicians from 'above' who call for a more active and firm Polish *Ost-Politik* and actively support the centre in its demands that Brussels adopt a clearer EU *Ost-Politik*, which, they believe, does not exist at the moment (on this, see Wolczuk, 2001b).

The strong criticism of Schengen does not imply, however, that the borderland community condones instability and crime at the borders. In fact, on the contrary, it is in the local people's interest to keep the borderland regions safe. This not only affects the quality of their everyday life, but also has an impact on economic development in the region (tourism, business investment). Therefore, the borderland community is searching for a form of border protection that would reduce crime, especially by organized groups, but at the same time would not create a barrier to cross-border cooperation. They believe a border based on such a model already operates in the case of Poland and Germany, and they would welcome something similar in the eastern borderlands.

CONCLUSIONS

In the eastern borderlands, the three outlined processes – democratization, decentralization, and NATO/EU enlargement – were accommodated 'below' and effected a transition in ethnic relations. Firstly, democratization sparked the process of ethnic revival, which was reflected in the rapid growth of numerous political and cultural activities on the part of ethnic minorities. This ethnic activism met with a negative response from the local Poles, who feared losing their dominant, privileged position secured in the past. In this sense democratization 'from below' resulted in opposition of the local Poles and cultural and political confrontation among ethnic groups.

Secondly, decentralization, although it developed slowly, prompted joint inter-ethnic initiatives, which contributed to a new process of social integration. In particular, cross-border cooperation played a special role, changing perceptions of both Poland's eastern neighbours and of the ethnic minorities in the borderland regions, and allowing them to be viewed in a more positive way. This suggests that decentralization may help to moderate longstanding historic animosities between ethnically diverse communities, by creating a stronger sense of regional belonging.

Finally, the process of European integration and the prospect of the Schengen *aquis*, although uniting Poles and ethnic minorities in the short term, is likely to generate new sources of tension, which may threaten stability not only in the borderland region, but also in Poland's relations with its eastern neighbours once Poland joins the EU. It is evident that inter-ethnic relations in the eastern borderlands generally are very vulnerable to political changes coming largely from outside. Therefore, there is a need to work out consistent, long-term policy that would prevent confrontation or opposition between ethnic groups, and encourage cooperation and accommodation. This issue should be addressed not only at the local and domestic level, but also internationally. The EU could play a special role in improving regional and inter-state relations in Central and Eastern Europe in the light of the forthcoming eastwards enlargement. The question arises, however, of how far the EU and its member-states are ready to understand this role.

NOTES

1. Initially the exchange was supposed to have a voluntary character; however the right to be resettled in Poland was not granted to Ukrainians, Belarussians or Lithuanians who used to have Polish citizenship. There were also restrictions on the resettlement of Polish nationals, e.g. Poles in Kazakhstan.
2. Interviews with minority groups in Warsaw, Kraków, Przemyśl, Białystok and Sejny, November December 1999.
3. Interviews with minority representatives, see n.2.
4. The re-vindication of property included: in Przemyśl, properties belonging to the Greek Orthodox Church e.g. church building, grammar school, orphanage (see Fenczak and Gąsiorowska-Czarny, 1995); in Kraków, the Association of St Wlodzimierz Rusi Kijowskiej received property in a prestigious part of the city Kanonicza Street; in Białystok and surroundings the Belarussian minority reclaimed an Orthodox church and estates connected to it in Supraśl. It was also given places to accommodate ethnic organizations and schools; in Sejny and Puńsk the Lithuanian minority was given a number of schools.
5. Interview with the Director of the *Instytut Poludniowo-Wschodni*, Przemyśl, November 1999.
6. Conflicts arose particularly around monuments erected for Ukrainian Upsurgent Army members in Przemyśl region; in Białystok the monument commemorating Belarussians who died during the Second World War; and in Sejny around a monument which commemorated Polish soldiers who died in battle with Lithuanians in 1919 and a monument erected to bishop Baranowski; see also Wilk, 1998: 31; Szulc, 1999: 84–5; Wilczak, 1999: 32–3; *Przegląd Sejneński*, March 1999, Special Edition; *Przegląd Sejneński*, September 1999.
7. Interviews with representatives of the Belarussian Democratic Association and Belarussian Association in the Polish Republic, Białystok, December 1999. Author's interviews with the Director of Instytut Poludniowo-Wschodni; Chairman of Przemyśl Business Centre; head of the Meduza Ukrainian cultural association; head of the Ukrainian school, Przemyśl, November 1999).
8. See *Gazeta Wyborcza*, 25 February and 14 May 1999; *Polityka*, 13 March 1999.
9. See www.um.szczecin.pl/reforma/kryteria: 3
10. See www.um.szczecin, 1998
12. See www.szczecin: 4, 1998
13. Interview with President of Przemyśl, November 1999.
14. Interviews with the head of the Ukrainian School in Przemyśl; head of the 'Meduza' Ukrainian Cultural Association; research fellow at *Instytut Poludniowo-Wschodni*, Przemyśl, November 1999.
15. Interview with the Chairman of the Lithuanian Association in Sejny; see also *Przegląd*

Sejneński, No.12, 1998, pp.4–5.
16. Interview with the Chairman of the Centre for Business Initiatives, Przemyśl, November 1999.
17. See n. 16.
18. Interview with the Director of the *Instytut Południowo-Wschodni* in Przemyśl, November 1999.
19. Interview with Dr Eugeniusz Mironowicz, Białystok, December 1999.
20. Interview with the Chairman of the Ukrainian Association in Poland, Warsaw, December 1999.
21. Interview with the vice-head of Podłaskie province, Bialystok, December 1999.
22. Interview with the Director of *Instytut Południowo-Wschodni*, Przemyśl, November 1999.
23. Interviews with the head of the Ukrainian School and the head of the 'Meduza' association of cultural organizations in Przemyśl, November 1999.
24. Interviews with Dr Mokry, Krakow, and head of the *Instytut Poludniowo-Wschodni*, Przemyśl, November 1999.

REFERENCES

Amato, G. and J. Batt (1998), *Minority Rights and EU Enlargement to the East*. Florence: Robert Schuman Centre Policy Paper no 98/5, European University Institute.
Amato, G. and J. Batt (1999), *Border Regimes and Border Protection in the Enlarged European Union*. Florence: Robert Schuman Centre Policy Paper 99/6, European University Institute.
Babiński, G. (1995), 'Regionalism versus Nationalism? Toward a Theory of Ethno-Regional Movements', in B. Synak (ed.), *The Ethnic Identities of European Minorities. Theory and Case Studies*. Gdańsk: Wydawnictwo Uniwersytetu Gdańskiego.
Babiński, G. (1998), *Pogranicze Polsko-Ukraińskie. Etniczność. Zróżnicowanie Religijne Tożsamość*. Kraków: Nomos.
Bachman, K. (1998), 'Unijny Szlaban na Bugu', *Rzeczpospolita*, 10 February, No.34.
Bailes, A. (1999), 'The Role of Subregional Co-operation in Post-Cold War Europe: Integration, Security, Democracy', in A. Cottey (ed.), *Subregional Co-operation in the New Europe. Building Security, Prosperity and Solidarity from the Barents to the Black Sea*. Basingstoke: Macmillan.
Bertrand, A. (1973), *Basic Sociology*. Louisiana: Louisiana State University Press.
Bonusiak, W. (1999), 'Granice i mentalność (na przykładzie stosunków polsko-ukraińskich)', in W.Bonusiak (ed.), *Polska-Niemcy-Ukraina w Europie. Model dla Euroregionów Środkowowschodniej Europy. Jak wychowywać dla Europy*. Rzeszów: Wydawnictwo Wyższej Szkoły Pedagogicznej.
Brubaker, R. (1996), *Nationalism Reframed*. Cambridge: Cambridge University Press.
Chałupczak, H. and T. Browarek (1998), *Mniejszości narodowe w Polsce 1918–1995*. Lublin: Wydawnictwo Uniwersytetu Marii Curie-Skłodowskiej.
Chlebowczyk, J. (1975), *Procesy narodowotwórcze we Wschodniej Europe Środkowej w dobie kapitalizmu (od schyłku XVIII do początku XX w)*. Warszawa, Wrocław, Kraków: PWN.
Dąbrowski, M. (1998), 'Dlaczego bronię bazarów. Skutki ustawy o cudzoziemcach', *Gazeta Wyborcza*, 17 February, No.40.
Davies, N. (1981), *God's Playground. A History of Poland*. Oxford: Clarendon Press.
Davies, N. (1986), *Heart of Europe. A Short History of Poland*. Oxford: Oxford University Press.
Fenczak, A.S. and N. Gąsiorowska-Czarny (1995), *Ukraińska Mniejszość Narodowa w Województwie Przemyskim w latach 1989–1993*. Fraza: Pismo Literacko-Społeczne: Rzeszów.
Filipowicz, M. (1992), 'Gente Polonus, Natione Ruthenus', *Tygodnik Powszechny*, No.34.
GUS (1998), *Podstawowe dane o województwach*, via www.polska.pl/gus
Heliński, P. (1997), *Euroregion Karpacki: Cele, Działalność i oczekiwania społeczne*, Biuletyn 3, Przemyśl: Instytut Południowo-Wschodni.
Kłoskowska, A. (1991), *Sąsiedztwo kultur i trening we wzajemności*. Warsaw: Kultura i

społeczeństwo.

Kłoskowska, A (1993), 'Wielokulturowość regionów pogranicza', in K. Handke (ed.), Region, regionalizm – pojęcia i rzeczywistość. Warszawa: Slawistyczny Ośrodek Wydawniczy.

Kurcz, Z. (1999), 'Pogranicza: modelowe euroregiony czy tereny tradycyjnej rywalizacji?', in Z. Kurcz (ed.), Pogranicze z Niemcami, a Inne Pogranicza Polski. Wrocław: Wydawnictwo Uniwersytet Wrocławski.

Kwaśniewski, K. (1982), Zderzenie kultur. Tożsamość, a aspekty konfliktów i tolerancji. Warszawa: PWN.

Łossowski, P. (1966), Stosunki polsko-litewskie w latach 1918–1920. Warszawa: Instytut Historii Polskiej Akademii Nauk.

Łukomski, G. (1995), 'Konflikt polsko-litewski o Suwalszczyznę 1918–1928', in Lithuania (Warszawa), Vol.2, No.15, pp.125–47.

Mach, Z. (1993), Symbols, Conflict and Identity. Essays in Political Anthropology. New York: State University of New York Press.

Mach, Z. (1997), 'Heritage, Dream and Anxiety: The European Identity of Poles', in Mach Z. and D. Niedźwiecki (eds.), European Enlargement and Identity. Kraków: Universitas.

Mach, Z. (1998), Niechciane Miasta. Migracja i Tożsamość Społeczna. Kraków: Universitas.

Michta, A (1997), 'Democratic Consolidation in Poland after 1989', in Dawisha K. and B. Parrot (eds.), The Consolidation of Democracy in East Central Europe. Cambridge: Cambridge University Press.

Miłosz, Cz (1980), Rodzinna Europa. Paris. Instytut Literacki.

Misiło, E (1993), Akcja 'Wisła'. Warszawa: Archiwum Ukraińskie, Zakład Wydawniczy 'Tyrsa'.

Mniejszości narodowe w Polsce. Informator 1994, (1995). Warszawa: Wydawnictwo Sejmowe, Warszawa.

Mokry, W. (1997) (ed.), Problemy Ukraińców w Polsce po wysiedleńczej akcji 'Wisła' 1947. Kraków: Szwajpolt Fiol.

Motyl, A. (1980), The Turn to the Right: The Ideological Origins and Development of Ukrainian Nationalism, 1919–1929. Boulder, CO: East European Monographs.

MSWiA wini białoruskie przepisy celne, Rzeczpospolita, 10 February 1998, No. 34.

Nikitorowicz, J. (1995), Pogranicze. Tożsamość. Edukacja Międzykulturowa. Białystok: Trans Humana.

Olechowski, A. (1998), 'Nie uciekamy od naszych sąsiadów', Gazeta Wyborcza, 18 February, No.41.

Orlof, E. (1999), 'Związek Międzyregionalny Euroregion Karpacki i jego znaczenie', in W. Bonusiak (ed.), Polska, Niemcy, Ukraina w Europie. Rzeszów: Wydawnictwo Wyższej Szkoły Pedagogicznej.

'Podwójny Paszport, Kto może być obywatelem Polski', Polityka, 28 March 1998.

Policja kontra kupcy. Blokada przejs'cia w kuz'nicy białostockiej, rzeczpospolita, 10 February 1998, No. 34.

Sadowski, A. (1992), 'Socjologia pogranicza', in Pogranicze: Studia społeczne. Białystok: Uniwersytet Warszawski filia w Białymstoku.

Sadowski, A. (1995), Wschodnie pogranicze w perspektywie socjologicznej. Białystok: Ekonomia i Środowisko. Fundacja Ekonomistów.

Słomkowski, Z. (1993), 'Spór o euroregiony w zwierciadle prasy', in Słomkowska, A. (ed.), Kontrowersje wokół transformacji prasy polskiej (1989–1992). Materiały pomocnicze do Najnowszej Historii Dziennikarstwa, t. XXIII. Warszawa: Instytut Dziennikarstwa, Uniwersytet Warszawski.

Smolicz, J (1990), Kultura i nauczanie w społeczeństwie wieloetnicznym. Warszawa: PWN.

Sosnowska, D. (1995), 'Stereotyp Ukrainy i Ukraińca w literaturze polskiej', in Wallas, T. (ed.), Narody i Stereotypy. Kraków: Międzynarodowe Centrum Kultury.

Stępień, S. (1998), 'Granica polsko-ukraińska w ostatnim półwieczu. Kwestie związane z delimitacją, statusem prawnym, akceptacją społeczną i funkcjonowaniem', in Biuletyn Południowo-Wschodniego Instytutu Naukowego w Przemyślu, No.4.

Szulc, A. (1999), 'W Pawłokomie Apokalipsa', Polityka, No.44, 30 November, pp.84–5.

Tatarkiewicz, A. (1978), 'Dwuznaczny Urok Galicji', Polityka, No.17.

Vakar, N. (1956), *Belorussia: The Making of a Nation*. Cambridge, MA: Howard University Press.
Wilczak, J. (1999), 'Otwarta mogiła', *Polityka*, No.48, 27 November, pp.32–3.
Wilk, E. (1998), 'Tłok na cokole', *Polityka*, No.18, 2 May, p.31.
Wolczuk, K. (2001) 'Polish-Ukrainian Borderlands: the Case of Lviv and Przemyśl', in Krzysztofek, K. and A. Sadowski (eds.), *Ethnic Borderlands in Europe: Harmony or Conflict*, Białystok: University of Białystok.
Wolczuk, K. (2001b), *Poland's Relations with Ukraine in the Context of EU Enlargement*, ESRC One Europe or Several? Briefing Note 4/01.
Zaucha, J. (1999), 'Regional and Local Development in Poland', in E.J. Kirchner, (ed.), *Decentralization and Transition in the Visegrad*. Basingstoke: Macmillan Press.

Transcarpathia:
Peripheral Region at the 'Centre of Europe'

JUDY BATT

No one writing about Transcarpathia can resist retelling the region's favourite anecdote: A visitor, encountering one of the oldest local inhabitants, asks about his life. The reply: 'I was born in Austria-Hungary, I went to school in Czechoslovakia, I did my army service in Horthy's Hungary, followed by a spell in prison in the USSR. Now I am ending my days in independent Ukraine.' The visitor expresses surprise at how much of the world the old man has seen. 'But no!', he responds, 'I've never left this village!' In fact, this tale considerably understates the convolutions of Transcarpathia's trajectory: in the course of the twentieth century it underwent no fewer than 17 changes of political status. These included not only annexation and re-annexation by the states mentioned above (with varying degrees of autonomy under each); occupation by Romania (in 1919–20) and Nazi Germany (in 1944); but also two brief periods of independent existence. Always an economic and political backwater, Transcarpathia nevertheless bore the full brunt of twentieth-century Europe's travails.

Transcarpathians insist on their 'Central European' identity, 'officially' confirmed by the Viennese Geographical Society, which in 1911 identified the 'Centre of Europe' in the Carpathian foothills just above Rahiv, a small town in the east of the region. A monument marks the precise spot. One of the more endearing inconveniences of everyday life in Transcarpathia today is the local insistence on using Central European time – one hour behind official Kiev time – quietly asserting where the province feels it belongs. Indeed, it conforms nicely to Milan Kundera's celebrated characterization of 'Central Europe' as:

> a condensed version of Europe itself in all its cultural variety, a small arch-European Europe, a reduced model of Europe made made up of nations conceived according to one rule: the greatest variety within the smallest space (Kundera, 1984: 33).

The ethnic composition of the region is indeed complex. The last (1989) Soviet census recorded a large majority of Ukrainians (78.4 per cent) alongside a significant minority of Hungarians (12.5 per cent), and small, but locally concentrated minorities of Russians, Romanians, Roma,

Slovaks, Germans and others. The once large Jewish communities, in the inter-war period accounting for some 12–13 per cent (and 30–40 per cent in the major cities), have almost disappeared as a result of wartime extermination and subsequent emigration. But they left their mark on the region's architectural heritage, notably the Užhorod synagogue, commissioned from leading Hungarian architects at the turn of the century, whose flamboyant Moorish-Byzantine style won favour with Jewish communities in the main cities of the Habsburg Empire (Németh, 1991: 46–7).

Transcarpathia's demographic proportions are still in flux as various groups re-identify themselves in response to new circumstances. The main issue is the resurfacing of Rusyn (traditionally in English, Ruthene) identity, by which the local East Slavic-speaking and mainly Uniate (Greek Catholic) population was known before 1945, when Rusyns were officially reclassified as Ukrainians. Ethnic re-identification has taken place among other groups too, especially over the past half-century (see Tables 1 and 2). Most Transcarpathians, especially in urban areas, are bilingual if not polyglot; intermarriage has been fairly widespread, especially among co-religionists (Roman Catholic Hungarians, Germans and Slovaks), and linguistically close Slavs (Ukrainians, Rusyns, Russians and Slovaks). Multiple identity has been an invaluable means of survival in the face of invading armies and bureaucrats from the states that have successively bludgeoned Transcarpathians into ill-fitting national categories. Moreover, Roma culture and identity have been recently revived with the support of international human rights organizations and donors such as the Soros Foundation, and many may now abandon their previous Ukrainian or Hungarian 'cover' and declare Roma identity in the next census.

Transcarpathia's contested position at the junction of no fewer than five states (today Ukraine, Poland, Slovakia, Hungary and Romania) has ensured its exposure to the nationalizing efforts of the rival states that claimed it over the course of the twentieth century. What is remarkable, however, is the local atmosphere of goodwill and pragmatic accommodation among the various ethnic groups. Neither during the Second World War, nor when the Soviet Union collapsed, did Transcarpathia see the kind of inter-ethnic tensions and conflict that occurred elsewhere. In this respect too, Transcarpathia can claim to have lived up to Kundera's ideal of 'Central European' multiculturalism rather well. The vicissitudes of history have engendered a sense of common Transcarpathian identity. Locals take pride in preserving peace among themselves, and have resisted the dubious appeals to their various national loyalties pressed by the neighbouring 'mother countries'.

At the turn of the twenty-first century, Kundera's 'Central Europe' is finally escaping 'tragic' subjection to the 'East' by acceding to NATO and the EU, while Transcarpathia's central geographical location, on the other hand, threatens to become one of multiple peripheralization. It has always been the most remote, inaccessible, economically backward region of whatever state it has belonged to. A tortuous 18-hour train journey across the Carpathians separates it from Kiev ('Transcarpathia is as far from Kiev as it is from God', as the local saying has it), the venal and near-bankrupt Ukrainian capital. But it is now also in danger of being cut off from its western neighbours as they join the EU and so fall in line with the EU's tough external border and visa regimes.

Today, it is still the poorest region of independent Ukraine (see Hesli, 1995). In the Soviet period, about 30 per cent of its labour force would leave to find work over the mountains in Ukraine or Russia. With the break-up of the Soviet Union, and the ensuing economic crises, such opportunities have dried up, as has local employment in military-related transport and services as the region lost its strategic role as the westernmost outpost of Soviet military projection into Central and South-Eastern Europe. Transcarpathia's rural economy is weak. The lowlands, chronically starved of investment, are vulnerable to regular inundation from the wide, sluggish Tisza river; highland farmers struggle in isolated communities whose way of life was hardly touched by the twentieth century. Average wages (about $20 per month) are below subsistence level. Since the early 1990s, Transcarpathians have become increasingly dependent for economic survival on crossing the borders westwards, chiefly into Slovakia and Hungary. Permanent emigration is the ambition of many, especially the young, the better qualified, and those with family and ethnic ties in neighbouring states or North America.

Where does Transcarpathia belong, and what political configuration might best provide for the security and welfare of its peoples, satisfy their sense of a special, shared historical predicament, their 'Central European' vocation, and their diverse ethnic identities? Unfortunately, there is no clear answer to these questions.

The Soviet Legacy

Transcarpathia fell before the westward advance of the Red Army in October 1944 into Nazi-occupied Hungary. Instead of returning the province to Czechoslovakia, the Soviets reconstituted it as 'Transcarpathian Ukraine', and Stalin persuaded the Czechoslovak president-in-exile, Edward Beneš, to transfer it to the USSR. In June 1945, it was incorporated into the Ukrainian Soviet Socialist Republic as *Zakarpatska oblast'* (Transcarpathian region). Like the other newly acquired western territories, Transcarpathia underwent a traumatic period of political purging as the Soviet NKVD rooted out 'class enemies'. Many of the former regional elite had already fled, but remaining local Hungarians and Germans were stigmatized as 'fascist nations', and lived under constant threat. Meanwhile, an influx of Russians and Ukrainians staffed the sovietized administration. Russians were few, but overrepresented in the regional communist party, forming 12.8 per cent of the membership in 1985 (see Duleba *et al.*, 1995: 210). Russification, in the sense of linguistic assimilation, remained low (see Hesli, 1995: 100); nevertheless, Russian became accepted as the *lingua franca* among different ethnic groups. The minorities learned Russian, rather than Ukrainian, at school.

By the 1980s, the Transcarpathian political elite was but a provincial offshoot of the (strongly russified) Soviet Ukrainian elite, itself marked by deep ideological conservatism that long resisted Gorbachev's reforms. In contrast to Galicia (the *oblasti* of western Ukraine north of the Carpathians), there was little sign here of democratic and Ukrainian-nationalist ferment. However, *nomenklatura* ambitions emerged in 1987–90, coinciding with economic collapse and the disintegration of the Soviet Union. The regional elite put forward proposals for 'economic autonomy' to exploit the potential of the region's location in a 'Zone of Common Entrepreneurship'. This, they hoped, would attract foreign investment and 'accelerate and deepen the integration of the region and the rest of Ukraine into European economic structures' (quoted in Duleba *et al.*, 1995: 213). This early adumbration of the idea of Transcarpathia's mission as Ukraine's 'gateway to Europe' was presented to the Ukrainian Supreme Soviet in early 1991, but sank without trace. In the meanwhile, the very survival of the Soviet Union had come on to the agenda. The sluggish elite of Soviet Ukraine was evolving a *nomenklatura* separatism of its own, in uneasy alliance with the radical Ukrainian nationalists of Galicia. When the August 1991 coup took place, they seized the opportunity to declare Ukrainian independence.

Transcarpathians shared the general enthusiasm of the time for Ukrainian independence, and the province returned a 92.6 per cent vote in favour in the December 1991 referendum. More significant was the referendum organized simultaneously by the Transcarpathian elite, asking voters whether they wished Transcarpathia 'to have the status of a special self-governing administrative territory' within an independent Ukraine. 78 per cent of the voters supported this proposal (see Solchanyk, 1994: 62–3), but again the initiative was buried by the subsequent 'state-building' preoccupations of the Ukrainian government (see Wolczuk's contribution).

The 'Rusyn Question'

In parallel to the *nomenklatura*'s efforts, demands for self-government began to be articulated on behalf of the Rusyn 'nation'. Probably the majority of the population recorded as Ukrainian in the last Soviet census in fact still regarded themselves as, in some sense, Rusyns. What Rusyn identity actually consists in, and, further, what its political implications are for Transcarpathia, remain obscure to say the least. The very name given the province is a highly charged issue: 'one of those political controversies so exciting to Central Europe and so difficult for Western Europe to follow', as C. A. Macartney noted in 1937 (Macartney, 1937: 200, fn). The name used today – *Zakarpattya*, Transcarpathia – was introduced after 1945, along with the Soviet regime, and implies the province's attachment to a centre 'over', that is, *east* of the mountains. The more radical Rusyn nationalists prefer 'Sub-Carpathian Ruthenia', the pre-war designation, implying a natural gravitational field drawing it *westward* (as also implied in the Hungarian name of *Kárpátalja*).

The Rusyn revival was not confined to Transcarpathia, but has been in evidence since 1989 all over former Habsburg East/Central Europe: in Poland, Slovakia, Hungary, Yugoslavia, and, albeit to a lesser extent, Romania, wherever minorities officially designated as 'Ukrainian' are to be found. A helping hand in this ethnic revival has come from émigré Rusyn communities in North America, led by the Toronto-based historian Professor Paul Magocsi (see Magocsi, 1993). The largest group of potential Rusyns is, however, in Transcarpathia, where, in contrast to the neighbouring countries, they have been refused official recognition as a 'minority' by the new Ukrainian state, which regards Rusyns as a sub-group of the Ukrainian nation. 'Rusynism' therefore tends to be regarded as a parochial confusion, or even as a foreign-inspired plot to undermine the territorial integrity of Ukraine.

The Rusyn revival that took place in Transcarpathia in the last years of Soviet rule was often stridently anti-Ukrainian. The 'Society of Carpathian Rusyns' formed in February 1990 demanded recognition of the Rusyns as a separate nation and proposed the restoration of 'Sub-Carpathian Ruthenia' as an 'autonomous republic' with rights according to the 1938 Czecho-Slovak federal constitution, which, it is argued, were part of the legal terms of the province's cession to the Soviet Union in 1945. Some Rusyns would have advocated re-annexation to Czechoslovakia, but this option collapsed in 1992–93 along with the Czecho-Slovak Federal Republic itself. The prospect of an independent Ukraine, dominated by the nationalist agenda of the Galician *Rukh* movement, and by a political elite rooted in the old communist *nomenklatura*, fired the separatist Rusyn tendency. After Kiev's brusque rejection of Transcarpathian self-government, in May 1993 radical Rusyns set up a 'Provisional Government of Sub-Carpathian Ruthenia', appealed for Russian support, and declared their intention to join the Commonwealth of Independent States independently of Ukraine. This confirmed Ukrainian hostility to the Rusyn cause, and was hardly likely to win Western sympathy either.

Why the Rusyn radicals should adopt this confrontational and ill-judged posture, and why this tendency has since been eclipsed by a more 'moderate', culturally oriented approach that leaves the question of the Rusyns' political future open, requires some historical explanation. It runs against the pattern of progression from 'cultural group' to politically self-conscious 'nation' demanding self-government that has been characteristic of most of the rest of Central and Eastern Europe since the late eighteenth century (see Hroch, 1995). The extraordinarily complex history of the region has bequeathed doubt, confusion and fatalism among the Rusyns about their identity. These undermine their capacity and collective will to assert themselves as a political community, without diminishing their inchoate longings for some form of autonomy.

Ruthen, in German, was the term used to refer to diverse East Slavic groups within the Habsburg Empire, who called themselves *Rusyns,* or sometimes *Rusnaks.* Originally Orthodox, from the seventeenth century onwards, under Polish and Habsburg rule, they were induced to accept the authority of Rome, while retaining the eastern rites and liturgy. Thus was formed the Uniate (Greek Catholic) Church, which by the late eighteenth century became dominant in what was then known as Hungarian Ruthenia (*Kárpátalja* in Hungarian) and in Galicia, north of the Carpathians. In Galicia, Rusyn intellectuals by the late nineteenth century identified themselves as Ukrainians against their Polish overlords, and *rutenstvo* (Rusynism) became a byword for extreme conservativism and provincialism. Galician Ukrainians looked eastwards to their Orthodox kinsfolk languishing under Russian rule, and took up the task of building a united Ukrainian nation (see Subtelny, 1994: 218–19). But Rusyns south of the Carpathians remained almost completely untouched by these developments.

Insofar as a Rusyn intelligentsia developed at all in Hungarian Ruthenia, it looked in quite different directions. The literary language used was Church Slavonic, not Ukrainian. The Uniate Church was heavily dependent on Vienna, but the Rusyns of Hungary were to prove hard to mobilize for the Imperial cause in 1848 against the insurgent Magyars. Many of the Uniate clergy succumbed to the temptations of assimilation into the dominant Magyar language and lifestyle, and showed little interest in fomenting a Rusyn national revival comparable to those of the Romanians, Serbs and Slovaks elsewhere in Hungary.

However, the encounter with Russian Imperial troops invading Hungary in 1849 on behalf of the Habsburgs persuaded some Rusyns in Ruthenia of their 'ethnic brotherhood' with the Great Russians. For a time Russian was adopted as the literary language, and Muscovite Pan-Slavism promised support against the Magyars. This attracted only a minority, and Macartney reports enthusiasm for Magyarization among the urban middle classes before the First World War. The 1910 Hungarian census discovered only 542 'intellectuals' of Rusyn mother-tongue, of whom the bulk were clergy. There were only 21 teachers, and a single person in 'literature and the arts' (see Macartney, 1937: 211).

Meanwhile, 'unmoved by the rival blandishments of Russian and Ukrainian, the Ruthene peasants continued to be Ruthenes, and hardly even that' (Macartney, 1937: 210–11). Probably around 90 per cent illiterate, they spoke a multitude of dialects, close to Ukrainian but strongly influenced locally by Polish, Slovak or Magyar, with traces of Old Church Slavonic and Russian. A standardized Rusyn language was codified only in 1995. Distinct local identities, ambivalent even towards the Rusyn identity – namely the Hutsuls, Lemkos and Boikos – persist to this day. Representatives of the latter groups are also still to be found in Poland.

The 'Ukrainian idea' penetrated Ruthenia only when Ukrainian nationalist emigrés arrived after the Russian Revolution. Joined by visiting agitators from Galicia (now part of Poland), they freely propagated the national cause in the new Czechoslovak Republic's eastern province of 'Sub-Carpathian Ruthenia' (seen from Prague, it was this side of – under – the mountains). Their efforts, especially against the pro-Magyar elements in the clergy and middle classes, were not unwelcome to Prague, fearing post-Trianon Hungary's revisionist claims. But Ukrainian agitation was countered by that of 'White' Russian refugees in Czechoslovakia. The rival Ukrainian and Russian propaganda had little impact on the Rusyns. While some reconversion to orthodoxy took place, about half of the province's total population remained Uniate. One can only speculate whether this indicated dogged attachment to local ways, if not inertia, rather than the Rusyns' pro-Magyar sympathies.

The Czechoslovak period was nevertheless a formative one, regarded by many Rusyn intellectuals in Transcarpathia today as something of a 'Golden Age' of enlightened democratic rule, when the diverse ethnic identities of the province were respected and mother tongue education was promoted for the Rusyns, who hitherto had been educated, if at all, only in Hungarian. A Rusyn nationalist activist explained to the author (interviewed in Užhorod, April 2000) that under Czechoslovakia, the province made 'truly European' strides forward: a 'high moral culture' pervaded public affairs; order and cleanliness became established norms of everyday life, exemplified by the neat, well-cultivated gardens that, for him, demonstrated Transcarpathia's essential 'Europeanness', in contrast to the 'Asiatic' slovenliness to be found the other side of the mountains.

This historical link is still appreciated in Prague, where elderly professors are said to look kindly on students from Transcarpathia as 'fellow-countrymen' and a 'Society for Sub-Carpathian Ruthenia' aims to revive cultural links and channel aid to the province. Czech sentiment is well expressed by the poet Miroslav Holub:

> In Czechoslovak nostalgia, Sub-Carpathian Ruthenia is something like a pearl resting at the bottom of the ocean, something barely found before again being lost, a sixth finger amputated before we had learnt to use it. And we are still feeling the phantom pain. By our standards it is a wild country, 'beautiful in its poverty' as a poet put it, a land that could have been closer to us than to any of its rulers. (Holub, 1999: xii)

The vexed question of *who* the Rusyns are has bedevilled the determination of their rightful political place. Upon the collapse of Austria-Hungary, three 'national councils' were set up in the region. One, based in Užhorod, negotiated with the the Hungarian government of Mihály Károlyi to remain in Hungary as an autonomous *Russka Krajina* (Rusyn Land); another, based in Chust, advocated union with the emergent independent Ukraine. In late 1918, the Hutsuls declared their own 'Körös Country Hutsul Republic'. The Hungarian and Ukrainian options collapsed with Bolshevik takeovers in both countries. Meanwhile, representatives of émigré Rusyns in the USA (numbering some 300,000), failed to secure international support for an independent state (uniting Ruthenia with Galicia and Bukovina) and then negotiated with Thomas Masaryk to join the new Czechoslovak Republic as an 'independent state' within a federation. The Paris Peace Conference, recognizing the Rusyns as 'racially and linguistically a distinct nationality' in need of a 'national home', but sceptical of their capacities to constitute an independent state, accepted this proposal, *faute de mieux*. It was subsequently approved by a third Rusyn national council based in Prešov in eastern Slovakia (see Macartney, 1937: 212–21).

Leading Rusyn politicians of the inter-war period found the Czechoslovak experience disillusioning (see Shandor, 1997). A particular bone of contention with Prague was the provincial border between Slovakia and Sub-Carpathian Ruthenia, drawn up provisionally at the Peace Conference along the Ung river, which left large numbers of Rusyns in mixed areas of eastern Slovakia. Subsequently Prague was unwilling to antagonize the Slovaks by changing it. The Rusyns shared the Slovaks' frustration with the tutelary role assumed by incoming Czech officials in what turned out to be a unitary state, regarded by them as a betrayal of promises of federation made in 1918.

The opportunity to rectify the situation came with Nazi-German expansion into Central Europe. At Munich in September 1938, France and Britain agreed to Germany's annexation of the *Sudetenland*. The rump Czechoslovakia was briefly reconstituted as a federation, with self-government for Ruthenia. In March 1939, the Nazis occupied Bohemia-Moravia, turning it into a 'Protectorate', and a nominally independent Slovak Republic emerged. Pro-Ukrainian Rusyns set up an 'Independent Carpatho-Ukrainian Republic', and appealed for Nazi support. Instead, within hours, it was occupied by the troops of Horthy's Hungary, and an aggressively anti-Ukrainian, and pro-Rusyn, policy followed. The 'Carpatho-Ukrainian' pretenders fled to North America, and this brief interlude of independence seems more significant today to their descendants than to Rusyns in Transcarpathia.

The Rusyn separatism of the early 1990s, promoted by the Society of Carpathian Rusyns, appears to have collapsed – for the time being. Kiev's earlier antagonism towards the Rusyn question has abated as Ukrainian statehood has gradually consolidated. The government launched a campaign of counter-propaganda against 'Rusynism' at home and abroad in 1996 (see 'Plan of Measures', 1996). More insidious methods appear also to have been employed: the leading Rusyn nationalist, Professor Turianitsa, has been discredited among his people by a scandal that bears all the traces of a political stitch-up by the local Transcarpathian elite, by now pliant dependants of Kiev.

The Ukrainian authorities have also responded to pressure from Western minority rights organizations to open dialogue with the Rusyns (see ECMI report, 1999). Rusyn cultural organizations, including the Society of Carpathian Rusyns, are now represented on the Transcarpathian *oblast*'s council for minority affairs. In 1999, after assurances that Ukraine's territorial integrity would not be questioned, the Ukrainian authorities permitted the Fifth World Congress of Rusyns to take place in Užhorod. There are even hints that the 'Rusyn' option will be included on the menu of ethnic identities presented in the next census (although probably only as a Ukrainian 'sub-ethnos' rather than a 'nation minority' or 'nationality' in its own right).

How many Rusyns will avail themselves of this opportunity, if presented, is nevertheless uncertain. They have long treated Rusyn identity as a purely private matter, invoked only among family and close friends. 'Historical fatigue' saps the will of older generations to take any risky step. Younger people show little interest in the 'Rusyn question' and seem comfortable with Ukrainian identity. As one of their more cynical representatives summed up the state of the Rusyn movement in April 2000 (in an unmistakably local idiom!): 'The dog barks, but the cow does not move.'

It is not known how much mass support there ever was for the Rusyn 'national revival', but for now it is clear that Rusyns have reverted to political apathy, profoundly mistrustful of any plot to implicate them in a no doubt fruitless quest for control of their own destiny. However, the first line of the national anthem: 'Ukraine is not yet dead!' may also apply to the Rusyns. There remain a number of lively and well-supported Rusyn cultural societies, conducting a vibrant musical and choral life with links to Rusyn organizations in neighbouring countries. The Duchnovych Society has for many years been dedicated to 'constructing the scientific basis' of Rusyn identity, as one of its leading lights explained to the author. The aim is to build up the identity from below, by 'organic work' among the masses (recalling Masaryk's strategy for inter-war Czechoslovak nation-building). The Institute of Carpathian Studies at Užhorod University is researching Rusyn history. As one member of their staff told me, self-government need not imply territorial change, and was the common aspiration of most regions of Ukraine; moreover, 'on a European level this is considered normal' (interview, April 2000). Tellingly, he concluded, 'We think in Central European terms, whether we like it or not. We are not against the Ukrainians, but we *are not* Ukrainians.'

Hungarian Autonomism

The Hungarians are not afflicted with such perplexities. They constitute the largest ethnic minority, some 12.5 per cent of Transcarpathia's population, concentrated in the lowlands of the south-west bordering on Hungary, especially in Berehove district (Beregszász in Hungarian), where they make up 67 per cent of the population (Orosz and Czernicskó, 1999: 29). For the Hungarians, Transcarpathia has a special place in the national history. It was at the Verecke Pass in the mountains that the Magyar tribes first crossed into 'Europe' in the legendary year 896, abandoning their original homeland on the steppes north of the Black Sea. They first pitched camp at what is now Mukacheve (Munkács in Hungarian), before moving on to establish their 1,000-year rule in the Carpathian basin. The site, a volcanic plug, developed into a fortress, refashioned as an elegant Renaissance palace by the Rákoczi family, Princes of Transylvania, and so played a key role in the early eighteenth century Hungarian rebellions against the Habsburgs.

Hungarians were the dominant landowning aristocracy of Ruthenia until 1918. There was also a sizeable class of Hungarian peasants on the plains, whose descendants remain there today. Most of the Hungarian upper classes left for Hungary after 1920. Those who remained became *déclassés* as a result of the Czechoslovak government's programmes of 'nostrification' which removed 'aliens' from the administration and replaced them with Czechoslovaks; and land reform, which targeted the Hungarian estates. The Hungarian share in the towns declined, and the overall social structure of Hungarians became more egalitarian, mainly rural, peasant farmers and small town dwellers. In 1939–45, when the province was reoccupied by Hungary, the Hungarian population increased due largely to an influx of military and administrative personnel, but possibly also due to re-identification (especially urban Jews) as Hungarian.

Hungarian identity, however, became a curse at the end of the war. In October 1944, the Nazis occupied Hungary and replaced Horthy by a more 'trustworthy' Arrow Cross (fascist) regime. Thereafter, nearly all of the more than 90,000 Jews of Ruthenia were delivered up to the gas chambers of Auschwitz (see Braham, 2000). Then, as the Soviet Army advanced and took control of the province, the Hungarian middle classes fled. All Hungarian and German men between the ages of 15 and 50 were ordered to report, and were deported for forced labour, mainly to the Donbas in eastern Soviet Ukraine (see Kócsis and Kócsis-Hodosi, 1998). About 30,000 men were involved, of whom only half returned. Many died, but scattered remnants survive today in the cities of the Donbas (where the main Hungarian minority organization in Ukraine claims some 2,000 members). Many of those Hungarians left in the province (along with the small German 'Schwab' communities) hid their identity, replacing it with a safer one. This may account in part for the otherwise surprising rise in numbers of Slovaks between the 1941 and 1959 censuses (see tables).

All contact with Hungary – despite its becoming a communist 'fraternal ally' of the Soviet Union – was cut off until 1960, when a few family reunions were permitted. Hungarian-language education at secondary level restarted only after 1953. No publications in Hungarian were allowed until 1967. Religious persecution of the Roman Catholic and Evangelical Churches, to which nearly all Hungarians belonged, was maintained throughout the communist period. The Uniate Church also counted some 10,000 Hungarian-speakers among its congregation, who were not only berated by the Soviet authorities as renegade Orthodox, but also regarded as targets for 're-Ukrainianization'.

The Gorbachev period provided the impetus for a national revival among the Hungarians (see Reisch, 1992). In April 1988, a visit of the then Soviet head of state, Andrei Gromyko, to Budapest opened the way for increased travel and cultural contacts between the Hungarian minority

TABLE 1

POPULATION OF TRANSCARPATHIA ACCORDING TO MOTHER TONGUE AND
NATIONALITY RESPECTIVELY (1880–1989) (IN ABSOLUTE NUMBERS)

	1880	1910	1921	1930	1941	1959	1970	1979	1989
Hungarians	102,219	184,789	111,052	116,975	233,111	146,247	151,949	158,446	155,711
Ruthenians*	239,975	334,755	372,278	446,478	500,264	–	–	–	-
Russians	–	–	–	–	–	29,599	35,189	41,713	49,458
Ukrainians	–	–	–	–	–	686,464	808,131	898,606	976,749
Germans	30,474	63,561	9,591	12,778	13,222	3,504	4,230	3,746	3,478
Romanians	–	–	–	–	–	18,346	23,454	27,155	29,485
Slovaks**	7,849	6,344	19,632	34,700	6,847	12,289	10,294	8,914	7,323
Jews	–	–	80,117	91,845	–	12,169	10,857	3,848	2,639
Gypsies	–	–	–	–	–	4,970	5,902	5,586	12,131
Others	20,763	13,325	19,772	31,531	97,145	6,585	7,515	7,745	8,638
TOTAL	40,1280	602,774	612,442	734,315	850,589	920,173	1,056,799	1,155,759	1,245,618

* 1880–1941 together with the Russians and Ukrainians
** 1921–30 and 1959–79 together with the Czechs

TABLE 2

POPULATION OF TRANSCARPATHIA ACCORDING TO MOTHER TONGUE AND
NATIONALITY RESPECTIVELY (1880–1989) (IN PERCENTAGES)

	1880	1910	1921	1930	1941	1959	1970	1979	1989
Hungarians	25.47	30.66	18.13	15.93	27.41	15.9	14.4	13.70	12.50
Ruthenians*	59.80	55.54	60.79	60.80	58.81	–	–	–	-
Russians	–	–	–	–	–	3.2	3.3	3.60	3.97
Ukrainians	–	–	–	–	–	74.7	76.5	77.75	78.41
Germans	7.59	10.54	1.57	1.74	1.550	0.4	0.4	0.32	0.27
Romanians	1.86	1.90	–	–	1.83	2.0	2.2	2.34	2.36
Slovaks**	1.96	1.05	3.21	4.73	0.80	1.4	1.0	0.76	0.58
Jews	–	–	13.08	12.51	9.25	1.3	1.0	0.33	0.21
Gypsies	–	–	–	–	0.14	0.5	0.5	0.48	0.98
Others	3.32	0.31	3.23	4.29	0.19	0.6	0.7	0.66	0.69
TOTAL	100	100	100	100	100	100	100	100	100

Notes:
* 1880–1941 together with the Russians and Ukrainians
** 1921–30 and 1959–79 together with the Czechs

1880 and 1910: according to mother tongue.
From 1921: according to nationality.

Census data before 1959 concern the territory of today's Transcarpathia, too.

The 1880, 1910, 1941 data based on the Hungarian census; the 1921, 1930 data on the Czecho-Slovakian census; and the 1959, 1970, 1979, 1989 data on the Soviet census.

Source: Orosz and Csernicsko (1999), pp.14–15.

and its 'motherland'. In March 1989, the need for visas, official invitations and other documentation in order to travel was abolished. The opening of the border led to a surge of visits in both directions, greatly assisting the revival of independent cultural and political activity among the Transcarpathian Hungarians, who today seem the most effective of Transcarpathia's ethnic groups (see *Report on the Situation of Hungarians in Ukraine*, 1997). The Carpathian (*Kárpátaljai*) Hungarian Cultural Association, claims 27,000 members, and returns one of the province's six deputies to the Ukrainian parliament. This may be the largest independent association in the province. New Hungarian schools have opened, and as of 1996/97, there were 98, including three run by the Evangelical Church. A Hungarian Teachers' Training College has been set up in Berehove/Beregszász, with assistance from the university of Nyíregyháza in eastern Hungary (see Orosz and Csernicskó, 1999: 44–51).

Nevertheless, emigration, especially among the young and better educated, has become a matter of concern to local community leaders, as well as to Hungary itself. The primary reasons for this are economic. Most Hungarian respondents in a poll agreed that Ukrainian independence had 'brought more bad than good'. Over 75 per cent expressed 'very little' or 'no attachment' to Ukraine at all – even fewer than towards the former USSR, to which 69 per cent expressed very little or no attachment. On the other hand, the sense of attachment to Hungary was strong for 37 per cent, and very strong for 27 per cent; and even more towards 'Europe', to which 28 per cent felt attached, and 35 per cent strongly attached. But local loyalties were found to be the most important, with 63 per cent strongly and 29 per cent attached to Transcarpathia (see Orosz and Csernicskó, 1999: 60).

The relatively benign situation for the Hungarians *as an ethnic minority* has been assisted by favourable inter-state relations between Hungary and Ukraine. Hungary was first to recognize Ukraine as a sovereign state in 1991, and a 'Treaty on Good Neighbourliness and Cooperation' was signed as early as 6 December 1991. This speedy action was the result of steadily growing collaboration between the two sides even before the collapse of the USSR, in which Hungary offered its support for Ukraine's aspirations in exchange for satisfactory treatment by Ukraine of its Hungarian minority. The Treaty confirmed the binding status of the 'Declaration on the Principles of Cooperation between the Hungarian Republic and the Ukrainian SSR in the field of Guaranteeing the Rights of National Minorities' issued in May 1991. Thus the Hungarians were able to secure what has since eluded them in similar bilateral treaties with Slovakia and Romania – their partner's commitment to recognize the 'collective rights' of minorities, in addition to the individual rights of their members (see 'Treaty', 1991; and Vogel, 1996).

What 'collective rights' entail, in the Hungarian view (promoted from Budapest by the government's Office for Hungarians Beyond the Borders, and pursued by all the main Hungarian minority organizations in the neighbouring states), is 'autonomy'. This includes not only cultural autonomy – the right to independent, self-governing cultural and educational facilities – but also territorial autonomy, a more radical demand legitimated, in the Hungarian view, by *Recommendation 1201(1993)* of the Council of Europe's Parliamentary Assembly:

> *Article 11*: In the regions where they are in a majority the persons belonging to a national minority shall have the right to have at their disposal appropriate local or autonomous authorities or to have special status, matching the specific historical and territorial situation and in accordance with the domestic legislation of the state.

This commitment was not embodied in the Council of Europe's 1995 *Framework Convention for the Protection of National Minorities*, but nevertheless has continued to be promoted by the Hungarian government and Hungarian minorities both at international fora and in dealings with Hungary's neighbours. It has proved contentious not only internationally, especially in the Hungarian minorities' countries of residence, but even on occasion among the Hungarian minority communities themselves. This is because of the divergence of interests and perspectives arising between Hungarians living in territorially compact masses as a local majority, often in rural areas, and those living as a minority, and/or in a more ethnically pluralistic environment, often in larger cities. The Transcarpathian case is no exception.

A Hungarian demand for 'autonomy' surfaced early. Alongside the two referenda of December 1991 – on Ukrainian independence, and on Transcarpathian self-government – the Berehove/Beregszász leaders also initiated a referendum on turning their district into a Hungarian Autonomous Region. In the district, this won the support of 81.4 per cent of voters (thus included a proportion of the non-Hungarians). However, the initiative provoked a rift in the Carpathian Hungarian Cultural Association between a group of the leadership concerned not to take any actions that might be construed as 'anti-Ukrainian', and the Berehove/Beregszász leaders, who continued to press for special treatment for their district as a Hungarian majority area. The latter group left CHCA and founded their own organization in 1993 (see Dyba, 1994: 19).

Nevertheless, the CHCA has not abandoned the idea of a self-governing territory for the Hungarians. As the CHCA parliamentary deputy, Miklós Kovács, told the author in an interview in April 2000, while the 1996 Ukrainian constitution ruled out the creation of

'Autonomous Regions', it was still possible to redraw local administrative boundaries. He proposes creating a large single district encompassing most of the 89 per cent of Transcarpathia's Hungarians who are now divided between four adjoining districts along the banks of the Tisza, next to the border with Hungary (Berehove, Užhorod, Mukacheve and Vinohradiv). Special rights and competences are not being asked for, he explained, just the possibility for Hungarians to live together under a common self-government, conducting their public business in Hungarian. His correspondence with the office of the Ukrainian president has so far elicited little appreciation of the merits of the plan.

The Carpathian Euroregion

Transcarpathia's sense of its 'Central European' vocation as Ukraine's 'gateway to Europe', and its earlier plans for a 'special economic zone' prepared the ground for its early and enthusiastic response to the project of the 'Carpathian Euroregion' (CER), initiated by the New York-based Institute for East–West Studies. The CER, founded in Debrecen in February 1993 by the foreign ministers of Hungary, Poland, Slovakia and Ukraine in the presence of the Secretary General of the Council of Europe, united three Hungarian counties, five Polish *wojwódstwa*, the 13 districts of the former East Slovakian region, six Romanian counties, and five Ukrainian *oblasti*. Transcarpathia found itself in a gratifyingly central position in this massive new entity with a total population of nearly 10 million (see Map 2).

The CER was the first Euroregion in East-Central Europe, modelled on the hundred or so similar examples found mainly in Western Europe (and more recently, along Germany's and Austria's eastern borders with their Central European neighbours). It shares the same wide-ranging goals of promoting cross-border trade and cooperation, cultural contacts, mutual understanding and historical reconciliation between peoples divided by international frontiers. As the CER's main financial backer, the Carpathian Foundation, explains in its brochure:

> It [the CER] is unique among the hundred plus transfrontier cooperative structures in the world, and is truly a microcosm of the New Europe. Although wide diversity defines the region in terms of language, religion, and ethnicity, the zones of each country belonging to the Euroregion share as many similarities as they do differences. A common history and geography, similarities in economic development, and common aspirations for economic prosperity and integration create a sense of community and a willingness to work together among local leaders and the larger population (Carpathian Foundation, 1995–97: 9).

But the CER has not lived up to its ambitions; nor has Transcarpathia been able to assert itself as a key player. The reasons for this are many, and instructive. Firstly, the very fact that the initiative came from outside, from the IEWS, suggested that the CER would find it difficult to fly unaided. It very rapidly became clear that it was too big, and did not rest on adequate interest and existing contacts 'from below.' Above all, the transport and communications infrastructure is woefully inadequate for the purposes of regional integration (see Dánc, 2000). As one CER representative told the author in April 2000, it is almost certainly quicker to get from Baia Mare (in north-eastern Romania) to New York than to Przemyśl (in south-east Poland). The over-extension of the project was in part a result of political factors. In the case of the Polish and Hungarian participants, there was an irrepressible urge on the part of regions even quite distant from the frontiers to clamber on board; in the case of Ukraine, it seems clear that Kiev, wary at the start of the CER's potential as a vehicle for 'separatism', pressed for the inclusion of the impeccably nationally minded *oblasti* of Galicia in order to keep an eye on what the Transcarpathians were getting involved in. On the other hand, the wariness of the Slovak and Romanian governments (up to 1997–98) about the CER as a vehicle for Hungarian ambitions in the Carpathian basin led them at first actively to obstruct the formation of the CER, and later severely constrained the participation of their respective regions.

But more prosaic obstacles were littered across the CER's path. The economic systems of the participant countries have become more and more diverse over time. Poland and Hungary are steaming forward in their economic transition, while Romania was deemed by the European Commission's progress report on its accession preparations to be 'not a functioning market economy' (see European Commission, 2000). The Russian financial collapse of 1998 dragged Ukraine even further down into the economic mire, from which it is still struggling to recover. Even if the economic conditions were more propitious, the legal and administrative conditions are not. The participant regions, districts, *oblasti*, etc., all have different powers and competences within their own constitutional systems and thus find it difficult to work together. Most of the participant states have barely started the process of defining regional development policies and the institutional framework for them. The need to refer almost every aspect of any planned cross-border cooperation back to the capitals of still, for the most part, highly centralized states, only adds to the complications – leaving aside the fact that those capitals are often the main source of nationalistic agitations directed against the neighbouring states. But nationalistic sensitivities are also readily aroused in the border localities, notably between Poles and Ukrainians, Romanians and Hungarians. In any case, all the participant local authorities suffer from their peripheral status in their respective states, and so tend to have weak administrative capacities, high dependency on the centre for budgetary transfers, and lack experience and even the will to cooperate with neighbouring border regions. In the Transcarpathian case, enthusiasm among the local former *nomenklatura* elite evaporated along with their economic autonomy projects by the mid-1990s. Rapidly disappointed in the CER as a lucrative source of ready cash, they have found more profit in the two small 'special economic zones' granted by presidential decree, no doubt as part of the political deal which reintegrated them into the Ukrainian elite, including its 'oligarchic' networks.

To prosper, the CER needed, and needs, more substantial political and financial backing. The IEWS has moved on to other projects, leaving behind the small Carpathian Foundation whose resources can only support very small cross-border initiatives under the CER (about $3 million was disbursed in the period 1995–99, of which $500,000 was allocated to about 70 projects in Transcarpathia). The Polish and Hungarian governments took up the CER with some degree of commitment at first, but the project fell rapidly down their list of priorities once the prospect of securing EU accession firmed up. Scarce human and financial resources have inevitably been diverted towards this hugely demanding, but compelling objective. A telling illustration of the atrophy of the CER came in late 1999, when the Tisza river, which runs right through the heart of its territory, was deluged with cyanide from a gold mine's leaking reservoir near Baia Mare. The CER should have been at the forefront of the clean-up operations, but not even a squeak was heard from its HQ. Instead, divergent interests came to the fore: between Baia Mare (anxious to protect employment in the Australian-owned mine), and the Hungarians and Ukrainians living along the Tisza, including their ruined fishermen. Recriminations flew in all directions and it was left to the national capitals to step in and sort the whole problem out.

The EU has not been helpful. EU support has proved difficult to secure, due not only to the bewildering complexity of applying for funding, but also in no small measure to poor coordination in Brussels between the PHARE and TACIS programmes, falling under different directorates (for Enlargement in the case of the accession candidate countries, for Foreign Relations in the case of the non-candidate Ukraine). But these are minor problems compared to what looms with Hungarian and Polish accession to the EU. As negotiations proceed, the increasingly touchy issue of the 'free movement of persons' within the future enlarged 'Area of Freedom, Security and Justice' has moved up the agenda. If the prospective new member states want their citizens to have the same unconstrained right to move about and work wherever they wish in the EU that citizens of existing member states now enjoy, they will be obliged to implement tougher controls, following the Schengen procedures, at their eastern borders, which will become the EU's external border. This border runs right through the heart of the CER.

Moreover, those furthest advanced in accession negotiations are already under pressure to implement the EU's common visa regime. This would mean introducing visas for visitors from Ukraine, thus reverting to the regime of the Soviet period. Hungary and Poland have stated that they regret this (see House of Lords, 2000); but nevertheless both are committed to taking this step in due course. Slovakia has already (since June 2000) implemented a visa regime with Ukraine, prompted by Prague which had done this earlier (on the pretext of pressure from the EU, but also strongly motivated by the desire to restrict the illegal importation of cheap Ukrainian labour, a matter of concern to the governing Social Democrats' working class constituency).

Schengen is seen by Transcarpathians as little short of an impending disaster. Even if the CER itself is flagging, cross-border activity by individuals is not, and has become a vital lifeline as Transcarpathians seek ways out of their dire economic predicament as the poorest people in the whole crisis-ridden Ukrainian economy. Very many, if not most, people cross daily or several times a month into Hungary or Slovakia, taking a carton of cigarettes or a suitcase of *bric-á-brac*. The author was told in April 2000 that a Transcarpathian teacher can double her official salary by crossing the border westwards two or three times a month with a full tank of petrol to siphon into the can of a waiting Hungarian motorist. As many as 270,000 Transcarpathians stay abroad for longer periods to work 'on the black', especially on construction sites in flourishing Warsaw, Budapest or further afield (the estimate is based on the numbers of permanent residents registered with the local authorities as temporarily absent). Schengen, for Transcarpathians, is the final blow. The prospect is prompting more and more to leave, while they still can, and for good. All those interviewed by the author in April 2000 – of whatever ethnic group – posed the question in similar, agonized terms: 'How can Europe do this to us? We are the *centre* of Europe, but Europe is betraying us.'

'Fuzzy Citizenship' –Hope on the Horizon or a Mirage?

Local Slovak minority leaders, interviewed by the author in Transcarpathia in April 2000, made a surprising statement: in the 2001 census, they expect the numbers of self-declared Slovaks in the province to rise to 80,000 from the 7,000 or so recorded in 1991. What could provoke such a sudden surge?

The author was told that the Slovak Foreign Ministry, in preparation for the new visa regime, had proposed to Kiev that some sort of special arrangement might be discussed to ease the conditions of travel for residents of Transcarpathia, given the historic ties, the Slovak minority's position, and the bustling cross-border economic activity. But Kiev, ever-sensitive to any proposal that might publicly concede a special status to Transcarpathia, turned the proposal down: Ukraine is and will remain a unitary state. Nevertheless, Slovakia remains interested in making some special arrangements for visitors from Ukraine (communication to the author from the Slovak Embassy, London, 19 January 2001).

However, in the meanwhile the Slovak government has in place a special provision for so-called 'external Slovaks'. Anyone recognized as a 'Slovak' can acquire from the Slovak Foreign Ministry an 'External Slovak card', on presentation of which the holder is not only exempt from the need for a visa and official invitation (where applicable), but also enjoys certain special rights when in the Slovak Republic (including the right to apply for admission to any Slovak educational institution; to be exempt from permits for long-term residence and work in Slovakia; to receive a pension; to buy real estate; as well as smaller concessions such as reduced fares on Slovak public transport for pensioners, etc.). The law was passed by the Slovak parliament in 1997, under the Mečiar government (see Zákon 70, 1997), and the regulations for obtaining this status are set out on the Slovak Foreign Ministry's website (www.foreign.gov.sk/page_slovaks.htm).

The law and regulations set out how one may become a 'foreign Slovak'. The applicant has to present a birth certificate and valid ID card or passport as proof of personal identity. Then to prove himself a 'Slovak' by nationality or ethnic origin, the applicant must produce an official document (birth or baptismal certificate, extract from the official register, proof of state citizenship or of permanent residence of any of the successive Czechoslovak republics) referring to himself or an ancestor to the third generation (Zákon 70, 1997: I:2:4). If unable to furnish such proof, written testimony from a Slovak minority organization in the applicant's place of residence, or, in the absence of that, two local 'External Slovaks' who know him, can serve instead (Zákon 70, 1997: I:2:5). In practice, Slovak ambassadors may exercise a wide discretion in approving applications – as one told me, 'We know who the Slovaks are locally, they keep in contact with us'. Finally, the applicant must also demonstrate 'Slovak cultural-linguistic consciousness [*povedomie*]', namely, 'at least passive knowledge of the Slovak language and basic familiarity with Slovak culture,' and activity in his local Slovak minority organization (Zákon 70, 1997: I:2:6 and 7).

Given the new visa regime, interest in obtaining such a document intensified sharply in 2000. Visas are costly (at $18, a sizeable part of the average monthly wage). They are inconvenient and time-consuming to obtain, even if a new Slovak Consulate has opened in Užhorod. An 'External Slovak' card comes free of charge, with unlimited validity, and, to judge from the wording of the law, could be quite easy for many people to obtain. Slovaks living as minorities outside Slovakia are typically quite flexible and undogmatic about their identity. A key marker of Slovak identity is adherence to the Roman Catholic Church, and Slovaks have readily associated and intermarried with local German 'Schwabs' and Hungarians of the same confession. But they also mix freely with Rusyns on account of the closeness of the two languages. There are thus very many people in Transcarpathia who can claim some Slovak ancestry, and even more who are descendants of former Czechoslovak citizens. It is not improbable, therefore, that the local Slovak minority will find its numbers burgeoning (although by end 2000, the Slovak Embassy in Ukraine reported that only about 1,000 had applied for and been granted 'External Slovak' cards – communication to the author from the Slovak Embassy, London, 19 January 2001).

In the meanwhile, Hungarian governments have been wrestling with a similar possibility for 'Hungarians Beyond the Borders', long advocated (in light of the obstacles to dual citizenship as a solution) by the Hungarian minorities and Budapest-based organizations concerned with their fate. The difficulties lie in the web of conflicting priorities. Hungarians are torn between an emotional sense of responsibility (also enshrined the constitution) for kinsfolk cut off by Treaty of Trianon; their sense of the need to avoid antagonizing the neighbouring 'successor' countries of the former Hungarian Kingdom, ever alert to Hungarian 'revisionist' designs; and their concern not to introduce anything that might impede the progress of their EU accession, in this case, by contradicting the *acquis* on border control and migration. Two practical problems have emerged. Firstly, defining what rights the 'Hungarian card' will give to non-citizen ethnic Hungarians when in Hungary raises inescapable financial issues for a government hard-pressed to provide adequately for its own tax-paying citizens' healthcare, welfare, pensions and education. And secondly, who should have the right, and on what grounds, to determine who is in fact a 'Hungarian': should the Hungarian state authorities have the final say, can or should this be left in the hands of the registered Hungarian minority organizations, and/or their churches and other registered civic organizations? At bottom the whole proposal raises issues of fundamental importance for the concepts of state sovereignty and citizenship. Creating a special status for ethnic

Hungarians that is compatible with both the Hungarian constitution and European legal norms will be tricky.

A Standing Commission on the question, chaired by a representative of the Hungarian Ministry of Foreign Affairs, and including representatives of the parliamentary parties and the Office for Hungarians Beyond the Borders, has been struggling for some years to produce a workable draft law. A draft law was indeed finalized in December 2000 (see Final Statement, 2000) and passed by the Hungarian parliament in June 2001. The law is notably silent on the question of the future visa regime, and therefore presumably will have to be amended when Hungary accedes to the EU. The main purpose of the law is to keep the Hungarians beyond the borders in their homelands, and, to that end, offers them the right to apply for certain grants, benefits and concessions that serve to strengthen their links with the 'mother country', and at the same time to preserve and develop the cultural heritage of Hungarian communities in the neighbouring countries. Access to a 'Hungarian card', the key to accessing the proposed benefits in culture, educational and social welfare, depends upon the recommendation of local Hungarian minority organizations recognized by the Hungarian state authorities; but ultimately the authority to issue the card remains with the Hungarian authorities. The law passed with the support of all the Hungarian parliamentary parties except the Alliance of Free Democrats. Given the compromises already made in its drafting, and the careful scrutiny of analogous legislation existing, or being reformed, in current EU member states (notably Germany), the question of its compatibility with Hungary's eventual accession to the EU remains open (see Fowler, 2001).

CONCLUSION

Transcarpathia simply does not fit into a Europe of nation-states, and yet the emerging Europe that promises to transcend their most inhumane aspects does not seem to have room for this most 'central' of 'Central European' regions either. Paradoxically, this predicament could in future propel the Rusyns, even against their inclinations and better judgement, towards a more assertive nationalism, because without a state of 'their own' they will remain forever in political limbo. Yet it is precisely the Rusyns' reluctance hitherto to engage in the murderous politics of ethnic exclusivism that has enabled inter-ethnic peace to be preserved within Transcarpathia. Rusyns may be the majority in this province, but they are not the only ethnic community for whom it is a long-established homeland. Moreover, a Rusyn 'nation' ultimately cannot be imagined without also embracing the large numbers of newly self-conscious Rusyns who exist beyond its borders, especially in Slovakia and Poland, but also, although fewer in numbers, in Hungary, Romania and Yugoslavia.

REFERENCES

Braham, R. (2000), *The Politics of Genocide. The Holocaust in Hungary.* Detroit, MI: Wayne State University Press.
Carpathian Foundation (1997), *Report 1995–97* (Košice); see also www.carpathian.euroregion.org
Dánc, L. (2000), Keleti kapu és elszigeltség. Az elzártság kérdése és a határon átnyuló kapcsolatok esélye az északkelet-álföldi határ mentén, *Tér es Társadalom*, 2–3, pp.275–84.
Draft Law (2001), T/4070 törvényjavaszlát a szomszédos államokban élő magyarokról (March), online at www.mkogy.hu/irom36/4070/4070.htm
Duleba, A. *et al.* (1995), *Zakarpatsko.* Bratislava: Slovak Academic Press/Slovenský Inštitut Medzinárodných študii.
Dyba, O. (1994), 'Zakarpattia: a "Doubling" of the Hungarian Factor"', *Demos*, Vol.1, No.2 (17 October).
ECMI – European Centre for Minority Issues (1999), *Inter-Ethnic relations in Transcarpathian Ukraine: Užhorod, Ukraine 4–7 September 1999* (ECMI Report No.4, September)
European Commission (2000), *2000 Report from the Commission on Romania's Progress towards Accession* (8 November), www.europa.eu.int/comm/dgs/enlargement/romania/index.htm
Final Statement of the December 13–14, 2000 Session of the Hungarian Standing Conference (2000), www.htmh.hu/archivum/hsc3.htm
Fowler, B. (2001) *Fuzzing Citizenship, Nationalizing Political Space: A Framework for Interpreting the Hungarian 'Status Law' as a New Form of Kin-state Policy in Central Eastern Europe*, One Europe or Several? Working Paper no. 40/02, January.
Government Office for Hungarian Minorities Abroad, *Report on the Situation of Hungarians in Ukraine* (1997), www.htmh.hu/dokumentumok/repukr-e.htm
Holub, M. (1999), 'Introduction', in Olbracht I., *The Sorrowful Eyes of Hannah Karajich.* Budapest, Central European University Press.
Hesli, V. (1995), 'Public Support for the Devolution of Power in Ukraine: Regional Patterns', *Europe–Asia Studies*, Vol.47, No.1, pp.91–121.
Hroch, M. (1995), 'National Self-Determination from a Historical Perspective', in S. Periwal, (ed.), *Notions of Nationalism.* Budapest: Central European University Press.
House of Lords Select Committee on the European Union, (2000), *Enlargement and EU External Frontier Controls.* London: The Stationery Office, HL Paper 110.
Illés, I. (1999), *The Carpathian (Euro)Region.* Occasional Papers No.6. Tübingen: Europaisches Zentrum für Föderalismus-Forschung.
Köcsis, K. and E. Köcsis-Hodosi (1998), *Ethnic Geography of the Hungarian Minorities in the Carpathian Basin.* Budapest: Geographical Research Institute, Research Centre for Earth Sciences and Minority Studies programme, Hungarian Academy of Sciences.
Kundera, M. (1984), 'The Tragedy of Central Europe', *New York Review of Books*, 26 April, pp.33–8.
Macartney, C. A. (1937), *Hungary and Her Successors.* London, Oxford University Press/Royal Institute of International Affairs.
Magocsi, P. (1993), 'Rusyns of Transcarpathia', in *Minorities in Central and Eastern Europe*, Minority Rights Group Report, London, May, pp.23–6.
Németh, A. (1991), *Kárpátalya.* Budapest: Panorama.
Orosz, I. and Csernicsko, I. (1999), *The Hungarians in Transcarpathia.* Budapest, Tinta Publishers.
Plan of Measures *for Resolving the Problem of Ukrainian-Rusyns, State Committee of Ukraine for Nationalities and Migration*, Kiev, 7 October 1996.

Reisch, A. (1992), Transcarpathia's Hungarian Minority and the Autonomy Issue, *RFE/RL Research Report*, 7 February, pp.17–23.

Shandor, V. (1997), *Carpatho-Ukraine in the Twentieth Century*. Cambridge, MA: Harvard University Press for the Ukrainian Research Institute, Harvard University.

Solchanyk, R. (1994), 'The Politics of State-Building: Centre-periphery Relations in Post-Soviet Ukraine', *Europe–Asia Studies*, Vol.46, No.1, pp.47–68.

Subtelny, O. (1994), *Ukraine. A History*. Toronto: University of Toronto Press.

Treaty (1991) – Szérződés a jószomszédság és az együttmuködés alapjáirol a Magyar Köztársaság es Ukrajna között, www.htmh.hu/dokumentumok/asz-uk-h.htm

Upravlinnia u spravakh natsional'nostei ta migratsii zakarpatskoi oblastnoi derzhavnoi administratsii (1999), *Natsional'no-kul'turni tovaristva Zakarpattia* (Užhorod, Gosprozrakhunkovii redaktsiino-vidavnichii viddil komitetu informatsii).

Vogel, S. (1996) 'A kétoldalú kisebbségvédelmi jogeszközök rendszere' in *Külpolitika* Vol.2, No.1, pp.23–44.

Wolczuk, K. (2001), 'Catching Up with "Europe": Constitutional Debates on the Territorial-Administrative Model in Independent Ukraine', *One Europe or Several? Working Papers*, W20/01, February.

Zákon, 70 zo 14. februára 1997 o zahraničných Slovákoch a o zmene a doplnení niektorých zákonov, *Zbierka zákonov* (Bratislava), Vol.30, pp.390–92.

Reinventing Banat

JUDY BATT

The region that today claims the name of 'Banat' comprises two counties (*judeţ*) of the borderlands of south-western Romania: Timiş and Caraş-Severin. These make up only about two-thirds of the historical Banat, which was part of the Kingdom of Hungary until 1920, when the Treaty of Trianon divided it between Romania and the Kingdom of Serbs, Croats and Slovenes (later Yugoslavia), leaving only a fraction in Hungary to the south-east of Szeged. The region's capital is the city of Timişoara (*Temesvar* in Hungarian and *Temeschwar* in German), where in December 1989 a popular uprising began that turned into the nationwide revolution against the Ceauşescu regime. Post-communist Romania's 'transition to democracy' has been marked by the re-emergence of a potent Romanian nationalism, mobilized by former communist *nomenklatura* elites and assorted disreputable demagogues, but also permeating the fragmented and poorly coordinated anti-communist 'democratic' forces.

Throughout Central and Eastern Europe, 'national revivals' have been accompanied by increased tensions at the local level, as the opening up of political life exposed a long-suppressed and ignored ethnic diversity, challenging the complacent hegemony of the hitherto dominant groups. These can be especially intense at the borderlands of nation-states. As Marzena Kisielowska-Lipman describes in her contribution, the local Poles found it hard to adjust to the newly assertive minorities, and resorted to the language of majoritarian nationalism to reject their claims as a threat to the integrity of the Polish national state. In contrast, Romanian Banat has chosen to reinvent itself as a 'multicultural' and quintessentially 'Central European' region, at odds with the prevailing trend of Romanian nationalist discourse. The visitor to the region is repeatedly told that this region's 'multicultural identity' and traditions of inter-ethnic harmony make it special. These have become the source of a deep regional patriotism that is alienated and frustrated by the centralism and inertia of Bucharest policy-making.

It comes as something of a surprise, however, to discover that Banat today is more homogeneous than it has ever been, with over 82 per cent declaring themselves Romanian in the last (1992) census (see Table 1). In the light of this, and the prevailing nationalist discourse elsewhere in Romania, it is also surprising to find that it is the local Romanians who are

TABLE 1

ETHNIC COMPOSITION OF BANAT (TIMIŞ AND CARAS-SEVERIN)

Absolute numbers:

	1930	1956	1966	1977	1992
Romanians	511,083	768,650	591,758	802,784	885,897
Hungarians	97,839	147,427	85,358	85,554	71,271
Germans	223,167	173,733	133,197	118,271	38,826
Russians	1,598	576	484	424	209
Ukrainians (including Rusyns and Hutans)	3,892	4,825	5,427	7,363	10,854
Serbs, Croats and Slovenes	40,503	44,683	38,535		
Serbs	27,250	24,884			
Croats/Caraşovans			8,766	4,024	
Bulgarians	10,012	9,350	7,617	7,214	6,623
Czecho-Slovaks	14,096				
Czechs		8,887	6,829	4,326	4,060
Slovaks		11,893	3,592	2,584	2,866
Poles	592	691	443	204	142
Jews	11,248	12,990	3,099	1,961	698
Gipsies/Roma	17,919	10,726	6,769	155,459	22,953
Others	7,201	1,128	742	887	3,473
Undeclared	808	245	168	48	55
TOTAL	939,958	1,195,804	884,018	1,223,095	1,076,835

In per cent:

	1930	1956	1966	1977	1992
Romanians	54.37	64.28	66.94	65.64	82.27
Hungarians	10.41	12.33	9.66	6.99	6.62
Germans	23.74	14.53	15.07	9.67	3.61
Russians	0.17	0.05	0.05	0.03	0.02
Ukrainians (including Rusyns and Hutans)	0.41	0.40	0.61	0.60	1.01
Serbs, Croats and Slovenes	4.31	3.74	4.36	0.00	0.00
Serbs	0.00	0.00	0.00	2.23	2.31
Croats/ Caraşovans	0.00	0.00	0.00	0.72	0.37
Bulgarians	1.07	0.78	0.86	0.59	0.62
Czecho-Slovaks	1.50	0.00	0.00	0.00	0.00
Czechs	0.00	0.74	0.77	0.35	0.38
Slovaks	0.00	0.99	0.41	0.21	0.27
Poles	0.06	0.06	0.05	0.02	0.01
Jews	1.20	1.09	0.35	0.16	0.06
Gipsies/Roma	1.91	0.90	0.77	12.71	2.13
Others	0.77	0.09	0.08	0.07	0.32
Undeclared	0.09	0.02	0.02	0.00	0.01
TOTAL	100.00	100.00	100.00	100.00	100.00

Source: Census data

the most enthusiastic proponents of the Banat 'multicultural model' among all the ethnic groups who live there. To explain why this apparently paradoxical myth has taken hold, we need to begin by delving into the history of the region. In the absence of a systematic history of Banat in English to which to refer the reader, the following background sections are rather longer than those in other chapters of this volume, and they by no means cover the full story. But they are necessary in order to expose the rich and complex seams laid down by the past for today's Banaters to mine in their efforts to define where they belong and how they should be governed.

The Origins of Banat's 'Multi-cultural Society'

'Year Zero' of the modern history of Banat can be dated precisely to 1716, when the Habsburg forces, led by the military genius Prince Eugene of Savoy, besieged the Turkish garrison at Timişoara, forcing the surrender of this last stronghold of Ottoman rule in Hungary. The Treaty of Passarowitz of 1718 brought to an end 164 years of Ottoman control of the 'Vilayet of Temesvar', a distinct rectangular area naturally bounded on three sides by the rivers Maros, Tisza and Danube, and in the east by the south-western foothills of the Carpathian mountains, where they reach the Danube at the rapids of the 'Iron Gates' (see Map 1). Most of the Hungarian population by this time had fled, but impoverished Romanian (then known as *Vlach* or Wallachian) mountain-dwellers, Aromanian merchants and Serbs had moved in continually from the east and south, along with Sephardic Jews and gypsies (Roma) from the Ottoman lands. However, the impact of the protracted military campaigns between 1683 and 1716 devastated the region. Towns and villages were destroyed, the rich and fertile land neglected, and the population dispersed. 'Wide territories of quite unoccupied land confronted the Austrian conquerors when they first penetrated southern Hungary', McNeill notes (McNeill, 1964: 165). The lowland area in the west, in the centre of which stands Timişoara, reverted to an inhospitable and insalubrious swamp, among the worst conditions in Europe (see Sugar, 1977: 108). The last of a series of bubonic plague epidemics would sweep Timişoara as late as 1738–39. However, the region occupied a vital strategic position in the Habsburg's southern defences against the continuing Ottoman threat. The urgent task of reconstructing Banat presented the bureaucratic modernizers, military planners and Catholic proselytizers of the Imperial regime with irresistible challenges.

Instead of returning Banat to Hungarian control, it was proclaimed *terra neo-acquisita* (newly acquired territory) and placed directly under the *Hofkriegsrat* (Military Council) in Vienna. Land along the three rivers was incorporated into the southern Military Border, and was subjected to the same special military regime as applied in south Slavonia and the Croatian *Krajina* (see Rothenburg, 1960). As in the latter, the *Grenzer* regiments in the Banat drew heavily on Serbian recruits, who had fled from Ottoman-controlled Serbia, culminating in the legendary exodus led by the Patriarch of Pecs in 1690. Romanians were also recruited into an 'Illyrian-Wallachian' regiment stationed in the south-eastern Banat, and a German regiment was formed in the west (Drace-Francis, 2000). Recruits were granted land, and exempted from serfdom and taxation. The Serbs in addition had special privileges, which promised them religious freedom and self-government, and granted their Orthodox Church full spiritual and temporal authority over the affairs of all Orthodox believers (thus including the Romanians of Banat) within the former Hungarian lands apart from Transylvania (see Adler, 1976–77 and 1979). These special conditions were to have an enduring impact on the region. As Macartney reported from his visit in 1937, 'among the Germans and even the Serbs and Romanians of the Banat, and especially of the military frontier, a strong tradition of local independence lives on, and memories of the old Austrian rule are still fresh' (Macartney, 1937: 386).

Meanwhile, the rest of Banat, now an autonomous Crownland with a governor appointed by Vienna, became the 'scene of the most elaborate colonisation scheme which had, perhaps, ever been attempted' (Macartney, 1937: 384). Although the Banat's geographical position had ensured that it always had a mixed population, it was the Habsburg colonization that laid the basis of today's 'multi-cultural' society. Unwilling to allow the politically unreliable Hungarians to return to their ancestral lands (a revolt of the Calvinist Magyar nobility of Transylvania having only just been put down), the Habsburgs first turned to demobilized Austrian soldiers and convict labour, both of whom proved unsatisfactory (see Mitchell, 2000). After 1730 some Hungarians, provided they were Catholics, were allowed to resettle. But the authorities had to look beyond the borders of the Empire for suitable and willing recruits. They found them mainly among the stoutly Catholic German peasants of lands to the north, known generically, but inaccurately, as 'Schwabs' ever since; but also French-speakers from Luxembourg, Lorraine and Belgium, along with Italians, Catalans and others, who were enticed by free transport, land grants, start-up capital and tax breaks to sign up for three great waves of planned settlement in the course of the eighteenth century. A small group of Bulgarian Catholics, converted by fourteenth-century Franciscan missionaries to Bulgaria, who had fled north of the Danube to escape persecution, were rewarded with the special affection of the devout Empress Maria Teresa, as was another small group of Catholic south Slavs settled in several villages centred on Caraşova. The Empress' benevolent protection was also extended to the Lippovans, 'Old Believer' schismatics from the Russian Orthodox Church of the Tsarist Empire. At the height of the colonization, seventeen different languages were spoken in Banat (Ingrao, 1994: 141).

Later, after Banat's reversion to Hungarian control in 1778, Magyars returned to reclaim their estates, bringing with them Slovak peasants from Upper Hungary (today's Slovakia). The Jewish presence in the towns revived with influxes from Hungary and Galicia. Land hunger in the early nineteenth century brought Magyar peasants from the Great Plain, Czechs from Bohemia, and Rusyns from Hungarian Ruthenia (today's Transcarpathia) and Maramaros. Thus was created the 'multi-cultural' Banat recorded in 1840, with a total population of over one million, including 200,000 Germans, 570,000 Romanians, 60,000 Magyars, and 200,000 Serbs (see Vultur, 2000: 22). Although, as we shall see, the ethnic proportions have since changed substantially, the extraordinary fact is that not only the four main ethnic groups, but also all the smaller ethnic groups can still be found in Banat today.

The explanation of how this came about throws light on the nature of 'multi-culturalism' as practised in pre-twentieth century Banat, which does not quite conform to the image conveyed by today's Banat patriots. For the persistence of separate identities over such a long period suggests a history not of close contact and intermingling of ethnic groups, but rather a sustained pattern of mutual exclusivism and separate development. The latter in fact underlay both the social organization and the planned physical reconstruction of Timişoara after the expulsion of the Turks. The inhabitants were organized into two separate communities under 'magistracies' or local councils comprising mayors and councillors: one Catholic, dominated by the Germans (who were the majority of the city's population by 1730s), and one Orthodox, dominated by the Serbs (Cuţara, 1999: 11–12).

The city itself was razed to the ground and built anew from its foundations, obliterating not only the Turkish, but also the medieval heritage (which included the castle, in the early fourteenth century the seat of the Hungarian king). The new city was rationally planned and rebuilt in brick and stucco. At its centre was a rectangular grid pattern of streets and squares on which were erected blocs of austere, neo-classical barracks, and administrative buildings in the elegant high Baroque style so characteristic of this period of triumphal self-confidence sweeping right across the Habsburg domains. What is unique, however, is Timişoara's Main Square (today *Piaţa Unirii*), where, on the east side, the splendid Roman Catholic Cathedral, the *Dome*, built in 1736–54 by the Viennese Josef Emanuel Fischer von Erlach the younger, looks across to the fine

Serbian Orthodox Church of the Ascension, built in neo-romanesque style in 1744–48.

The inner city was surrounded by polygonal fortifications, with four main gates. Beyond these, the Bega river was channelled as part of a huge programme of land drainage and flood control. Outside the city, military exercise grounds, an industrial district (still called *Fabrik*) at the centre of which today can be found a baroque Serbian orthodox church, and a late nineteenth-century synagogue and Hungarian Catholic church in close proximity. Further suburbs were built, each centred on a church, forming purpose-built residential quarters for the different denominations. The *Mehala* district was designed for the Orthodox; from 1760 there was a Jewish quarter with a synagogue ('proving that the inhabitants of Timişoara have never had anti-semitic feelings', as a contemporary guide explains: Cuţara, 1999: 70). Other quarters had explicitly ethnic names such as *Deutschestadt*, or *Wallachischestadt*. This pattern was added to gradually over the next two centuries, ensuring a high degree of cohesion within, but also separation between, the communities.

A similar approach was taken to settling the colonists in rural areas, where villages were planned and laid out for each ethnic group, often in clusters connected by roads to markets, which provided the main, if not sole, point of contact for their respective inhabitants. The component parts of these linked settlements were identified ethnically – so, for example, on a map based on the 1890 Hungarian census of the region, we find clusters of villages such as *Szerb* (Serbian) *Csanád*, *Német* (German) *Csanád* and *Magyar Csanád*; or *Horvát* (Croat) *Kécsa* and *Román* (Romanian) *Kécsa*; as well as singular *Bolgártelep* (Bulgarian Settlement), *Kis-Orosz* (Little Rus), *Tót* (Slovak)-*Komlós*, *Új* (New) *Moldova*; and the presumably originally Italian *Alberti* and Austrian *Tirol* (see Jordan, 1999). Marriage across the confessions was officially and socially discouraged. Intermarriage among ethnic groups of the same confession (e.g. between Catholic Germans, Hungarians and Slovaks; Orthodox Serbs and Romanians) was inhibited by language and social class barriers.

The Germans were everywhere the leading ethnic group, and their overwhelming cultural hegemony can still be felt in Banat today. They drained the swamps, introduced innovative farming methods, viticulture and new crops such as maize, potatoes and tobacco, transforming 'empty grasslands and fever-ridden swamps into smiling fields within a generation' (McNeill, 1964: 214). They brought with them a work ethic and commitment to educating their children that were widely admired and set the standard for the whole province. Timişoara became a flourishing bourgeois centre of industry and commerce, boasting all the latest conveniences of modern life, including the first electric street lighting in

Europe, installed in 1884 (Cuțara, 1999: 15). The transport and communications infrastructure of the region became one of the densest in Central Europe. This advanced socio-economic level set Banat apart from the rest of Hungary, somewhat to the chagrin of the returning Magyar nobility, who found themselves looked upon by the locals as 'newcomers' to the region and their pretensions to leadership disregarded. The future Emperor Joseph II, visiting Banat in 1768, had early reported considerable mutual hostility between Germans and Magyars that continued, in more or less muted rivalry, thereafter (Seton-Watson, 1934: 184–5). The largest ethnic group, the Romanians, struggled under multiple disadvantages: in religious life, under the Serbian-dominated Orthodox church; in the towns, under the Germans; and in the countryside, under Magyar landlords. In Kann's view, in Banat 'Romanian national status was inferior even to that in Transylvania' (Kann, 1974: 299).

Banat Between Nationalisms and Nation-States

This heterogeneous region would be severely tested by the rise of nationalism in the nineteenth century, which led ultimately to the collapse of the Empire. The first great threat to the peaceful coexistence of the various ethnic groups came with the Revolution of 1848, when the Hungarians declared their independence from the Empire. Events here were confused as much by divisions within the ethnic groups as between them. The then mayor of Timișoara, a German, clearly sympathized with the liberal agenda of the Hungarians, declaring the city's adhesion to the revolution and renaming Prince Eugene Square as 'Liberty Square', the name it retains to this day. But other Schwabs sided with the Austrians against Hungary. Meanwhile, the Romanians, in contrast to their ethnic kin in Transylvania, 'did not form a coherent group bent on achieving power on ethnic grounds', and were remarkably quiescent (Drace-Francis, 2000: 12). This was not only due to their social backwardness and marginalization, but also because their most articulate leader, Eftimie Murgu, saw the Serbs as the main threat to the Romanians in Banat, rather than the Hungarians. The Romanians protested against Serbian domination of the Orthodox Church, and were bitterly opposed to the Serbs' demands for the restoration of their 1690 privileges and the transformation of a large area of southern Hungary, including Banat, into an autonomous Serbian ethnic homeland. In their opposition to the latter, the Romanians were assured of the support of the Hungarians, who would fight ferociously to preserve the unity of the Hungarian Kingdom. In this struggle, Hungarian and Serbian nationalist leaders incited the peasants against each other, with the result that people 'who had lived in peace for centuries … were massacring one another in the name of nationality'

(Deak, 1990: 220). One of the final battles of the Hungarian forces against the Austrians was fought at Timișoara in August 1849; shortly thereafter, the Hungarian revolutionary government, based at Arad on Banat's northern border, resigned, and their army surrendered. Thirteen of their leaders were executed at Arad by the Austrian General Haynau, an act of brutal revenge that shocked the whole of Europe (see Kontler, 1999: 258–9).

The Serbs, on the other hand, were rewarded for their loyalty to the Emperor with the establishment in 1849 of the 'Vojvodina of Temesvar and Serbian Banat'. But the promised self-government never materialized under the centralist regime that was installed after the revolution. Then, with the 1867 *Ausgleich* by which Vienna ceded self-government to the kingdom of Hungary, the Vojvodina was fully reincorporated into the Hungarian county system, and the Serbian privileges lapsed (see Adler, 1979: 280 ff). The most active Serbian national leaders left for Belgrade, which by now was the capital of the independent Serbian principality.

After 1867, Banat, like the rest of Hungary, was subjected to the 'nationalizing' regime of the triumphant Magyars, bent on transforming the Kingdom of which they constituted less than one half the population into a Hungarian national state. The Germans, according to Macartney, adapted willingly to the pressures to magyarize: 'Politically, they were as good Hungarians as any in the country, and seem always to have allied themselves with the Magyar elements against the Romanians and Serbs' (Macartney, 1937: 275). It was during this period that Banat flourished as one of the leading centres of economic development in the Dual Monarchy, its economy tightly integrated into the markets of Vienna and Budapest. Nevertheless, by the early twentieth century the Germans had clearly begun to chafe under the overweening Magyars, and, upon the collapse of Austria-Hungary, their representatives declared for union with Romanians in 1919, having abandoned the idea of autonomy within the collapsing Hungary and, meanwhile, Timișoara and the west of the region having been occupied by the Serbian Army (see Köpeczi *et al.*, 1994: 654).

The key issue now therefore was not whether Banat would remain part of Hungary, but how the rival claims of the Serbian and Romanian nation-states to it were to be settled. By a secret treaty of August 1916, the Western powers had promised the whole of Banat to Romania. As Seton-Watson argued,

> If this clause had been put into effect, the Jugoslavs would have looked across the river from the windows of their capital to Serbian territory which had been wrested from Hungary merely in order to

bc assigned to an ally who had never possessed it and had not conquered it. It is difficult to conceive a better method of turning two friendly neighbours into enemies than to provide such an obvious bone of contention (Seton-Watson, 1934: 537–8).

Notwithstanding Prime Minister Brațianu's intransigent insistence on Romania's claim to the whole, eventually the Peace Conference decided otherwise, and Banat was divided. The Serbs were given what they wanted, the predominantly Serbian south-west part, which joined the Kingdom of Serbs, Croats and Slovenes, and the rest was left to Romania. Germans were scattered in both parts, as were Romanians, Serbs, Slovaks and others.

Both parts of Banat in the inter-war period were affected by the nationalistic policies of the Serbian and Romanian regimes, neither of which was inclined to implement the commitments imposed on them by the League of Nations' Minority Treaties. Influxes of Serbs and Romanians were encouraged from elsewhere in the respective states to implement the national capitals' efforts to integrate the newly acquired territories. In Yugoslavia, Banat identity melted naturally into that of Serbian Vojvodina. The local dominance there of the nationally conscious Serbs, and the proximity to the capital, Belgrade, meant that there was no real basis for regionalist opposition to Belgrade. In Romanian Banat, however, the social and cultural dominance of the Germans persisted. Mass emigration of Serbian teachers and priests to Yugoslavia after 1920 deprived the local Serbs of their elite. The Hungarians' attitudes were uncompromisingly hostile, as Macartney reports in 1937:

> [They] regard themselves as simply part of unitary Hungary, cut out of its living body by an unjust frontier. There is no separate local feeling, no tradition of co-operation with the other local nationalities … They do not even attempt, as far as I could judge, to live on tolerable terms with the non-Magyars. Even a tennis club which was started in Timișoara failed because the nationalities could not play peaceably together (Macartney, 1937: 337).

The Romanians therefore took special care to privilege the German minority in order to prevent an alliance among the non-Romanian nationalities in the region, and especially between the Germans and revisionist Hungarians. Moreover, in the inter-war period, the importance of Germany as a trading partner for Romania was an additional reason for treating them carefully (see Komjathy and Stockwell, 1980: 103). Thus, by the 1930s, Banat's economic prosperity had revived, and Timișoara was 'the centre of a fat little world of its own' (Macartney, 1937: 341).

Nevertheless, the Germans remained dissatisfied with the failure of the Romanian government to live up to the promises of self-government made at Alba Iulia, and nationalistic sentiment grew among them.

Banat was by no means a haven of liberal multiculturalism in inter-war Romania: an important 'nest' of the Romanian 'Legionaries', a radical right-wing, anti-semitic nationalist movement, was active at the new Timişoara Polytechnic, established in 1920 to promote the development of a Romanian technical intelligentsia. The German minority party's older generation of pragmatic conservatives was gradually eclipsed by a radical 'Young Schwabian Movement' influenced by Nazi ideology, which young Schwabians had imbibed as students in Germany. After the abdication of King Carol in 1940, Nazi Germany's influence on Romanian politics increased dramatically, and a branch of the Nazi NSDAP became the sole recognized representative of the German minority, using the swastika as its emblem, much to the consternation of the Romanian nationalists and the Romanian government, who proved, however, unable to resist it (Komjathy and Stockwell, 1980: 121).

Most of the Banat Germans appear always to have had reservations about the drift of their organizations to the right and their eventual total subordination to the political dictates of the Reich. Anti-semitism appears to have been unwelcome, as many Jews regarded themselves, and were regarded by the Schwabs, as Germans; and the churches, always the centre of Banat German community life, opposed the basic philosophy of Nazism (Komjathy and Stockwell, 1980: 113). Banat Schwabs, deeply attached to their land, also received with dismay the news of the Führer's plans to resettle all the German communities in the Reich. While the Second Vienna Arbitration of 1940 may have satisfied the Romanian Germans' long-pressed demand for community self-government, it came at a price. Nazi Germany demanded ever-greater authority over their affairs, and this included increasing pressure on them to serve in the German army and Waffen SS. Some no doubt joined up out of conviction (this seems to have been more common among Transylvania's Saxons than in Banat); others may have preferred this to service in the corrupt and ill-disciplined Romanian army. But coercion was also necessary, particularly among the Banat Schwabs, who deserted in larger numbers than any other group of ethnic German minority recruits (Komjathy and Stockwell, 1980: 123).

In all, about 54,000 Romanian Germans served in the Waffen SS, and 15,000 in the Wehrmacht and 'Operation Todt'. Their losses during the war were heavy (Komjathy and Stockwell, 1980: 124). But worse was to come when the German retreat began, and Romania made its late switch over to the Allied side, after which a Soviet-backed regime was installed. In January 1945, 70,000 Romanian Germans were deported to the USSR for forced labour for one to five years, of whom many never returned (Vultur, 2000: 28). Many Banat Germans fled west over the border into German-occupied Yugoslav Banat, and left with the retreating German army. Nevertheless, the profound attachment of this mainly rural, farming people to their native soil appears within a short time to have drawn them back to Romania. Nearly 150,000 more Germans were found in Romania in the 1948 census than could have been expected from the figures on their enlistment, transfers and deportations during the war (see Schechtman, 1962: 269–70). While no mass expulsion of the Germans took place in post-war Romania (as happened in Poland, Czechoslovakia and Yugoslavia), they hardly received a warm welcome on their return. Between 1945 and 1948, German farms and enterprises were confiscated, and their homes were reallocated to new Romanian settlers from Moldavia and Soviet-annexed Bessarabia, and from Bulgarian-annexed Dobrudja.

By 1950, Romanians had become the absolute majority in Banat, a proportion that continued to grow steadily thereafter (see Table 1). In the years 1951–56, a systematic programme of deportations removed supposedly 'unreliable elements' from the region and deported them for forced labour in the Bărăgan region north of Bucharest. Serb villages near the border with Yugoslavia were cleared in response to the perceived threat of the 'Titoist heresy'. Recent Macedo-Romanian settlers from Dobrogea, now branded as 'nationalists,' joined them. The wealthier farmers – not only Germans, but also Hungarians and others – had their properties confiscated and were sent to Bărăgan. After 1956, many deportees returned to Banat: some to the land, but many to the towns where they could more easily lose themselves in the anonymity of urban life, change their identities and thus avoid the official opprobrium that continued to stigmatize the lives of former deportees and their children (interview with Ms Smaranda Vultur, December 2000).

In the Ceaușescu period of Romania's 'independent' foreign policy, at odds with the rest of the Soviet bloc, Romania cultivated good relations with Israel, as a result of which those Jews who had survived the Second World War were allowed to leave. Then in 1978, Romania came to a profitable arrangement with West Germany, which paid substantial sums of hard currency for exit permits for Romania's Germans. Thus began an exodus of about 10,000 a year, culminating in 1990 when over 60,000 Germans left Romania. From 1977, when they had numbered about 159,000 in Banat, their community dwindled to about 40,000 by the 1992 census. The Ceaușescu regime was set on a course of 'national communism' that aimed at homogenizing Romanian society both socially and ethnically. In Banat, meanwhile, Romanians had become some 83 per cent of the population of the two Banat counties.

Rediscovering Diversity – Reinventing Banat

Banat's multi-cultural past had all but vanished from public life by 1989. Moreover, that past had been marked by inter-ethnic rivalry, inequality, and ugly episodes of violence. If a distinctive 'Banat identity' ever existed, it was more likely to have been experienced differently by the separate ethnic communities, rather than as an overarching, unifying identity. It was not an integrated 'multi-cultural society' valuing ethnic diversity and actively promoting inter-ethnic dialogue and equal participation. Only after 1989 could this begin to be the case, due to the new conditions that arose in the region that facilitated the self-assertion of some ethnic groups, and provoked others who had forgotten their ethnic origins to rediscover them. What is interesting about Banat is the Romanian majority's participation in the reinvention of Banat as a 'multi-cultural society' whose constituent ethnic groups all emphasized their differences from the rest of Romania, and their shared regional identity.

The starting point can be found in the events of December 1989 in Timişoara (the best account in English is Siani-Davies, 1995). The trigger for the events was the local communist authorities' attempted eviction of the Hungarian pastor, László Tökés, from the manse of the Reform Church (see Tökés, 1990). The small gathering that came to support him mainly comprised his Hungarian parishioners, but rapidly swelled so that the crowds that later seized control of the city were overwhelmingly young Romanians and striking workers. It was indeed a rare moment of unity among all the people of the city, and a formative one for the 'Banat myth'.

In March 1990, dismayed at the 'hijacking' of the Romanian revolution by a group of former communists around Ion Iliescu, the 'Timişoara Society', a group of local intellectuals, produced the *Timişoara Declaration* that set out for the first time all the basic ingredients that have since crystallized into a distinctive Banat identity:

- pride in Banat's 'first place' in Romania, and resentment at Bucharest's failure to recognize their achievements;

- affirmation of the region's 'European' identity and mission to lead Romania's 'return to Europe;'

- commitment to the value of pluralism, and rejection of divisive tactics intervening to disrupt the social and ethnic unity of the region;

- 'unity in suffering' as the historical basis of shared values and interests;

- the special economic position of the region, arguing for decentralization, and for the possibility of faster progress in Banat.

The Timişoara Declaration is permeated by pride in the fact that the revolution started in Timişoara. Its final paragraph declared, 'we are grieved and revolted by the central policy of minimizing our revolution' (Mihalcea, 1994: 47), exemplified by the selection of 22 December (the day of Ceauşescu's fall from power in Bucharest) rather than 16 December (when the demonstrations began in Timişoara) as the national day commemorating the revolution. Subsequently the new government's recourse to communist-era tactics had betrayed the unity of the people, fighting for the essentially 'European' ideals espoused by the Timişoara's revolution:

> In Timişoara people did not die so that the second and third rank communists should go to the front line, or that one of the participants in the mass murders should be promoted by the latter as Minister of the Interior. People did not die so that the social and national feuding, the personality cult, the censorship of the mass media, misinformation, written and telephone threats, and all the other communist methods of coercion should be practised openly, while we are requested to stay passive on behalf of social stability (Mihalcea, 1994: 47–8).

The aim of Timişoara's Revolution had represented 'the return to the genuine values of European democracy and civilization', and, it was asserted, 'The idea of political pluralism has been and is among the most cherished values of the people of Timişoara' (p.43), now threatened by old 'divide-and-rule' tactics. The 'multi-cultural' theme of 'unity in suffering' first appears in paragraph 4:

> Side by side with the Romanians, there were Hungarians, Germans, Serbians, members of other ethnic groups who sacrificed their lives for the cause of the Revolution. They have been coinhabiting our city in peace and goodwill for centuries. Timişoara is a European city where all the nationalities have rejected and reject nationalism. All the chauvinists of the country, no matter whether they are Romanians, Hungarians or Germans, are invited to come to Timişoara to a re-education course in the spirit of tolerance and mutual respect, the sole principles reigning in the future European House.

Finally, the Timişoara declaration touched on the economic issues. Here again, the aim is 'to Europeanize Romania', by embracing 'private initiative': 'We shall never have political pluralism without economic pluralism' (pp.45–6). Moreover, 'Timişoara is determined to take economic and administrative decentralization seriously' (p.46), and had prepared a model for market reform, utilizing local expertise and aiming to attract foreign capital. This drew the most hostile reaction from Romanian TV, which interpreted it as a demand for full-blown autonomy, thus raising the old bugbear of 'dismemberment' of the unitary Romanian national state (Gallagher, 1995: 151). Reactions of this sort to initiatives originating in Banat were to become a regular irritant in dealings with the capital, and helped cement the sense of cultural distance and political alienation from the capital, as we shall see.

The task of articulating Banat identity was taken forward by the local intelligentsia. The Timişoara university professor, Victor Neumann, whose Western contacts gave him the opportunity to propagate the 'Banat story' among an international audience, writes: 'Banat was a model of peaceful co-existence between 1800 and 1950, an example to others of mutual understanding and the creation of interethnic and interconfessional relations' (Neumann, 1997: 21). This somewhat selective reading of history rapidly became accepted as standard in Banat, and was mobilized behind the region's claim to a 'special mission': 'The multiple identity of Banat may contribute ... to rebuilding the bridges between Eastern Europe and the "civilised" world' (Neumann, 1997: 27), as well as to Romanian–Hungarian reconciliation (p.28); and 'stimulate an individual and collective wish for integration in a Europe of regions' (p.29). The Banaters' reviving sense of their 'European' heritage was encouraged by an award-winning Timişoara TV programme in 1998 called *Timişoara – Little Vienna*. This drew on the rich architectural heritage of the city to demonstrate its intimate links, via Vienna, to a 'Central European' cultural space, a heritage long allowed to rot under the communist regime and still woefully neglected (see Armanca and Raţiu, 1998).

Banat has projected its 'European' and 'multi-cultural' image abroad. For example, the local tourist office promotes Banat as Romania's 'gateway to Europe'. The county Economic Development Agency describes Timiş as 'a Looking Forward [sic] Romanian County in Europe'. The websites of the Prefectures of Timiş and Caraş-Severin both draw attention to the ethnic diversity of the counties. Timiş Chamber of Commerce's information pack also highlights ethnic diversity and the 'open mentality' as local assets that explain the tradition of receptiveness to innovation. The point is reiterated by the editor of *Timişoara What, Where, When* magazine, who, in the August/September 2000 edition, describes the city as ' a great spiritual gateway to novelty'. The main publication on Timişoara for foreign consumption, on the other hand, stresses continuity: 'The city has always kept its old cosmopolitan charm due to its harmonious ethnical [sic] diversity', and explains:

As they were hardworking, for centuries accustomed to more advanced workskills, given their Occidental mentality and behaviour, the people of the Banat succeeded in keeping a higher standard of living and a more decent specific mode of existence than the other Romanians (Cuţara, 1999: 23).

A more scholarly approach was pursued by the 'Third Europe' Foundation in Timişoara, set up in 1996 by academics to coordinate research activity on Timişoara and the Banat region, drawing in postgraduates in the fields of literary studies, political sociology and history. The group's information leaflet affirms the local tradition: 'Being a multiethnic and multilingual area, the region has cultivated the concept of intercultural dialogue based on its specific model of civic conduct and on a highly acclaimed level of research'. The research agenda includes the aim 'to encourage Romanian participation in the European dialogue, as well as to emphasise Romania's natural sense of appurtenance to this cultural sphere'.

The historians of 'Third Europe' have collected oral testimonies among the older generations of Banat's ethnic groups to produce an 'anthropology of memory' that analyses the way in which the older generations have come to terms with the traumatic experience of the deportations in 1951–56 to Bărăgan, and the way in this shaped local identities:

> Far from being a simple informative act, the act of narration develops additional functions linked to the cathartic power of confession... Telling the story of deportation and of his life, testifying about them, give the narrator the opportunity to evaluate things, to size them up, to redress a trauma, to forget a mental wound. All these justify his life, get him adjusted to the deviations of an individual or collective fate, recreating his image and identity (Vultur, 1997: 384).

The extraordinary, terrible experiences uncovered by the research also show how memories of 'unity in suffering' in the 1950s contribute to the emergence of Banat identity after 1989, and how the experiences of ordinary villagers confirm the 'Banat myth' articulated by Timişoara intellectuals. In the labour camps of Bărăgan, the interviewees report that differences between ethnic groups were effaced. Banat identity became the key, as the deportees were kept separate from the local Bărăgan population, warned by the communist authorities that the new arrivals from Banat were dangerous criminals. Whole families were deported together, which helped them survive. The Banaters describe how they set to work in Bărăgan: their relentless work, their industry and their achievements – they had been dumped in a desert, but they made it flourish. Their stories uncannily replicate the language and themes of the original Schwab myth of the eighteenth-century colonization of Banat, emphasizing their work ethic, honesty and resourcefulness, in comparison to the 'backward' and hostile local population. The Schwabs suffered alongside the others, providing not only practical lessons in survival, but also a mythological model for making sense of, and retrieving some value from, the shared experience. The invented 'tradition of inter-ethnic harmony' expunged from their memories any historic episodes of inter-ethnic tension in Banat itself (interview with Ms Smaranda Vultur, December 2000).

The Schwabs, now reduced to a fraction of their former numbers, have nevertheless recovered their traditional status in Banat because the cultural attributes for which they are recognized seem especially advantageous for the post-communist social and economic transformation to which the region aspires. Their position was also boosted by their links with Germany, admired throughout Central Europe as post-war Europe's great success story, as well as the key source of both moral and financial support for would-be members of the European Union. German government aid to the Schwabs has flowed in to stem the flood of emigration that became a source of concern to the German Länder and public opinion by the mid-1990s. Since 1990, a total of about DM170 million has been provided to the German communities in Romania by the German Foreign and Interior Ministries, the largest part of which has gone to Banat (where about 29 per cent of Romania's Germans live: see *Auswärtiges Amt* website; and direct communication from the German Embassy in Bucharest). While this aid is explicitly targeted to the German minorities, in practice other ethnic groups feel the benefit. The aim of German policy is to secure the full integration of the German minorities as respected members of their local communities. The Institute for Foreign Affairs (financed by the German Foreign Ministry) actively promotes inter-ethnic projects in Central and Eastern Europe, and in the case of Romania, the German communities' high prestige is felt to make them 'an appropriate starting point for the IFA's multiethnic projects' (see *IFA* website).

Thus the German government funded a new German cultural centre in Timişoara, but also specified that the premises were to be made available free of charge for all the Banat minorities. Assistance provided under such conditions has encouraged the Schwabs to assume – informally – a leading role among the minorities in Banat, on similar lines to those Germany itself practises in its external relations: just as Germany promotes 'not a German Europe but a European Germany', so the Schwabs in Banat are encouraged to eschew national self-aggrandisement in the broader interest

of Banat's 'Europeanization'. That this self-effacing approach is already
well internalized was nicely illustrated by an exchange between the author
and an elderly couple of Schwabs at a winter festival for minorities held at
the German community centre in December 2000. Each minority group
turned up in traditional dress, and presented a table of their festive
seasonal dishes. The Schwabs' table was without doubt the best
provisioned, and I remarked on the glorious display of cakes and other
delicacies. But I was tactfully corrected: 'All the other tables are very fine
too, I think, *nicht wahr?*'

The 'Third Europe' oral history project has uncovered some
remarkable cases of the 'rediscovery' of ethnic identity by some groups
after 1989, in which external 'mother-countries' have played a role,
although not always as smoothly as in the Schwab case. For example,
following the collapse of Yugoslavia, the Caraşovans (those south Slav
Catholics cherished by Maria Teresa) were encouraged by a visit of the
Croatian President Franjo Tudjman to look to Croatia for support. The
Caraşovans, nearly all of whom had chosen to declare themselves as such,
rather than as Croats, in the 1992 census, seized the opportunity offered by
Tudjman to take Croatian citizenship, which they saw as a chance of easier
access to Europe. They sent their folk ensemble to Croatia, but were
dismayed to find their repertoire greeted with hostility, as their songs were,
to a Croat ear, unmistakeably 'Serbian' (interview with Ms Vultur,
Timişoara, December 2000). Nevertheless, with the lifting of the EU visa
restrictions on citizens of Croatia, the Caraşovans' new passports came in
handy, and the majority of families now have at least one member working
in Croatia, or (illegally) in EU countries, earning on average DM1.500 per
month, all of which is brought home and invested in their native village,
dubbed in a recent newspaper report Romania's 'Schengen village'. Only
one family has opted for permanent emigration, and loyalty to their
homeland remains strong. As the deputy mayor explained, 'Though we
have Schengen visas, we are still waiting for the moment when we will be
able to travel in Europe as Romanians' (Kaitor, 2001; and interview with
Mr Mihai Radan, MP, Caraşova, September 2001).

Meanwhile, the Bulgarian ambassador also paid a visit to the small
Bulgarian community, but his overtures were met with polite distance: as
Catholics, the Banat Bulgarians were by no means ready for the embrace
of their Orthodox would-be 'motherland'. Around the depressed industrial
town of Oţelu Roşu ('Red Steel,' formerly Ferdinandsburg), locals have
been unearthing evidence of their Italian origins from boxes of family
records long-hidden in the attics. Perhaps the most extraordinary story that
Ms Vultur's researches encountered was that of a small village, colonized
originally by French peasants from the Avignon region, who had

assimilated to German by the nineteenth century. German identity became highly disadvantageous at the end of the Second World War, and this village was able to document its French origins. Having learnt that Robert Schumann was also from Avignon, they appealed to him as a fellow-countryman for help. Schumann secured their safe passage from Romania to France, and they were resettled in deserted farms in the hills around Avignon, where Ms Vultur tracked them down in the 1990s. Listening to their life-stories, she recognized once again the recurrent theme of the 'Banat myth': we came to this deserted, derelict place, and by our efforts and hard work, we have made flourishing farms and rebuilt our community (interview with Smaranda Vultur, December 2000).

The Serbs of Banat have also had difficulties in their relationship with their 'mother country' since 1989. At the outbreak of the Yugoslav crisis, the Banat Serbs sided with the Milošević regime out of an instinctive reflex of 'my country, right or wrong'. Links with Yugoslavia were assiduously fostered by the Belgrade government via the consulate in Timişoara. Local Serbs greeted the international ostracism of Serbia, and then the NATO bombardment of 1999, with dismay: they felt 'as if their mother-country was being violated' (interview with Mr Svetislav Rotkov, secretary of the Union of Serbs in Banat, December 2000), and addressed protests to the local authorities. The Union of Serbs' MP spoke out in the Bucharest parliament against the Romanian government's support for the NATO action. Nevertheless, the Serbs found in Banat a rather supportive environment. The fact that public opinion among the Romanians was on their side confirmed for them the 'tradition of the Serb–Romanian friendship'. This solidarity helped ease the tensions among the Banat Serbian community. The mayor of Timişoara led a campaign to persuade the local Serbs that his party's, and the Romanian government's, support for the NATO action was not directed against the Serbs as a people, but against the Milošević regime. Representatives of the Serbian opposition to Milošević were invited to Timişoara, and such initiatives helped shift the Banat Serbs' attitudes, preparing the way for their turn to support Kostunica in 2000 (interview with Dr Ciuhandu, mayor of Timişoara, December 2000).

It is among the Magyars that one senses a certain scepticism towards the 'Banat myth', and a lingering sense of separateness. As a leading Banat representative of the RMDSZ(Democratic Union of Romanian Magyars) told the author: 'We always say that this is a multilingual region. It was – but it is not now.' The following points summarise his account. The Romanian language is overwhelmingly dominant, and Hungarian is used only in church affairs, not in the public sphere. In mixed marriages, the children grow up using Romanian as their mother tongue. Hungarian ethnic identity is less confidently asserted in Banat than in Transylvania, where culture, language and traditions are nurtured. Hungarians here live in diaspora, forming for the most part less than 15 per cent of the local population among whom they live, not in compact, homogeneous Magyar communities like the 'Szeklers' of Transylvania. Significantly, he noted that in Banat, ethnic identities had tended to become 'fuzzy' (*diffusa*), which he explained by the pragmatic local preoccupation with economic self-advancement.

For the Banat Magyars, therefore, the idea of 'territorial autonomy' (a priority for the influential Transylvanian Szekler group within RMDSZ) is not of much interest; instead they prioritize cross-border cooperation with Hungary, and are leading proponents of the Euroregion concept (see below). The prospect of Hungary's EU accession, and its implementation of the EU's visa regime and the 'Schengen' system of border management, are clearly worrying for the Banat Magyars. Nevertheless, my interviewee insisted that Hungary's EU accession would bring advantages to them. The prestige of Hungary, and therefore of Magyars everywhere, would rise; the residual hostility they still encounter in Banat, their sense of being 'second-class citizens' would melt away. Hungary's EU accession would make the local Magyars key intermediaries for EU programmes in Banat, like the Germans are today, he argued. Indeed, the other minorities would become more inclined than they had been so far to recognize the Magyars, now much more numerous than Germans, as the 'natural leaders' of the minorities in their dealings with the local authorities (interview with Bódó Barna, December 2000).

Each of these cases points to the way in which the Banat minorities have regained their sense of identity, while at the same time finding both historical and practical justifications for insisting on a common, overarching Banat identity. Now we need to examine why the Romanian majority has also 'bought into' that identity, including its multicultural element. Firstly, they are not threatened by numbers or by 'separatism'. Historically, only the Hungarians ever pursued a revisionist agenda, but this had little impact in Banat. Banat did not change hands in the Second World War, unlike Transylvania, which was partitioned between Hungary and Romania with enduring consequences for inter-ethnic relations in that region. The Banat Magyars today seem fully reconciled to the territorial *status quo*, and are, moreover, ruefully aware that Banat is of much less interest to Hungary than Transylvania. From the Romanian point of view, the Magyars have effective counterweights in Banat's Schwab and Serb communities, neither of which is perceived as a threat. 'Multiculturalism' in this context can be regarded by the local Romanians not only with equanimity, but also with positive enthusiasm insofar as it brings in German resources to the benefit of the region as a whole.

A major role in shaping the local Romanians' attitudes to 'others' has undoubtedly been played by the Metropolitan of the Romanian Orthodox Church in Timişoara, described to me by a representative of a Timişoara NGO involved in inter-cultural relations as 'a quite outstanding individual'. The problem of Greek Catholic church property, taken over by the Orthodox church in 1948, was rapidly solved in Banat by the Metropolitan's immediate decision in 1990 to return it (mainly the cathedral in Lugoş). The Church has taken the initiative in fostering ecumenical dialogue and regular interaction with all confessions, thus setting the tone for a whole region in which the churches remain the pivot of community life.

The Romanians share in the pride of the region in being the most 'advanced' and 'European' part of Romania. These claims for 'the Banat way of life' seem to be most valued by the local Romanians, including recent incomers. The 'Banat myth' is above all the story of a society of immigrants, and thus is, in principle, open to all who come to share in its relative prosperity and advantageous border location, providing they are seen as adopting the local 'work ethic' as their own. This latter proviso is significant. As more than one of my interviewees suggested, 'economic exclusivism' is much more important than ethnic exclusivism in Banat: there is a pronounced hostility to 'outsiders' – mainly identified as Moldavians – who come in seeking to improve their lot but 'do not understand that prosperity only comes with hard work'. As is characteristic of immigrants elsewhere, it is the most recent newcomers who most anxiously guard their gains. 'Banat identity' may therefore also express such anxieties, and justify unsympathetic attitudes to more recent arrivals.

Institutional Tensions

For quite different reasons, the 'Banat identity' has also crystallized at the level of the (overwhelmingly Romanian) local political and administrative elites, in reaction against the centralism of successive governments in Bucharest, institutionalised in an *étatiste* constitutional model that still bears the marks of its nineteenth-century, *Code Napoléon* prototype, including government-appointed Prefects, who, in the contemporary Romanian context, are usually members of the ruling party rather than professional administrators (see Campbell, 1996: 86 ff; and interview with Viorel Coifan, MP, Timişoara, September 2001). The uncompromising definition of Romania in the first article of the constitution, pushed through in 1991 by the first Iliescu government, as a 'unitary and indivisible National State' can be read as a sign of mistrust not only of national minorities (chiefly the Hungarians), but also of potentially centrifugal regions, like Banat as well as the higher-profile Transylvania. As one Romanian politician warned a visiting western academic in 1993, 'The popular idea of the "Europe of the Regions" is not only simplistic but very dangerous, particularly if applied in the Balkans. We need to understand this if we are to avoid a repeat of the Yugoslav case' (quoted in Campbell, 1996: 86).

In the period 1990–96, the government in Bucharest was dominated by the former communist Ion Iliescu and his Party of Social Democracy of Romania (PDSR), whose policies and political style early stimulated Timişoara's opposition, as we have seen. Timiş county and Timişoara city councils in this period were strongholds of the anti-Iliescu and anti-communist Christian Democrats and National Liberals. Direct political clashes with the Prefect were not usual, mainly due to the relatively weak legitimacy of the Prefect as a non-elected, Bucharest appointee as compared to the Timişoara mayor and county council President; and to the fact that in practice real power remained with the deconcentrated offices of central ministries over which the Prefect exercised a nominal 'coordinating' function (interview with Mr Viorel Coifan, MP, Timişoara, September 2001). During that period, local politicians report that Bucharest authorities displayed systematic political bias against the Banat counties. Arad county, they claimed, was always favoured because of its PDSR and Democratic Party ties. However, party-political differences are not the whole story. Matters did not improve as expected under the subsequent government coalition of 1996–2000, which included both the Christian Democrats and the National Liberals. An illustrative case is provided by the 'Euroregion' experience.

The Timişoara elites have invested great hopes and much energy in the Danube-Körös-Máros-Tisza (DKMT) Euroregion, a project initiated in 1992 between Timiş and Csongrád county over the border in Hungary. This later expanded until by 1997 it embraced four Romanian counties (Timiş, Caraş-Severin, Arad and Hunedoara), four Hungarian counties (Csongrád, Békés, Bács-Kiskun and Jász-Nagykun-Szolnok), and the Yugoslav province of Vojvodina. Like other Euroregions that have mushroomed since 1989, its aims are to foster cross-border cooperation in economic affairs, infrastructure and environmental improvements, and culture, education, health, sport and tourism (see *DKMT* website). The Timiş elite's efforts have not been well rewarded. One obvious problem for its functioning has been posed by the inclusion of Vojvodina, with which economic links were paralysed during the international embargo on Yugoslavia, and whose representative on the Euroregion council (a Milošević supporter) was assassinated in May 2000 while holding the Euroregion's presidency. Another problem was the lukewarm interest shown by the Hungarian government, which only began to take interest in its potential once its new regional policy identified the south-east counties as priority development areas. On the Romanian side of the border, having overcome Bucharest's initial fears of 'separatism', the Timiş local authorities report Bucharest's preferential treatment of Arad county, which, as noted above, is explained in Timişoara by the party-political factor. Timiş county lobbied hard in Bucharest for years to speed the opening of a new crossing point in the county at the border with Hungary, directly connecting the cities of Timişoara and Szeged, the motors of the Euroregion project. The fact that all traffic between the two cities had to pass through the Arad checkpoint made the journey about 80 km longer than necessary. Three new crossings to Hungary were opened in the 1990s, all in Arad county. Even with political allies in government in Bucharest, it was not until October 2000 that the Cenad-Kisszombor border post was finally opened. This demonstrated to the Timiş officials, the sluggishness 'Byzantine inefficiency' and self-centredness of the capital.

This is not an isolated complaint. The Director of Timişoara TV explained to me at length her intense frustration in her endeavours to secure a regional frequency so that the TV station can provide a genuinely regional service for the Banat community, which it has all the necessary equipment, personnel and resources to do. After four years, she has nothing but a 'a whole archive' of correspondence (including declarations of support from the President and government) to show for her efforts. She explains this remarkable lack of progress in the same terms as the Timiş officials (interview with Ms Brînduşa Armanca, December 2000). Timişoara Chamber of Commerce – the first new regional Chamber to be set up after 1989 – has been effective in promoting the Banat internationally, and especially active in the 'Euroregion' project. Apart from the obvious difficulties with Yugoslavia, their main complaint is the slow progress of the Romanian government in reducing customs barriers and passing the necessary legislation and regulations to permit them to take the project forward at the pace they would like and know they can sustain. They get little help, moreover, from the national-level Chamber of Commerce, which they see as a holdover from the communist era and still marked by its legacy. Even in the secretariat of the Metropolitan of Timişoara, there is little attempt to disguise that their ecumenical activities in Banat are not accepted by the Orthodox Church elsewhere in Romania as a model to be followed.

One Banat or Several? The Fragility of 'Multi-Culturalism'

A major shock to Banat's self-image was delivered by voters in the elections of November and December 2000. Votes for the far right in the parliamentary election more than doubled over the 1996 level in Timiş, and trebled in Caraş-Severin. Two of Timiş' four senate seats, and three of its 10 parliamentary deputies, were filled by the Greater Romania Party (PRM). Votes for Vadim Tudor, the PRM leader, as President were well above the national average in both first and second rounds of the election in Caraş-Severin (34.5 per cent and 46.3 per cent), and in the second round in Timiş (38.5 per cent). Vadim Tudor and his party are known for their xenophobic, anti-minority, extreme Romanian nationalist stance, and thus hardly conform with the 'multiculturalism' professed by Banaters, and strongly suggest the fragility of the 'Banat myth'.

Nationally, the swing to the right reflected a general popular frustration with the enduring economic difficulties. One early Romanian analysis suggested a strong tendency to vote for the PRM among 'poor people in rich areas' (see SAR website), and thus could clearly apply to Banat. A major factor everywhere was the perceived incompetence, disorganization and corruption of the Bucharest political class, sentiments fully shared in Banat. Students also showed a propensity to vote 'Vadim' out of a sense of alienation from politics in general. Other Romanians in Banat seem to have felt profound disillusion with the governing National Liberals and Christian Democrats (who, moreover, ran an exceptionally disorganized campaign), while at the same time finding it unacceptable to vote for the ex-communist Iliescu. Many of these abstained (the turnout in the second round was only about 44 per cent in Banat). Others, however, were receptive to Vadim Tudor's diatribes against the corruption and incompetence of the national political elite. In all of these cases, the motive appears to have been protest, rather than endorsement of the PRM's xenophobic, anti-minority agenda. As a perceptive Timişoaran explained to the author:

> It's Central Europe, the space of mixtures. It has two centres: Vienna of culture and Auschwitz of extermination. Two hearts, still alive. A mentality quite flexible, so flexible that people bear abnormalities hoping they would mend by themselves. The Habsburg way of life was quiet, things went automatically within a sober order. When order is overthrown, people wait. And wait. Lately they realise: 'Hey this is not natural. Somebody is not serious here. Let's make him disappear'. I guess it is a sort of ancestral thinking that says 'Things should work'. And if they don't, people find who's guilty and exterminate him. Vadim was not seen as a leader but many saw him as an extermination tool. The elections were a warning signal for the region.

The 'Banat myth' has not collapsed, and the warning seems already to have been heeded: the very insistence with which my Banat interviewees emphasized their 'multi-cultural tradition' strongly suggested their underlying awareness of its fragility. Multi-culturalism cannot be taken for granted, and many Banaters seem determined to work to preserve it, no matter what happens elsewhere in Romania.

ACKNOWLEDGEMENT

Part of this paper is based on interviews in Timişoara and Caraşova in December 2000 and September 2001. I am grateful to Claudiu Mesaroş for helping me arrange and conduct the interviews, and to Cordula Greinert for research assistance on German government policy towards the German minorities.

REFERENCES

Adler, P. (1976–77), 'Serbs, Magyars and Staatsinteresse in Eighteenth Century Austria: A Study in the History of the Habsburg Administration', in *Austrian History Yearbook*, Vols XII–XIII, Part 1, pp.116–47.
Adler, P. (1979), 'Nation and Nationalism among the Serbs of Hungary', in *East European Quarterly*, Vol.XIII, No.3, pp.271–85.
Armanca, B. and D. Raţiu (1998), *Timişoara – Little Vienna*. Timişoara: TVR Timişoara (video).
Campbell, A. (1996), 'Local Government and the Centre in Romania and Moldova', in Hanson, P. and J. Gibson (eds.) *Transformation from Below: Local Power and the Political economy of Post-Communism*. Cheltenham: Edward Elgar.
Cuţara, A. (1999), *Timişoara – an Artistic Monograph*. Timişoara: Amarcord.
Deak, I. (1990), 'The Revolution and the War of Independence 1848–1849', in Sugar, P., P. Hanak and T. Frank (eds.), *A History of Hungary*. Bloomington, IN: Indiana University Press.
Drace-Francis, A. (2000), 'Cultural Currents and Political Choices: Romanian Intellectuals in the Banat to 1848', paper to conference *Nation and Community in the Vojvodina and Banat*, School of Slavonic and East European Studies, University College, London, 28–29 April, MS.
Gallagher, T. (1995), *Romania after Ceauşescu*. Edinburgh: Edinburgh University Press.
Ingrao, C. (1994), *The Habsburg Monarchy 1618–1815*. Cambridge: Cambridge University Press.
Jordan, P. (ed.) (1999), *Atlas Ost- und Südosteuropa*. Vienna: Österreichisches Ost- und Südosteuropa-Institut, map number 2.8-H/R/YU1 A Development of Ethnic Structure in the Banat 1890–92, Part A: 1890.
Kaitor, M. (2001), 'Satul Schengen', in *Banateanul*, No.16, 18–24 September, p.14
Kann, R. (1974), *A History of the Habsburg Empire 1526–1918*. Berkeley, CA: University of California Press.
Komjathy, A. and R. Stockwell (1980), *German Minorities and the Third Reich*. New York: Holmes and Meier.
Kontler, L. (1999), *Millennium in Central Europe. A History of Hungary*. Budapest: Atlantisz.
Köpeczi, B. *et al.* (1994), *History of Transylvania*. Budapest: Akadémiai Kiadó.
Macartney, C. A. (1937), *Hungary and Her Successors. The Treaty of Trianon and Its Consequences*. London: Oxford University Press for the Royal Institute of International Affairs.
McNeill, W. (1964), *Europe's Steppe Frontier 1500–1800*. Chicago: Chicago University Press.
Mihalcea, F. (ed.) (1994), *Proclamaţia de la Timişoara 11 martie 1990*. Timişoara: Societatea Timişoara.
Mitchell, B. (2000), 'The Habsburg Conquest', paper to conference *Nation and Community in Vojvodina and Banat*, School of Slavonic and East European Studies, University College, London, 28–29 April, MS.
Neumann, V. (1997), 'Multicultural Identities in a Europe of the Regions. The Case of Banat County', in *European Journal of Intercultural Studies*, Vol.8, No.1, pp.19–35.

Rothenberg, G. (1960), *The Austrian Military Border in Croatia, 1522–1747*. Urbana, IL: University of Illinois Press.
SAR (2000), *Political News and Forecasts from the Romanian Academic Society (SAR)*, e-mail newsletter, 9 December, sar@starnets.ro.
Schechtman, J. (1962), *Postwar Population Transfers in Europe 1945–1955*. Philadelphia: University of Pennsylvania Press.
Seton-Watson, R. (1934), *A History of the Roumanians*. Cambridge: Cambridge University Press.
Siani-Davies, P. (1995), *The Romanian Revolution of 1989: Myth and Reality – Myth or Reality?* London: School of Slavonic and East European Studies, University of London (PhD Thesis).
Sugar, P. (1977), *Southeastern Europe under Ottoman Rule, 1354–1804*. Seattle, WA: University of Washington Press.
A Treia Europă (1998), No.2, Timişoara; POLIROM.
Tökés, L. (1990), *With God, For the People*. London: Hodder and Stoughton.
Vultur, S. (1997), *Istorie trăită – Istorie povestită. Deportarea in Bărăgan, 1951–56*. Timişoara: Editura Amarcord.
Vultur, S. (2000), *Germanii din Banat, prin povestirile lor*. Bucharest: Paideia.

Internet Sources

Auswärtiges Amt: www.auswaertiges-amt.de
Caraş-Severin County Prefecture: www.sorostm.ro/pjcs
CCIAT – Timişoara Chamber of Commerce: www.cciat.ro
DKMT Euroregion: www.dkmt.csongrad-megye.hu
IFA – Institut für Auslandsbeziehungen: www.ifa.de/i/dirumaen.htm
Romanian election results: www.election.ro
Timiş County Prefecture: www.banat.ro/prefectura/index.html

Conclusion:
Identities, Regions and Europe

KATARYNA WOLCZUK

The disintegration of all three communist multinational federations in 1991–93 finally, in the troubled history of Central and Eastern Europe, made the nation-state the ubiquitous form of 'national self-determination'. But the fall of communism also presaged far-reaching internal change in the newly 'sovereign' nation-states. In particular, decentralization was not only demanded by regional and ethnic minorities, but championed as a way of jettisoning the communist legacy and 'returning to Europe'. Decentralization was viewed as an antidote to the communist-era legacies of rigid centralization resulting from the uniform institutional design, modelled on the system of soviets pioneered in the Soviet Union, imposed throughout the Soviet bloc after the Second World War. This centralized administrative-territorial model not only ruled out democratic self-government but was also in practice characterized by fragmentation at the regional level and, as a result, inefficiency. The end of the communist regimes prompted top-down institutional reform under the banner of decommunization, promoting democratization as well as greater efficiency. Yet this reform was limited in the early years of transformation to re-instituting genuine self-government at the local level. Reform of the regional tier evoked more controversy and hence in most cases was put on the backburner until the late 1990s.

Simultaneously, Central and Eastern Europe have been exposed to powerful external stimuli, a corollary of the 'return to Europe'. In practical terms, this 'return' signalled a drive to join European institutions, especially the European Union. Following the acknowledgement of this aspiration by the EU in the mid-1990s, the 'return to Europe' has taken on the technocratic form of implementing the *acquis communautaire*, comprising more or less precisely specified prescriptions. The EU's demands for the creation of sub-state, regional-level administrative institutions within the applicant states came when regional reform was otherwise mostly stalled, so the accession process opened the applicant countries up to influences from external actors in areas which have traditionally belonged to the realm of national sovereignty for EU member-states.

The drive to decommunize and 'Europeanize' coincided with a 'bottom-up' revival of minority and regional identities, which inspired calls for greater regional autonomy. The removal of the communist political straitjacket dispelled the myth of national and territorial homogeneity propagated by many communist regimes. As was pointed out in the Introduction to this volume, the resurgence of minorities and regionalism was hardly surprising in light of Central and Eastern Europe's ethnic and regional diversity, a well-known legacy of belated state-formation and frequent border changes.

Among the issues of decommunization, 'Europeanization' and the resurgence of ethnic and regional identities, only the first two have attracted adequate scholarly attention. The literature on decentralization in Central and Eastern Europe remains weakly linked to wider post-communist issues of state transformation, and in particular, to the interface between institutional change and identity politics. This is somewhat surprising as the collapse of the communist federations highlighted the role that institutions play in creating and sustaining identities and becoming platforms for political mobilization; equally, identities were shown to have the potential to profoundly transform state institutions. There has been little reflection on how identity politics continued thereafter, when major institutional changes in centre–periphery relations were embarked on, and intensive debates on the notions of nation, state, sovereignty and 'Europeanization' ensued. This volume was inspired by the idea that identity politics, especially in their spatial context, deserve more attention in Central and Eastern Europe. On the one hand, the question is how national-level processes are affected by (perceptions of) sub-state developments and external influences, and, on the other, how the sub-state politics of identity are shaped both by national-level developments and by the dynamics of EU enlargement. By examining the discourses which surrounded the reform of the meso-level institutions, as well as the perspective from the regions on the transformation of statehood after communism, this volume has unearthed the dynamic nexus between regional and minority identities, the policies of the national capitals, and the diverse meanings of and influences that 'Europe' brings to bear.

Resurgence of Minority and Regional Identities and Decentralization

As was pointed out in the Introduction, all post-communist states can be regarded as in some sense 'new' states as all of them, bar Hungary, were bequeathed regional and ethnic diversity and thus, after the collapse of communism, were confronted with fundamental questions about how the state should be structured to cope with this diversity. In all of the states covered in this volume, most ethnic minorities are regionally concentrated (with the important exception of the Roma minorities: see Guy, 2001).

The size of the minorities in relation to the ethnic majority, however, varies significantly: in Poland minorities account for approximately 5–7 per cent of the population, whereas in Estonia, they comprise about 40 per cent of the population. A no less important but often overlooked phenomenon is the persistence of regional diversity. As a result of frequent border changes, Central and East European states are often made up of regions that were once part of different empires, resulting in divergent political, social, economic and cultural traces that continue to make themselves felt today. Despite the homogenizing policies of communist regimes, distinct regional identities survived within and across Central and Eastern Europe states. All the historical regions examined in this volume – Banat, Upper Silesia, and Transcarpathia – formed parts of other states at certain points in their history. The opening up of public space after the collapse of communism prompted a resurgence of regional identities, often combining historic elements with a more recently discovered ethnic distinctiveness. Therefore, with the exception of Hungary, all the post-communist states in our selection of cases confronted some 'bottom-up' pressure for the recognition of ethnic and regional diversity.

These developments delivered a blow to the cherished ideal of 'national unity' and bred a sense of insecurity stemming from the fear that centrifugal forces may lead to territorial disintegration. In particular, states with historical regionalisms and concentrated ethnic minorities have been wary of reconstituting and empowering historical regions as these could gravitate towards their 'kin-states', even if few claims for territorial revisionism have been made officially in the region (apart from the obvious case of war-torn Yugoslavia, Romania's claim on Ukraine is one example). In particular, in the new states, ethnic and regional diversity has been a major factor militating against political regionalization: Ukraine and Estonia have eschewed regionalization, and Slovakia's regional reform debates have revealed the concern of some to 'dilute' the territorial concentration of the Hungarian minority. Such fears inspired continued reliance on a centralized territorial-administrative model in line with the nineteenth-century assumption in Western Europe that concentrating power in a single centre would afford the state better control and more efficient administration.

Estonia and Ukraine inherited large Russian and Russian-speaking minorities. The perceived security threats from secessionist regions and ethnic minorities had some substance in the early years of establishing independent statehood and redefining relations with Russia, even if these have now largely abated. While rejecting calls for territorial autonomy for Narva region where the Russian-speaking minority is concentrated,

Estonia pursued a path of accommodating ethnic heterogeneity by adopting the law on (non-territorial) cultural autonomy for minorities. Yet the right to exercise such autonomy belongs only to citizens of Estonia and does not apply to the majority of the Russian-speaking population, who have either taken up Russian citizenship or have the status of permanently resident 'aliens'. Ukraine refrained from re-constituting historical regions and retained directly elected institutions at the meso level defined by the existing *oblasti*. Yet being a communist-era creation, the *oblasti* were deprived of any significant political autonomy. Democratic self-government is thus effectively restricted to the local level, which poses little challenge to the highly centralized distribution of state power. This outcome was determined primarily by the acute awareness of the fragility of Ukrainian national identity and the corresponding fears of regional centrifugalism; but at the same time it enabled self-interested ex-*nomenklatura* elites to retain control over the levers of power in independent Ukraine.

Slovakia is more advanced towards political decentralization, although the passage of legislation in July 2001 has not put an end to acute controversy, likely to continue at least in part because of the disappointment of the regionally concentrated Hungarian minority in the final version of that law. But, as Bitušíkova argues, the tortuous process of regional reform also has much to do with the uncertainties and divisions among the Slovaks themselves as to their identity and national cohesion.

Even in Poland, which embarked on political decentralization, some concerns over supposed threats to territorial integrity were voiced throughout the 1990s (see Kowalczyk, 2000; Bokajlo, 2000: Buczkowski, 1998). As Kisielowska-Lipman points out, decentralization evoked such concerns in the regions as well. However, the strength of Polish national identity and the small size of the minorities mitigated such concerns to the extent that the imperatives of decommunization and 'Europeanization' prevailed. In the case of Hungary, different forces were at play. In the absence of regionalist demands, the arguments of efficiency and limiting corruption have been cited at the state centre to justify the retention of a more centralized model and the establishment of purely administrative regions with limited functions. Undoubtedly, as Fowler demonstrated, the entrenched political position of the historical counties and the lack of a clear push for political decentralization from the EU help to account for this outcome.

As the essays in this volume demonstrate, so far, most states still appear satisfied with decentralization to the local (municipal) level, as implemented in immediate post-communist reforms. The unitary state model, enshrined in national constitutions, commanded favour across the region (with the exception of Crimea in Ukraine, which was designated a federal component in an otherwise unitary, centralized state). Only Poland and Slovakia opted for far-reaching devolution of power to restructured regions; how fast and how far the intentions of the champions of the devolution legislation will be realized remains to be seen. The newest states among those considered here – those formed in 1991–93 upon the collapse of communist federations – turned out to be particularly wary of the dangers of centrifugalism emanating from sub-state regions and hence put a premium on unity and cohesion embodied in a centralized model of statehood.

Overall, nowhere in the region were debates on sub-state reforms couched explicitly in terms of the recognition of ethnic and regional diversity. Where political devolution to the meso level was implemented (Poland) or is planned (Slovakia), it is *despite* rather than *because of* the resurgence of regional and ethnic identities. Democratization, administrative efficiency, fiscal considerations, EU accession requirements and so forth were cited as the compelling reasons for regionalization, rather than the accommodation of diversity. However, in new states such as Ukraine, the spectre of centrifugalism was explicitly used as one of the key arguments *against* the political empowerment of the regions.

Regionalization and 'Europeanization'

The imperative of 'returning to Europe', that is, gaining membership in European organizations, has been another factor shaping the dynamics of regionalization in Central and Eastern Europe. All the states examined in this volume are members of the Council of Europe, the organization that promotes democratic development at both national and sub-state levels; the latter is embodied in the European Charter of Local Self-Government. But the Charter applies only to the local level, whereas the Charter of Regional Self-Government, concerned with the meso tier of representative institutions, is still in preparation and there is little prospect of its rapid ratification. Thus, as regards reform of regional-level institutions, it is the European Union that has potentially far greater impact on applicant states, insofar as the strengthening of administrative capacity at the regional level in the candidate state is exhorted as one of the conditions of accession. However, the incentive to 'Europeanize' sub-state institutions is not equally compelling for all post-communist states as they have markedly different prospects of joining the EU. Moreover, even for the applicant states, EU conditionality does not offer consistent and clearly spelled out policy prescriptions on regionalization. Nevertheless, appeals to 'Europe' are a constant feature of debates on regionalization in Central and Eastern

Europe, while at the same time, as our studies demonstrate, 'Europe' denotes different things to different people. As a result, the impact of 'Europeanization' is far from uniform across Central and Eastern Europe.

As noted in the Introduction, the traditional centralized model of the nation-state has lost its hegemonic position in the last 30 years among EU member states, as most have become more decentralized, but in very different ways. Thus if being 'European' means being similar to *any* EU member state, Central and Eastern Europeans can choose from among a wide range of models to emulate in the name of 'Europeanness': from the traditional French model of a centralized nation-state through Spanish asymmetrical devolution to Austrian and German federalism. These models themselves are, of course, often in a state of flux.

The traditional, centralized model of the nation-state retains considerable appeal, especially for new states in Central and Eastern Europe. Thus, Ukraine could equate its 'European choice' with the creation of a sovereign nation-state capable of unifying and consolidating disparate historical regions through a uniform set of sub-state institutions subordinated to the centre. Ukraine's interpretation of the traditional European trajectory of state-building was thus legitimized as a means of 'returning to Europe'.

The prospects of membership in a supra-national European organization for Central and Eastern European states determine their interpretation of what constitutes 'Europeanness'. In particular, different positions *vis-à-vis* the EU result in diverging impacts of European integration across the region. Poland, Estonia and Hungary, which entered into accession negotiations with the EU in 1998, belong to the so-called 'first wave', and this is not unconnected with faster progress in settling the question of regional reform. Slovakia's valiant efforts to make up lost ground after the change of government in 1998 provide the background to the increasing urgency with which regional reform was pursued. Romania, now relegated to the back of the queue of new EU entrants, has been both less radical in its approach to, and less consistent in implementation of, new regional structures. Ukraine remains an 'outsider', whose membership of the EU, despite Kiev's proclaimed aspirations, is not on the cards for the foreseeable future, if at all. So while for the frontrunners, debate over the external reasons for regional reform centres on the interpretation of EU conditionality, for Ukraine, it was the prescriptions of the Council of Europe, and in particular its emphasis on the local (municipal) level, which were the point of reference for defining 'Europeanness' when it came to sub-state institutional reform. Symptomatically, despite not being an EU candidate-state, Ukraine still sought to justify its institutional choices in the process of constitution-making by references to international norms, hence the importance of the Council of Europe as the standard-setting body.

Nevertheless, even for the candidate states, EU conditionality (enshrined in the *acquis communautaire*, the Accession Partnerships and the Commission's annual 'progress' reports) is far from unambiguous. EU legislation does not concern itself with sub-state institutions and does not envisage any particular model of regional-tier government or administration. Rather, the candidates are exhorted to 'strengthen their administrative capacity'. This involves establishing regional-level bodies capable of efficiently managing the transfer and use of structural funds following accession in line with the principles that are the main EU prescriptions in the regional policy field – subsidiarity, partnership and additionality. These regional bodies are to be established over the 'NUTS II' scale, itself not legally defined so far. But meeting these conditions can be achieved by purely administrative regionalization whereas *political* devolution of power remains a matter of choice for individual applicant states. This relatively 'soft' conditionality, in contrast to many other areas of the *acquis*, tends to be attributed to the Commission's desire not to interfere in a domain traditionally reserved for sovereign constitutional politics. Yet, the case of Hungary, where the issue of regionalization was almost wholly propelled by concern to meet EU accession criteria, illustrates the extent to which the EU Commission is concerned primarily with administrative capacity and not with political empowerment of the regions. The Commission prefers to deal with national rather than regional governments because of the fear of greater corruption and lack of administrative capacity at the sub-state level. So even if in general there has been progressive regionalization and decentralization amongst EU member states, the Commission's policy recommendations, however informal, have not always produced this result in Central and Eastern Europe.

It is thus hardly surprising that 'Europeanization' has taken diverse forms in Central and Eastern Europe. Both Poland and Hungary accepted regional reform as an organic ingredient of 'Europeanization', but with different results in the two cases. Driven equally by the imperative of democratization, Poland has instituted fully fledged political regions (*województwa*) with elected councils and wide-ranging competences, including the authority to conduct direct relations with regional units in neighbouring states. This latter feature partly reflects the pressure to create equal partners for powerful German Länder. However, although it borders on the similarly federal Austria, Hungary has so far established administrative and functionally specific regions that do not override the (similarly limited) competences of the historic counties of which they are composed. As Fowler argues, the counties were seen to have greater historical legitimacy in a state which, alone among the cases presented here, has no obvious larger, historical regions; the counties had also achieved political weight in the new post-communist state structures before the EU demand for regionalization had been felt. Yet another path was chosen by the third 'frontrunner' examined in this volume, Estonia. Because of its small size, the country can be treated as a single region for the EU's purposes, and so the demand to institute regions, for example to satisfy the inhabitants of Narva region, may be safely deflected.

Despite the ambiguity of external pressures for decentralization, the case studies in this volume amply illustrate the way in which frequent references to 'Europe' have been a ubiquitous feature of debates on the reform of the regional tier, while 'Europe' denotes a range of different things. Such indeterminacy regarding 'Europe' allows the concept to be 'domesticated' in national politics across Central and Eastern Europe and utilized as an extra legitimizing resource in domestic debates.

The Perspective From the Regions

Overall, the demands of regional and ethnic minorities have had a limited impact on the path of decentralization in Central and Eastern Europe (perhaps with the notable exception of Crimea, where the extent of mobilization induced Kiev to concede at least partially to regional demands in the 1996 constitution). This volume examines cases of regionalism based on both ethnic and historical grounds; that is, cases where either an ethnic minority demanded special provisions for self-government within a particular territorial unit, or a region's distinct history was invoked to justify such claims. There is a concentrated ethnic minority in Narva region, and a distinctive regional identity in Upper Silesia; whereas Banat, Transcarpathia and eastern Poland are distinctive in being multi-ethnic regions. Only Silesia had some tradition of autonomy in the pre-Second World War period, whereas a promise of autonomy for Transcarpathia never materialized in inter-war Czechoslovakia. So far all these regions' demands for the recognition of their specificities have been rejected by their host states, with the partial exception of Upper Silesia, which was institutionalized (albeit imperfectly) in a new *województwo*. This failure is not only due to the reluctance of national elites to concede political autonomy for historical regions and/or ethnic minorities in compact settlements. Most of all, it reflects relatively weak political mobilization at the sub-state level and the limited capacity of ethnic and regional 'entrepreneurs' to exert any influence on the process of territorial-administrative reforms. Yet the absence of sustained political mobilization does not mean that the sub-state, regional dimension can be ignored for its political irrelevance. On the contrary, all the regions examined in this volume are articulating their particular responses to national and European-level developments. The exploration of views from the periphery reveals lingering strains for nation-states in Central and Eastern Europe as they confront the challenges of EU enlargement.

The national elites do not have a monopoly on defining 'Europeanness' – indeed, the versions of 'Europe' that emanate from state peripheries differ from those in the national capitals. In several cases studied in this volume, regional distinctiveness is framed in terms of being more 'European' than the rest of the country, while calls for the recognition of diversity at the sub-state level are justified in terms of adopting European models and standards. This linking of regions with the idea of Europe illuminates the way that domestic dynamics are intertwined with the external dimension, something which makes the distinction between national and international politics increasingly blurred.

In defiance of nationalist agendas, regional activists do not recognize or identify with the entire territory of the national state as 'their own'. Instead, they propagate the notion of a collectivity bounded by sub-state regional boundaries, while at the same time, in their discourses, they reach out beyond the nation-state. The rejection of the nationalist paradigm of unified, homogeneous nationhood and territory in the cases of Upper Silesia, Banat and Transcarpathia is accompanied by claims of intrinsic 'Europeanness'. Even if, unlike Banat or Upper Silesia, Transcarpathia cannot claim economic prosperity as one of its 'European' credentials, peaceful multi-ethnic co-existence, mutual tolerance and lack of any form of militant mobilization along ethnic or political lines are cited as unique characteristics of Transcarpathia, which, in the view of Rusyn activists, set the region apart from the rest of Ukraine. In particular, multi-culturalism – which is proclaimed the norm in inter-ethnic relations in all the historic regions examined in this volume – is pointed to as a unique feature that sets them apart within their respective nation-states, but which at the same time brings them closer to 'Europe'. Thereby, these regions' inherent connection with Europe is emphasized, bypassing the nation-state.

As Smith argues, in the case of Narva region, populated by an ethnic Russian and Russian-speaking population, 'Europe' is seen as a factor that is expected to relax the dominance of the Estonian nation-state over the region. Even if calls by the Russian minority for autonomy have subsided (something which reflects the lack of a coherent identity amongst the inhabitants of the region and the minority's preoccupation with residential status and citizenship), the Russians of Narva look towards 'Europe' in the hope of greater territorial autonomy once Estonia joins the EU.

'Europe', however, does not only evoke benign associations; it is also a source of threat for the regions, insofar as all of them, bar Upper Silesia, will be affected by changes in the status of their external borders resulting from EU enlargement. They will find themselves either on the immediate inside or immediate outside of the enlarged Union (**see maps**). Thus, for these regions, the incongruity between discourses on 'Europe Whole and Free' and policies geared to toughening border controls at the instigation of the EU is thrown into sharp relief. Our regional case studies illuminate the deep concerns which exist at the prospect of the Schengen border, and its potential to disrupt inter-ethnic relations and the mutually beneficial economic and cultural contacts that have been built up between regions straddling it. While for the national capitals in the applicant states, the introduction of Schengen raises issues of foreign policy and regional economic development, for the border regions the prospect highlights the problem of day-to-day economic survival and the threat of marginalization, on whichever side of the border they will find themselves.

This is a particularly thorny question for the 'outside' regions. As our studies demonstrate, such regions' claims to 'Europeanness' are made regardless of the position of their respective states in the enlargement process. As the prospects of Romania, let alone Ukraine, joining the EU are dim or even receding, in Banat and Transcarpathia, exclusion from EU enlargement is depicted as nothing less than an impending tragedy. This is not just because exclusion threatens to disrupt vital, intensive economic exchanges across the border, and undermine the development of 'Euroregions'. It also breeds an acute sense of frustration at the 'betrayal' by 'Europe' itself of these regions' proclaimed European vocation. After enlargement, their claimed regional identities will not match the new geopolitical and economic boundaries of Europe, which are in many respects seen – both inside and outside the Union – as synonymous with the EU borders. Thus, the elites in these border regions draw their own unique discursive map of Europe. Banat and Transcarpathia (as well as Galicia in Ukraine, not covered in this volume) claim to belong to 'Central Europe' (see Batt and Wolczuk, 2001), a claim which for countries such as Poland or Hungary is by now largely *passé*. The notion of a Central European identity, which was revived in dissidents' discourses in the 1980s (see Schöpflin and Wood, 1989), was animated by the desire to oppose Soviet domination. By the mid-1990s, it had largely lost its vitality as 'Europeanness' began to be measured according to the terms of the Copenhagen criteria. Yet by emphasizing their 'Central Europeanness' as former subjects of the Habsburg monarchy, the border regions in Romania and Ukraine reinforce their intrinsic links with a wider Europe. So even if by now in official parlance 'Central Europe' denotes little more than an antechamber for EU applicants, the notion of a Central European identity is far from moribund: it has moved eastwards and is embraced in western regions of countries excluded from integration.

The prospect of exclusion breeds frustration not only with 'Europe' but, perhaps most of all, with the respective national capitals, for foot-dragging in preparing for the 'return to Europe'. Appeals to 'Central Europeanness' are designed not only to show organic ties with the wider Europe but also to contrast with the 'oppressiveness' of national capitals, i.e. Bucharest and Kiev, whose incompetence and corruption are attributed (at least in part) to their different, 'eastern' cultural traditions. This reveals the depth and potential strength of the lingering tensions between the centre and periphery which exist in these states, tensions which seem likely to be exacerbated by exclusion from EU enlargement. This has important policy implications for the EU's external relations in general and for its border management policy in particular. While the impact of enlargement on the new member-states will be profound, its impact on the stability of states left outside the future EU's border may be more difficult to predict, and in any case cannot be ignored by the EU.

REFERENCES

Batt, J. and K. Wolczuk (2001), 'Keep an Eye on the East', *Financial Times* (European Edition), 23 February.

Buczkowski, J. (ed.) (1998), *Jaka Europa? Regionalizacja a Integracja*. Poznan: Wydawnictwo Wyzszej Szkoly Bankowej.

Bokajlo, W. (2000), 'The Reform of Polish Local Government, and the Europe of the Regions', in Karl Cordell, (ed.), *Poland and the European Union*. London: Routledge.

Guy, W. (ed.) (2001), *Between Past and Future. The Roma of Central and Eastern Europe*. Hatfield: University of Hertfordshire Press.

Kowalczyk, A. (2000), 'Local Government in Poland', in Tamás M. Horváth (ed.), *Decentralization: Experiments and Reforms*. Budapest: Local Government and Public Service Reform Initiative.

Schöpflin, G. and N. Wood (eds) (1989), *In Search of Central Europe*. Cambridge: Polity Press.

Abstracts

Hungary: Patterns of Political Conflict Over Territorial-Administrative Reform
Brigid Fowler

This essay traces three forms of political elite conflict that marked the process of territorial-administrative reform in Hungary during the first post-communist decade: between government and opposition; 'decentralizers' and 'centralizers'; and supporters and detractors of different territorial tiers – the local, the county and the region. The study also discusses the way in which the notion of 'Europe' was used in these debates. It shows that, even in a territorially and ethnically homogeneous state, post-communist territorial-administrative reform in the context of the 'return to Europe' has elicited a rich set of political arguments about ways of arranging the state, driven by partisan interests and varying understandings of Hungary's pre-communist and communist pasts and post-communist experience.

Slovakia: An Anthropological Perspective on Identity and Regional Reform
Alexandra Bitušíková

This contribution deals with public administration reform in post-communist Slovakia from an anthropological perspective. It starts from the regional differentiation in Slovakia, which has resulted from its historical, political, social and cultural development in Central Europe, on the border between West and East. Regional differences have had a strong influence on local, regional and national identities. Regionalism still plays an important integrating role in people's lives and has an impact on the current transformation processes. Administration reforms have helped to fix regional differences. The essay mentions all the major administration reforms since the tenth century, with the main focus on public administration reforms after 1993 when the Slovak Republic was established after the 'velvet divorce' from the Czechs.

Catching up with 'Europe'? Constitutional Debates on the Territorial-Administrative Model in Independent Ukraine
Kataryna Wolczuk

Ukraine is a country with pronounced regional differences and a longstanding indigenous tradition of thinking on decentralization and federalism. Yet upon emerging as an independent polity, Ukraine failed to reform the territorial division inherited from the Soviet Union and opted for a centralized territorial-administrative system and territorial autonomy for the Crimean peninsula. The path of post-Soviet reforms can largely be attributed to a profound disagreement on what constituted the indigenous tradition and fear of centrifugal tendencies, which manifested themselves after independence. In the context of historical legacies of statelessness, the preservation of national unity and territorial cohesion was deemed of paramount importance. This would consolidate Ukraine's transformation into a truly European nation-state.

Narva Region within the Estonian Republic. From Autonomism to Accommodation?
David J. Smith

This essay examines the predominantly Russian-speaking city of Narva and its surrounding region of Ida-Virumaa within the framework of the independent Estonian state restored to being in 1991. From 1988 to 1993, the city became the locus of a movement for regional autonomy that challenged the emerging unitary and 'nationalizing' state order. The study assesses why the frequent parallels between Ida-Virumaa and the breakaway 'Transdniestran Republic' in Moldova during these years ultimately proved unfounded. It also suggests that, despite subsequent moves towards fuller political integration of the region into the state, 'Estonia's Narva problem' is still far from being resolved as the country prepares itself for entry to the European Union.

Upper Silesia: Rebirth of a Regional Identity in Poland
Luiza Bialasiewicz

The territorial decentralization of administrative competences has been a key focus of political debate in Poland since the fall of communism. The devolution of the functions of governance to localities and regions has been seen as an important step towards the consolidation of participatory democracy. Yet it has also become a key locus of cultural politics, with the rediscovery and revival of numerous local and regional historical-cultural identities in the post-1989 period. This essay focuses on processes of regionalization in Upper Silesia in south-eastern Poland, the home of some of the most vocal Polish regionalist movements in the past decade. It traces the ways in which the revival of Silesian identity has proceeded through the assertion of the region's historical and cultural difference from the remainder of the Polish state and the affirmation of the continuity of a distinct Silesian regional community through time.

Poland's Eastern Borderlands: Political Transition and the 'Ethnic Question'
Marzena Kisielowska-Lipman

This essay addresses two main questions: the extent to which Poland's transformation processes since 1989 have been accommodated 'below' in its ethnically diverse eastern borderlands; and the way in which these processes have affected inter-ethnic relations in the region. The author looks through the prism of three major processes: democratization, decentralization and NATO/EU enlargement, and comes to the conclusion that these processes are echoed in the eastern borderlands and, with various degrees of resonance, have impacted on the reshaping of inter-ethnic relationships in the region.

Transcarpathia: Peripheral Region at the 'Centre of Europe'
Judy Batt

Transcarpathia's special identity was formed by repeated annexations by rival states, of which it was always a remote backwater. The result was a multi-cultural ethnic mosaic, whose major groups all suffered under successive regimes. In the 1980s,

Rusyn ethno-national identity re-emerged to challenge the 'Ukrainianizing' efforts of the Kiev government, with, at times, the opportunistic support of the local former communist elite. Autonomy is also sought by the local Hungarian minority. 'Central European' identity is invoked to emphasize the region's cultural distance from the capital, and justify aspirations to a special regional status and closer links with the west. But the impending EU's Schengen border threatens these links, prompting many to emigrate. Those who remain feel 'betrayed' by the 'Europe' at whose 'centre' they lie.

Reinventing Banat
Judy Batt

Banat, a region in south-west Romania, has reclaimed its identity by emphasizing a 'multi-cultural tradition' at odds with the prevailing nationalist discourse in Romanian politics. The complex history of the region led to the immigration of an extraordinary mosaic of ethnic groups, but ethnic diversity was much reduced in the course of the twentieth century. It is notable that the Romanians, the overwhelming majority in the region today, seem as committed as the minorities to this myth, which provides a vehicle for expressing frustrations with the centralization of state power, corruption and the perceived incompetence of the Bucharest political elites.

Notes on Contributors

Judy Batt is Senior Lecturer in Central and East European Politics at the Centre for Russian and East European Studies/European Research Institute, University of Birmingham. She led the research team on the ESRC One Europe or Several? programme project, 'Fuzzy Statehood' and European Integration, which produced this volume.

Kataryna Wolczuk is Lecturer in Ukrainian Studies at the Centre for Russian and East European Studies, University of Birmingham. She has researched and published on institution building, constitutional issues and nationalism in Ukraine.

Brigid Fowler was a Research Fellow at the Centre for Russian and East European Studies, University of Birmingham, in 2000–2001, working on the ESRC-funded project *'Fuzzy Statehood' and European Integration in Central and Eastern Europe*. Now, as an Honorary Research Fellow, she is writing an ESRC-funded PhD there on the responses of Hungary's right-wing parties to European integration.

Alexandra Bitušíková works as a representative of the Slovak universities to the European institutions as well as a freelance researcher and lecturer in Brussels, where she is based. She was former Director of the Institute of Social and Cultural Studies, Faculty of Humanities of Matej Bel University in Banska Bystrica.

David Smith is Lecturer in the Contemporary History and International Relations of the Baltic States, Department of European Studies, University of Bradford.

Luiza Bialasiewicz is Lecturer in the Department of Geography at the University of Durham. Her research interests lie with the geopolitics of European integration and, in particular, the geographies of transformation in Central and Eastern Europe.

Marzena Kisielowska-Lipman was a Research Fellow on the ESRC-funded project 'Fuzzy Statehood' and European Integration in Central and Eastern Europe in 1999. She graduated from Tagiellonian University in Krakow.

Index